The Modern Sea Angler

by
HUGH STOKER

Sixth Edition

D1745605

ROBERT HALE · LONDON

First edition 1958
Second edition 1964
Third edition 1966
Fourth edition 1971
Reprinted 1972
Fifth edition 1977
Sixth edition (fully revised and reset) 1979

ISBN 0 7091 7580 9

Robert Hale Limited
Clerkenwell House
Clerkenwell Green
London, EC1

Photoset by Specialised Offset Services Ltd
Printed in Great Britain by
Lowe & Brydone Ltd., and bound
by Redwood Burn Ltd.

Contents

To
My Wife

Illustrations

PLATES

LINE DRAWINGS IN TEXT

Author's Note

I would like to thank the undermentioned persons, societies and firms for their willing assistance in the matter of technical information and illustrations: Dr G.A. Steven, Fisheries Naturalist, Marine Biological Association of the United Kingdom, Mr Gwion Davies, of the Fisheries Experiment Station, Conway; the Fisheries Laboratory, Lowestoft; Messrs Grice and Young, Ltd, Christchurch; ABU (Great Britain) Ltd, Clydebank, Dumbartonshire; The British Seagull Company, Ltd, Poole; The Bell Woodworking Co., Ltd, Leicester.

It might perhaps be advisable to mention also that I have no particular interest in any items of tackle described in this book. They have been chosen because they seemed most suitable for illustrating a certain point raised in the text, or were of a make and design that I have used for many years and found satisfactory.

H.S.

1

For Beginners Only

Let us begin this book on salt-water angling by imagining that you have just entered a tackle shop to buy your first sea-fishing rod. You mention your need to the dealer standing behind the counter, and he subjects you to a searching scrutiny in an endeavour to guess how much ready cash you are carrying in your pocket.

"A sea-rod, sir?" he says. "Why, certainly – what sort of a rod do you require?"

You gaze around at the visible stock-in-trade. What sort indeed! Wherever you look you see fishing-rods of every description – long rods and short rods; cheap rods and expensive rods; stout rods and thin rods; stiff rods and bendy rods; boat-rods and shore-casting rods ... The variety seems endless.

Obviously, my first job as author of this book must be to examine all these rods with you, as it were, so that you will become familiar with their more outstanding advantages and limitations.

The cost of a rod depends mainly on the materials and workmanship which have gone into it, and it is worth stressing that a good quality rod, chosen with care, will almost certainly prove cheapest in the long run. The fittings on any sea-rod should, of course, be designed to withstand the extremely corrosive effects of salt water, and on the average boat-rod one would expect to find chromed brass ferrules and screw-locking reel fittings, stainless steel or Sintox-lined rings, a cork handle or fluted plastic hand-grips, and possibly a gymbal-type brass butt cap fitted with an optional rubber end button.

In shore-casting rods the modern emphasis is on lightness and streamlined efficiency. Featherlight hard-chromed stainless steel rings are highly resistant to grooving through

line wear; whilst in many shorecasting rods the traditional
brass suction ferrule has been replaced by an internal spigot
joint that allows the rod to flex throughout its length.

The vast majority of present-day sea fishing rods are made
of fibreglass. This excellent material is capable of producing a
rod with a powerful snappy action, combined with a
remarkably even strength throughout its whole length. Also, a
fibreglass rod will retain its straightness, even after many
years of hard use, and it is proof against fresh or salt water rot,
worm and shrinkage.

Fibreglass rods come in two basic forms – solid or tubular.
The tubular type – commonly known as 'hollow glass' – is
more costly to produce, but has the great advantage of being
considerably lighter to handle. It also has a pleasanter and
more power-packed action when shore-casting or spinning.

For the boat or pier angler who is compelled to economise,
there are some reasonably-priced solid glass rods on the
market which do their job quite well. But I repeat – when it
comes to long-distance shore-casting there is really no
satisfactory *economic* substitute for hollow glass.

In recent years a new rod-building material, known as
carbon-fibre, has entered upon the sea angling scene.
Combining great strength with extreme lightness and steely
flexibility, it is an ideal material for long-distance surf-casting
rods. Unfortunately at the time of writing a carbon fibre
shore-casting rod costs approximately twice as much as a
comparable rod of hollow fibreglass construction. As a
compromise, some rod-makers have produced shore-casting
rods with a hollow fibreglass butt section and carbon fibre
reinforced tip. Such rods give a shade more casting power, but
– and this is probably more important – they also make it
easier to drive the hook into a fish when fishing at long range.

So much for the material from which salt-water rods are
built; now for the question of length. Ideally a rod used for
beach-casting should be fairly long, say 11 to 12 feet; whilst
the most popular length for boat fishing is in the region of $6\frac{1}{2}$
to 7 feet. For fishing from a pier or jetty a medium-length rod
of 8 or 9 feet will usually prove most suitable, although a
longer beach-caster can be used when there are no
obstructions or overhead power cables.

If you have decided to take up one kind of sea fishing, and

are convinced that you will be content to stick to it to the exclusion of all others, then choosing the length, strength and type of rod will be a fairly simple matter. But most newcomers to sea angling seem to hanker after a general-purpose rod, and precisely what form this should take has long been a debatable point. The truth is there is no such thing as a wholly satisfactory 'general-purpose' rod – although many fairly inexpensive solid glass rods are advertised as such. Usually they are about 9 feet long, because this length enables the rod to be used for short distance casting from a pier or steeply shelving beach; whilst at the same time being allegedly short enough to be used in a boat.

My own opinion is that such compromise rods are best left alone. It is far better to spend your money on a rod that has been specially designed for a particular branch of sea angling, because then it will remain a useful part of your equipment for the remainder of your life.

It is also worth stressing that some types of specialist rod are eminently suitable for other branches of sea angling. For example, an 11-foot shore-casting rod can be used for float fishing from a rock position, pier or harbour breakwater.

Likewise, a medium-powered two-handed 9-foot spinning rod can be used for float fishing, and also as a very sporting weapon when driftlining from a boat for pollack, black bream and bass.

The rod will, of course, need a reel. This should be of a size and weight to balance the rod, and the tackle dealer should be able to advise you on this point. The thing you must decide for yourself is the type of reel to buy.

The Centrepin reel is the simplest and cheapest sort, but it has its limitations and is not very widely used. However, it makes a satisfactory general-purpose reel for medium-depth boat fishing, and can also be used for pier and harbour wall fishing where long-distance casting is not usually necessary.

At one time centrepin reels were widely used for beach fishing, but on most parts of the coast they have been superseded by more sophisticated types capable of producing longer casts with less effort. However, because of its superior winching power, one sort of centrepin reel (the Scarborough) is still favoured by many east coast shore-anglers when cod fishing with heavy tackle amongst kelp beds and rocks.

Multiplier reels for shore and boat fishing are available in a wide range of designs and sizes. They possess the important advantage of providing a rapid rate of line recovery – the line spool being geared so that it revolves several times for every turn of the handle.

A multiplier reel is capable of producing very long casts – up to 150 yards or more in skilled hands. Some practice will be needed, however, before one can hope to achieve even half this distance without risk of tangles, but if the instructions contained in a later chapter of this book are followed carefully the art should be mastered without undue difficulty.

The multiplier is also the most popular type of reel with boat anglers. There are large and powerful models suitable for giant skate, conger and shark, but for general-purpose boat fishing the usual choice is a medium-sized multiplier capable of carrying about 250 yards of 30-lb. breaking-strain line.

The Fixed-Spool reel is another type which is very popular with shore anglers. At first glance it might appear to be a rather complicated piece of engineering, but it is in fact extremely simple to operate.

From the illustration on page 32 it will be seen that in this type of reel the line spool is so positioned that it lies at right angles to the rod-butt. When casting, this spool remains stationary, and the line spills in coils over its rim. Consequently, there are no moving or revolving parts to cause friction, inertia resistance, or line tangles, and this makes the fixed-spool reel particularly suitable for beginners, and for casting with light spinning baits.

One special consideration arises directly from the fact that the line leaves the fixed-spool in coils; for when those coils straighten out as they pass through the rod rings they become transformed into so many twists in the line. This difficulty, however, is automatically overcome by the reel mechanism, which reverses the process by guiding the line back on to the spool in coils when retrieving, so that the line is untwisted as it is wound on to the spool.

Other refinements incorporated in a fixed-spool reel include a geared retrieve to compensate for the small size of the spool; interchangeable spools so that lines of varying breaking-strain can be used for different types of fishing, and an adjustable slipping clutch which automatically yields line to a fish when it exerts a dangerously heavy strain on the line.

It should be stressed that the fixed-spool reel is primarily designed for shore-casting. It lacks the rugged winching power that is so essential when deep-sea bottom fishing, and for this reason its uses when boat fishing are normally limited to light tackle float fishing, and spinning with artificial lures. As previously mentioned, a multiplier reel is the most suitable choice for most other kinds of boat fishing.

The Side-Cast reel looks, at first glance, like an ordinary centrepin reel – except that the reel spool is comparatively shallow and has a dished rim on the side next to the handles. Although not widely used by British sea anglers, it does have its enthusiastic adherents on some parts of the coast, and is therefore worthy of a mention.

When retrieving line with a side-cast reel it functions just like an orthodox centrepin. Immediately prior to casting, however, the line spool is swivelled through 90 degrees, and this allows the line to spill over the rim on the fixed-spool principle. Very long casts can be obtained in this way, but in the process a lot of twists are put into the line as it coils over the rim of the spool.

These twists are not automatically removed during the retrieve, as is the case with the orthodox fixed-spool reel, and consequently the angler must take care to incorporate at least two free-running swivels in his terminal tackle in order to 'iron out' these twists. Failure to take this precaution will result in the line becoming hopelessly kinked and tangled after only a few casts.

The next job is to load the reel with line, and the modern sea angler is very fortunate in having a wide range of excellent synthetic lines at his disposal.

Nylon monofilament line is undoubtedly the most popular choice for shore-casting, light spinning and many types of boat fishing. As its name suggests, it consists of a single filament of nylon, and it is available in a wide range of breaking strains and colours. It is the cheapest type of synthetic line suitable for rod and line use, but its attractive price is not the only reason for its popularity.

Because it possesses a smooth surface, nylon monofilament flows off the reel smoothly when casting, and offers little resistance to waves and fast-flowing tides.

It does have one slight disadvantage, however. When under strain it stretches slightly, and this can make it difficult to drive the hook home when there is a lot of line between the rod-tip and fish.

This elasticity of nylon monofilament also imposes a considerable compressive strain on the reel spool – particularly when a 'stretched' line is wound back on to the spool before it has had time to contract again. In the case of a cheap, badly-designed reel, this may result in the spool bursting or becoming badly distorted.

Because nylon monofilament is smooth and springy, one must be careful when tying knots in this material. Elsewhere in this book you will find details of those knots most commonly used when making up salt-water fishing tackle, and you will be wise to use only these. Unorthodox knots are not only liable to fail under strain; they also create a serious point of weakness in the line itself.

Finally, it is worth mentioning that nylon lines are weakened by prolonged exposure to sunlight, so it is a wise precaution to store reels and spare spools of line well away from sunny windows.

Braided terylene or dacron lines are mainly used for deep-sea boat fishing. They are inert and pleasant to handle, and do not stretch to any noticeable degree under strain. They are therefore very suitable in situations where heavy and powerful fish have to be hooked in deep water. The lack of stretch not only makes it easier to drive the hook into the fish, but also minimises the compressive strain on the reel spool when the fish is being played up to the surface.

The main disadvantage of a braided line is that it is thicker than a nylon monofilament line of equivalent strength, and its surface is not so smooth. Consequently it offers more resistance to moving water, and this can present serious problems when fishing over a deep-water mark where the tidal current is flowing fast.

Twisted nylon line combines strength and cheapness with freedom from rot. It is unsuitable for use as a main reel line because it displays a tendency to come untwisted, but it does make an excellent and very cheap backing line for a large capacity big-game reel. Needless to say, a rot-proof line is essential for this purpose, because once a backing line has been introduced to the water it is liable to remain damp for long periods, owing to lack of ventilation.

Wire line is only used in a very few boat-fishing situations where fast tides, coupled with deep water, make it extremely difficult to hold bottom with ordinary monofilament or braided synthetic lines. By offering far less resistance to deep, fast water, a wire line enables the angler to maintain contact with the bottom without using so much lead that his rod becomes overburdened, and fishing ceases to be a sporting proposition.

Three basic types of wire line are used by sea anglers: monel metal; single-strand stainless steel; and multi-strand stainless steel. The multi-strand type is the easiest to use, being less springy and liable to kink; but at the same time it is the most expensive.

As wire lines do not stretch, the bite of a fish is transmitted to the rod-tip with surprising fierceness, even when fishing in 50 fathoms of water or more. For this reason it is customary to attach a 12-15-foot length of nylon monofilament betweeen the terminal trace and the end of the wire line to act as a 'shock absorber'.

Monel metal wire is best used on a centrepin reel with a large, narrow drum. The Pfleuger 'Pakron' reel is ideal for th. s purpose.

Stainless steel wire, both single and multi-strand, should preferably be used with a *narrow* spool multiplier.

It is also important to make sure the rod rings are robust enough to withstand the wear and tear of a wire line, and it is absolutely essential for the tip ring to be of the roller type.

It must be stressed that wire line can be very dangerous in unskilled hands. If, when boat fishing with a wire line, your tackle becomes snagged on the bottom, NEVER wrap the line around your hand or wrist in an effort to pull it free. A 50-lb. breaking-strain wire line is quite capable of slicing through flesh and bone. Instead, wind two or three turns of line around a gaff handle, and use this to pull your gear free.

The modern fashion in sea angling is to fish as 'light' as possible, using lines and traces with fairly low breaking-strains. The beginner, however, would be well advised to strike a happy medium in this matter, using a line that is neither too light for his limited skill nor too heavy for his rod. This last detail is worth noting. Far too many sea anglers, including many who have been fishing for years, and should know better, use tackle so badly balanced that the rod is the weakest link. Obviously, in the event of a big fish being hooked and becoming unmanageable, it is far better that the hook length or trace should be slightly less strong than the rest of the tackle, so that the encounter merely ends with a lost hook and a short length of snapped nylon, and not with a shattered rod-tip.

This brings us to hooks, traces, snoods, swivels and lead weights. These, when assembled in a variety of ways, are known to anglers as the terminal tackle, or the 'business end'. Hooks may be bought already tied to short nylon snoods, or else may be obtained loose for making up oneself. The second method is a good deal cheaper, and in some ways more satisfactory because one can then control the breaking-strain and length of the snoods.

A good assortment of hooks should be purchased, the range of sizes and patterns being governed by the kinds of fish which frequent the coastline in question. The hook sizes recommended later in this book for various species of fish may be taken as a fairly reliable guide; although variations are bound to occur according to the mood of the fish, local conditions, and the type of bait being used.

Certain kinds of fish, such as conger, have very sharp teeth which would quickly sever a nylon snood, and for this reason they have to be fished for with tackle carrying a length of flexible stainless wire next to the hook. If you are going fishing on a rocky coast where conger abound, you must therefore provide yourself with some strong conger hooks and traces. Practically every kind of sea fishing tackle should incorporate one or more brass swivels to prevent twists and tangles building up in the reel line, and a lead sinker to carry the hooks and baits down through the water to the fish. Elsewhere in this book you will find illustrated a selection of leads which should have a place in every all-round sea angler's tackle-box. The actual weight of the sinkers will depend on local conditions, but as the state of the sea varies considerably from day to day, and even from hour to hour, a fairly wide range should always be carried. For those who wish to economize, it is a simple matter to make most kinds of lead sinkers at home, and some hints on doing this will be found in the chapter entitled: "The Sea Angler's Workshop".

In the same 'do-it-yourself' section will be found hints on making up your own gaff. This item of equipment, consisting of a special gaff hook mounted on a 'broomstick' handle, is used to relieve the tackle of strain when lifting from the water the more bulky kinds of fish, such as skate, conger, ling and rays.

When fishing with light tackle for the smaller and more compact species, some form of landing net will normally be used instead of a gaff. From a lofty pier or harbour wall a drop-net, lowered on the end of the rope, will be found most serviceable; whilst for use at close quarters from a boat or waterside steps it is customary to use a hand-net. Among the latter, those fitted with a folding rust-proofed frame and lightweight handle are worthy of special mention. Shiny metal fittings and brightly coloured netting should be avoided, as these tend to scare fish as they are being guided gently towards the net, and may result in a last-second dash for freedom.

For removing hooks which have been swallowed deep, it is possible to buy very cheaply a special claw-shaped instrument known as a disgorger. However, a pair of long-nosed pliers will prove just as effective, as well as being useful for a number of other angling jobs.

Finally, no list of sea-angling equipment would be complete without mentioning bait-box, catch-bag, knife, bait-cutting board and tackle-box.

The bait-box should be made of wood or plastic – never of metal, which will react with salt water to kill live baits. It should be wide and shallow; and, for preference, fitted with partitions so that different kinds of bait can be kept separate. Sliding partitions, which can be lifted out of the box, are a great help when cleaning the container after use.

A sea angler's bait-knife should have a long, slender blade, and preferably it should also have a notched fish scaler on the back of the blade, and a buoyant balsawood handle. It should be kept well-honed and razor sharp, and reserved for such jobs as bait-cutting and filleting.

A heavy-bladed sheath knife, worn on a waist belt, makes a more suitable weapon for rugged jobs like removing hooks from shark jaws, slicing the wings from rays, and cracking open hermit-crab shells.

The tackle-box should be neat, easy to carry, and fitted with a number of separate compartments to prevent small items from becoming hopelessly jumbled up. For the rock fisherman, who often needs to be something of a mountaineer, a tackle-box is likely to be an encumbrance. A useful alternative is to wear an anorak with a large kangaroo pocket containing a selection of essential tackle spares.

2

Making up the Tackle

Strictly speaking, the term 'fishing tackle' covers all the paraphernalia of angling, from the most expensive rod to the most insignificant split shot. But usually when a fisherman talks about a certain *kind* of tackle he is referring to some special combination of hooks, trace, weights and swivels.

All told, there must be hundreds of these tackle combinations in use around the coasts of Britain today; although basically nearly all of them can be grouped under just a few convenient headings. We will consider them one by one.

The Paternoster. The distinguishing feature of this type of terminal rig lies in the fact that the lead is suspended below the hooks – usually one, two or three in number. Most present-day sea anglers use lightweight paternosters made up from lengths of nylon monofilament (see Fig. 1). The cumbersome brass wire booms and traces described in early sea-fishing books are rarely seen in use nowadays, except for a few forms of deep-sea boat angling.

An important advantage of the paternoster is that it minimises the risk of trace tangles when distance-casting from the shore, due to the fact that the baited hooks trail neatly behind the lead as it zooms seaward.

When shore fishing, a paternoster trace is normally allowed to lie more or less motionless upon the sea-bed. When boat fishing, however, the trace can be suspended on a tight line just above the bottom. Presented thus, with the baited hooks spaced out one above the other, and with boat and trace rising and falling with the motion of the sea, it is possible to fish more than one depth of water.

The leads used with a paternoster will vary according to local tidal or surf conditions, the type of fishing, and the

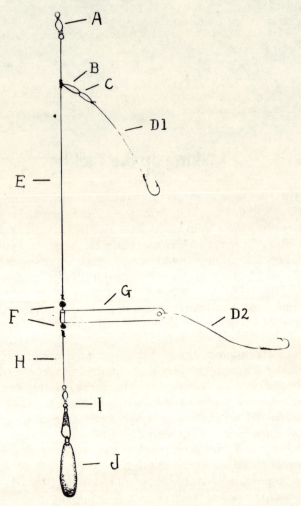

Fig. 1 Light Paternoster, made of Nylon Monofilament.

A: swivel to reel line; B: paternoster blood loop; C: see 'Joining Loop Knots' illustration at end of chapter; D1 and D2: nylon hook droppers (slightly weaker than main trace); E: main trace; F: small plastic beads held in position by blood knots; G: transparent plastic boom; H: nylon lead link (slightly weaker than main trace); I: swivel link; J: lead to suit local sea conditions.

NOTE: (a) The use of a trace boom is optional, but as a general rule booms are more widely used in boat fishing than shore-casting. (b) Do NOT omit swivel link (I) by tying the nylon lead link direct to the lead eye, as the nylon knot will quickly wear through when the tackle is being retrieved over the sea-bed.

Fig. 2 Stand-off booms are sometimes used when making up terminal tackle in order to prevent the trailing hook dropper becoming entangled with the reel line. Pictured here is a modern "Prospector" boom. In this type the hook dropper is threaded through a flexible plastic tube, which can be cut to any length to suit the local fishing conditions. Light and inconspicuous, it is far superior to the old-fashioned and cumbersome wire booms.

strength of the rod. For beach-casting under average conditions, a torpedo or bomb-shaped lead is often used, as the streamlined shape makes for longer and more accurate casts, and reduces the risk of snagging during the retrieve.

On the other hand, a shore angler casting out over a sandy bottom into a strong surf or powerful lateral tide would probably need to use a spiked anchor lead in order to hold bottom and prevent his baited tackle being washed inshore again.

Yet again, when shore-casting over rocky ground, a spoon-shaped lead is usually preferred, as this type tends to plane upwards over obstructions when retrieved rapidly.

In making up the paternoster, and other kinds of tackle, it is most important to use the correct knots, and these are described and illustrated at the end of this chapter.

Running Paternoster. This single-hook shore-casting rig is a favourite of bass fishermen. It differs from an ordinary one-hook paternoster by having the lead suspended from a swivel threaded on the reel line. Thus, when a fish grabs the bait, the resulting pull is transmitted direct to the rod-tip without encountering any resistance from the lead. This makes for a quick strike and positive hooking.

In fact this very popular rig is closely related to the free-running leger, described later in this chapter.

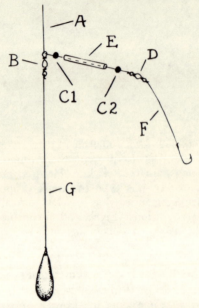

Fig. 3 Running Paternoster.

A: reel line running through eye of swivel B; B: swivel; C1 and C2: plastic "buffer" beads; D: swivel; E: 1¼ in. plastic tube; F: nylon hook link; G: nylon lead link (6)18 inches), slightly weaker than reel line.

Paternoster-trot. In this rig two or three hooks are arranged at intervals along a single flowing trace. It is mainly used by boat and pier anglers when fishing primarily for flatfish, but is useful also for various other species, including codling, whiting and rays. It is not recommended for use in situations where long-distance casting is called for, or where the sea-bed is snaggy.

Free-running Leger. This is normally used in the single-hook version shown here (see Fig. 5), but when boat fishing it is also possible to attach one or two up-trace dropper hooks as used in the *Paternoster-trot*.

When shore-casting with a free-running leger, the lead is usually attached to a swivel-clip threaded on the reel line.

When boat fishing, however, it is more satisfactory to attach the lead to a running Clements boom (see Fig. 64). Besides

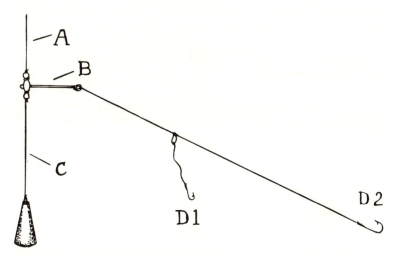

Fig. 4 Paternoster-trot.
A: reel line; B: revolving boom; C: nylon lead link (slightly weaker than reel line); D1 and D2: hooks.

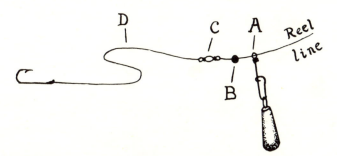

Fig. 5 Free-running Leger.
A: sliding lead attachment clip or Kilmore boom; B: plastic "buffer" bead; C: swivel; D: flowing hook link.

allowing leads to be changed quickly to suit the changing strength of the tide, the use of a Clements boom also helps to prevent the baited hook swinging up and tangling with the reel line when the tackle is being lowered swiftly into deep water.

The great point about a running leger, of course, is that a fish, on sampling the bait, is not deterred by any drag from the lead; and, when it is well and truly 'on', all its fighting power is transmitted direct from the hook to the rod-tip. For this reason it is an excellent form of tackle to use when fishing for suspicious or cautious-biting fish, such as reef bass, conger or rays.

Wessex Leger. In this terminal rig (see Fig. 6) there is one

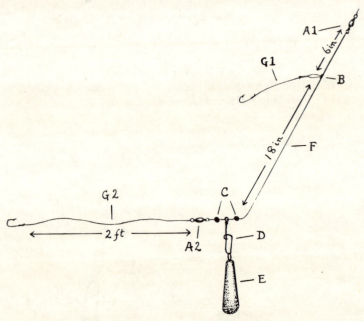

Fig. 6 Wessex Leger.

A1 and A2: swivels; B: paternoster blood loop; C; plastic "buffer" beads; D: sliding lead attachment clip made from stainless steel wire; E: lead to suit local conditions; F: main trace; G1 and G2: hook links (slightly weaker than main trace).

NOTE: The indicated trace measurements may be varied to suit local conditions.

hook on a flowing trace below the sliding lead, and another c
a short dropper above the lead. It thus combines tl.
advantages of the leger set-up with those of a paternoster. It i
a firm favourite with many West Country shore anglers -
particularly when fishing from beaches of mixed shingle anc
rock.

Drift-line Tackle, as its name implies, is allowed to drift
away on the tide from an anchored boat, or (where conditions
permit) from a pier or jetty. The tackle is simplicity itself,
consisting of a small swivel between line and trace, and a
single hook carrying a live or dead bait. The actual nature of
these baits, and their merits, vary according to local
conditions and the species of fish being sought, and this aspect
of drift-lining need not concern us at the moment.

In a strong run of tide some lead will be necessary to take
the bait down to the fish, and the most convenient position for
this is just above the swivel, which is usually about 4 to 6 feet
from the hook. However, when fishing in fairly slack water for
mackerel, bass, garfish and other mid-water or surface-feeding
fish, it is often possible to dispense with the lead altogether.

Of course, it must be borne in mind that the speed of the
tidal flow will vary considerably from hour to hour, requiring
frequent adjustment of the 'ballast'. Consequently, one must
go equipped with a good selection of leads, ranging from small
home-made fold-over leads to 1½ to 2-oz. spirals. In deep
water, or where tides run exceptionally fast, it will be
necessary to use much heavier leads – but always make a point
of using the minimum amount of lead possible, because in this
way you will obtain better catches and more exciting sport.

Needless to say, by adjusting the amount of lead it is also
possible to vary the fishing depth. Drift-line tackle presented

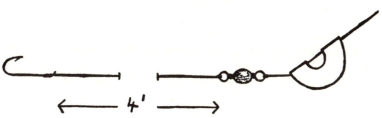

Fig. 7 Drift-line Tackle, with Fold-over Lead Attached.

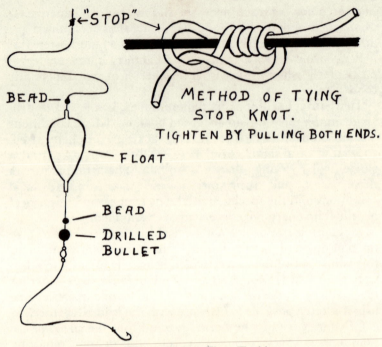

Fig. 8 Sliding Float Tackle.

The float is threaded on the reel line, and the fishing depth determined by the stop knot, which can be slid to any required position. In the inset, showing the method of tying the stop knot, the solid black line represents the reel line. The stop knot is tied with a few inches of thin nylon monofilament.

close to the sea-bed, or alongside a sunken wreck, is likely to produce pollack, sea bream and various other species which normally feed near the bottom; but the method is also very rewarding when a sandeel bait is fished in mid-water for shoaling bass and mackerel.

Float Tackle. Sometimes when sea angling it is necessary to keep the hook suspended in the water at a predetermined depth whilst at the same time allowing it to drift away from the spot where one is fishing. It is then that float tackle is brought into use, and Fig. 8 shows how it should be made up. When fishing at a depth greater than the length of the rod it is essential to use a sliding float, so that it shall not jam against

Shore-casting multiplier
reel.

Fixed-spool reel.

Cutaway view of a
fixed-spool reel.

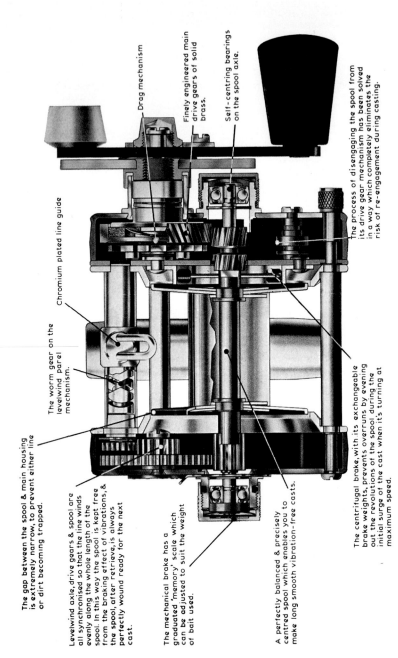

Drag mechanism

Finely engineered main drive gears of solid brass.

Self-centring bearings on the spool axle.

Chromium plated line guide

The worm gear on the levelwind panel mechanism.

The gap between the spool & main housing is extremely narrow, to prevent either line or dirt becoming trapped.

Levelwind axle, drive gears & spool are all synchronised so that the line winds evenly along the whole length of the spool. In this way the spool is kept free from the braking effect of vibrations, & the spool, after retrieve, is always perfectly wound ready for the next cast.

The mechanical brake has a graduated 'memory' scale which can be adjusted to suit the weight of bait used.

A perfectly balanced & precisely centred spool which enables you to make long smooth vibration-free casts.

The centrifugal brake, with its exchangeable brake weights, prevents overruns by evening out the revolutions of the spool during the initial surge of the cast when it's turning at maximum speed.

The process of disengaging the spool from its drive gear mechanism has been solved in a way which completely eliminates the risk of re-engagement during casting.

Inside view of a precision-built ABU casting multiplier reel.

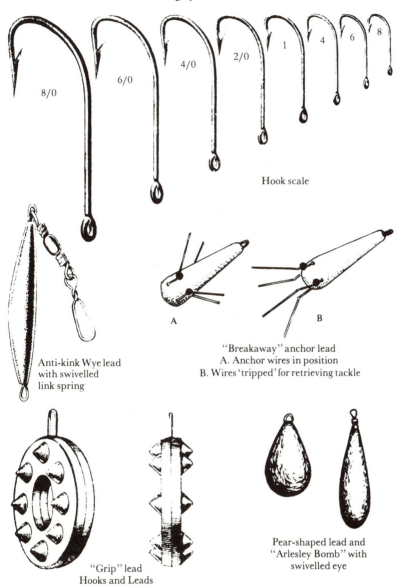

Hook scale

Anti-kink Wye lead
with swivelled
link spring

"Breakaway" anchor lead
A. Anchor wires in position
B. Wires 'tripped' for retrieving tackle

Pear-shaped lead and
"Arlesley Bomb" with
swivelled eye

"Grip" lead
Hooks and Leads

Fig. 9 Hooks and Leads: Hook scale; anti-kink lead with swivelled link spring; "Breakaway" anchor lead – A: anchor wires in position; B: wires 'tripped' for retrieving tackle; "Grip" lead; pear-shaped lead and "Arlesley Bomb" with swivelled eye.

the end-ring of the rod when reeling in.

The size and design of float will depend partly on the distance you need to cast, and partly on the amount of lead needed to get the bait down against the tide. Thus a medium cigar-shaped balsa float is usually a good choice for the open sea; whilst a small cork-bodied Avon-type float may prove preferable in a sheltered harbour or estuary.

Never use a float that is larger than is absolutely necessary. If a float is too large, or incorporates an unnecessary degree of buoyancy, it will present too much resistance to a taking fish, and is likely to arouse its suspicions so that it rejects the bait before the hook can be driven home. The amount of lead used should be just sufficient to cock the float nicely into the upright position.

For fishing at dusk, or on dull days, it is often a great help to use a float tipped with fluorescent orange paint. These floats may be obtained ready for use; or, alternatively, by obtaining a small bottle of the special paint from a tackle stockist it is possible to give a collection of ordinary floats the necessary treatment. However, there is one point you should remember. In order to obtain best results with fluorescent paint, it must be applied over an undercoat of white paint.

Spinning and Trolling Tackle. The art of spinning consists of drawing a baited or lure-decorated hook through the water in the hope that it will be attacked by a predatory fish. This means that the tackle must either be cast out repeatedly from some convenient vantage point, and then reeled in again; or else it must be towed behind a boat propelled by oars, motor or sail. This second method is generally referred to as 'trolling'. The term 'spinning' is reserved for the 'cast and retrieve' method, be it carried on from a beach or rock position, or from a *drifting* boat.

Although there are literally hundreds of artificial lures which may be used effectively for spin-casting from the shore or a drifting dinghy, the majority used by sea anglers fall into the following categories:

1. **Wobbling Spoons.** Shiny metal spoons which have an erratic wobbling or undulating action when retrieved through the water;
2. **Bar Spoons.** In this type of lure a light shiny or painted

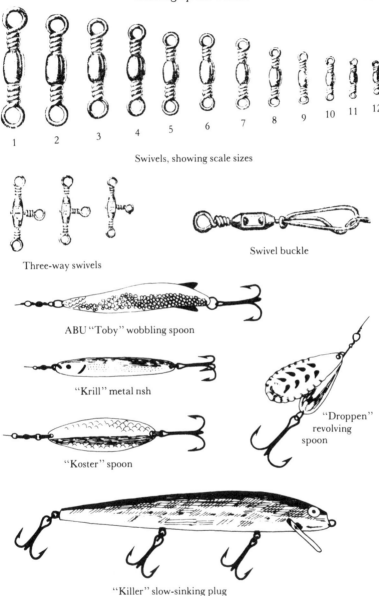

1 2 3 4 5 6 7 8 9 10 11 12

Swivels, showing scale sizes

Three-way swivels

Swivel buckle

ABU "Toby" wobbling spoon

"Krill" metal fish

"Droppen" revolving spoon

"Koster" spoon

"Killer" slow-sinking plug

Fig. 10 Swivels and Lures: swivels, showing scale sizes; swivel buckle; ABU "Toby" wobbling spoon; "Krill" metal fish; "Koster" spoon; "Dropper" revolving spoon; "Killer" slow-sinking plug.

metal blade revolves around a weighted central bar made of brass or lead. In a well-designed lure the blade starts to revolve at a surprisingly slow retrieve rate, and this makes it ideal when retrieving with a tidal current;

3. **Pirks.** Heavy metal lures, usually made of chromed brass, with little built-in action. Instead, the angler gives them a tempting appearance in the water by jerking the rod-tip, varying the rate of retrieve, etc. Also, this type of lure usually has numerous facets which reflect attractive glimmers of light, and these seem to arouse the predatory instincts of many fish. Available in various sizes, the smaller pirks lend themselves well to shore-casting (especially in windy conditions). Large pirks, weighing 7 oz. or more, are mostly used with a simple jigging or 'sink and draw' action from a boat, and are particularly effective against cod.

4. **Plastic sandeels.** Available in several designs, these very lifelike imitation sandeels are deadly for many species of salt-water fish, including bass, pollack, coalfish, mackerel – and even sea-trout in some areas. They are primarily designed for trolling, but with some up-trace lead they can also be used when spinning from the shore or a drifting boat. In areas where tides run fast they can also be worked sink and draw from an anchored boat in a drift-line fashion.

Equipped with a selection of the above lures, it is possible for the salt-water spinning enthusiast to enjoy good sport under most suitable conditions.

For shore spinning it is usually preferable to use self-weighted lures which require no additional up-trace lead. Not only can these be cast more easily, but when doing so there is less risk of the lure becoming entangled with the trace or reel line. Lures which merely wobble (like the ABU 'Toby' spoon in Fig. 10) can be attached direct to a small swivel-link on the end of the reel line; but those which spin in the water may need the use of an anti-kink vane or lead in order to prevent twists from being transmitted up the line.

The amount of lead used when trolling depends on the speed of the boat, the depth at which the lure is to be fished, and the thickness and submerged length of the line. Leads of the spiral Jardine pattern (see Fig. 11B) are well suited for this purpose, partly because they can be changed quickly, and partly because their streamlined shape reduces water disturbance to a minimum.

Natural baits for spinning can sometimes be mounted on an ordinary hook; but when the bait is a small dead fish the task may be simplified, and the results improved, by the use of a special spinning flight. A good pattern consists of a swivelled spike which is thrust through the body of the bait, and is then held in position by two or three triangle hooks.

The actual technique of spinning will be described later in this book when discussing the various species of fish which may be caught with this kind of tackle.

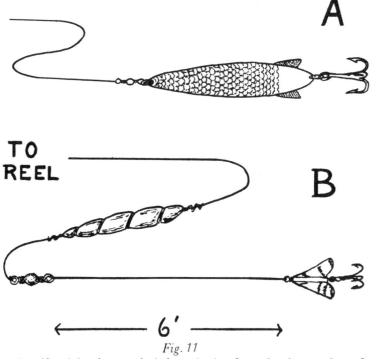

Fig. 11

A: self-weighted spoon-bait for spinning from the shore or boat. It is made of shiny metal and is attached direct to the reel line.

B: trolling trace for use from moving boat, with mackerel spinner, swivel and large Jardine lead. (Note: the lead will act as an anti-kink device if bent slightly between fingers and thumb.)

KNOTS

Before considering the various knots which may be used when making up tackle, it might perhaps be advisable to devote a few paragraphs to the special problems which crop up when tying knots in light modern lines. Many anglers, both novices and old hands, labour under the misapprehension that the only requisite of a knot is that it shall not become loose, or draw apart, when subjected to strain. They fail to appreciate the fact that the very act of knotting a line reduces its breaking-strain, and that quite often the firmest knots are, in fact, the weakest ones when considered from this second point of view.

As every angler discovers when he handles it for the first time, nylon monofilament line is tricky stuff to knot. It is slippery and somewhat springy, which increases the risk of carelessly-tied knots drawing apart under strain. There is, however, an added danger which is not so widely appreciated. When nylon is subjected to strain it stretches, and this naturally results in the line becoming thinner. When the strain is released the nylon contracts and becomes thicker again – resulting in a permanent 'nipping' action wherever the line is gripped tightly by the coils of a knot. Deformation of this sort is, to a certain extent, essential if a nylon knot is to be secure; but any knot which incorporates an exceptional and unnecessary degree of nip is a bad one, especially if it also causes a very sharp bend in the line.

Some anglers misguidedly use the single-turn overhand stop knot to fix the position of plastic beads or drilled bullets. Yet this is one of the worst knots it is possible to use; for when drawn tight it is capable of reducing the breaking strain of nylon monofilament by more than half. If a bead or drilled bullet has to be fixed, it is much better to do so with a blood

Fig. 12 Capable of reducing the strength of a fishing line by as much as 50 per cent, the Single-turn Overhand Stop Knot should be avoided at all costs.

knot (see Fig. 13), or with a couple of split shot. Even then, however, care must be taken to avoid nipping the line too fiercely when squeezing on the shot.

Remember, too, that overhand knots sometimes find their way into lines accidentally when tackling up. Often these knots are noticed only after the trace, hooks and baits have been attached, and then the temptation to tighten the loop and forget all about it can be very great. It is a temptation which should be resisted at all costs, however, if one is to avoid the disappointment of that 'big one that got away'.

The truth is that the knots which may safely be used with modern synthetic lines are strictly limited in number; although fortunately there is one for every purpose. Most are variations of the blood knot, which has long been the angler's favourite medium for joining two lengths of line together. In the form of a 'half' blood knot, however, it can also be used to connect a trace to an eyed hook, swivel, etc; and, in a few modified versions, to a hook shank.

Blood knots tied by the amateur generally include two or three turns, or twists, in each half (see Figs. 13 and 14). Although I cannot vouch for the accuracy of my non-scientific observations, it has always appeared to me that the three-turn blood knot, by 'spreading the load' of the coils over a wider area, causes less distortion to the line than the two-turn tuck-in knot. However, under rough boat-angling conditions, when one's fingers are cold and wet, and slimy with bait, tying a three-turn blood knot (containing six turns in all) can be a time-wasting business. That is why, in selecting the following knots, I have chosen both the standard three-turn version, and one very simple two-loop knot.

The Three-Turn Blood Knot. This is an excellent joining knot for lines of approximately similar diameter. It is free of sharp turns, and provides approximately 80 per cent strength. It is also widely used as a paternoster hook-dropper knot by leaving one of the free ends long. When used for this purpose the dropper has the advantage of jutting out from the trace at right angles.

The Two-Turn Tuck-in Blood Knot. A very easy knot to tie, because after the first half has been completed it can be pulled tight, thus allowing all one's attention to be devoted to making the second half.

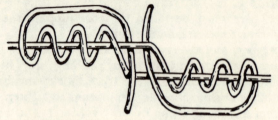

Fig. 13 Three-turn Cruciform Blood Knot.

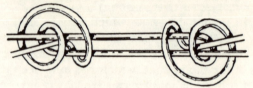

Fig. 14 Two-turn Tuck-in Blood Knot.

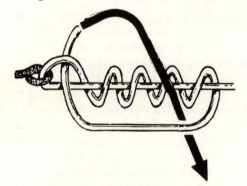

Fig. 15 Half-blood Clinch Knot.

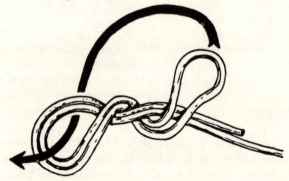

Fig. 16 Blood Loop Knot.

The Half-Blood Clinch Knot. A very strong knot, which may be used for attaching a line to any eyed item of tackle.

The Blood Loop Knot. A non-slip loop knot that is approximately 10 per cent stronger than the more widely used double-overhand loop knot (see Fig. 16).

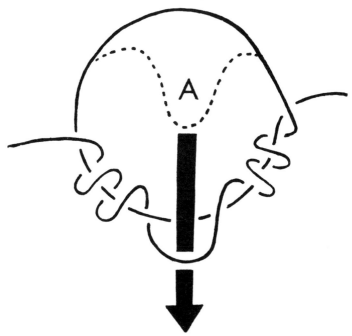

Fig. 17 (top) The solid black line represents the first stage in tying the Paternoster Blood Loop. To complete the knot the untwisted part of the line is pulled downwards to form the dotted bight A, and then taken through the gap in the coils.

(*bottom*) The completed Paternoster Blood Loop, after the knot has been drawn tight.

The Paternoster Blood Loop. A remarkably strong and neat-looking knot when completed, it is useful for making the looped dropper attachments on nylon monofilament paternosters – especially those which are to be used for beach fishing (see Fig. 17).

Joining Loop Knots. By joining loop knots in the manner shown in Fig. 18 it is possible to make changes in terminal tackle very quickly without tying or untying any knots.

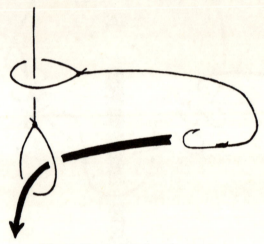

Fig. 18 How to join loop knots.

3

Baits

At the height of the holiday season it is often impossible for bait dealers in popular seaside resorts to cope with the heavy demands of visiting fishermen; whilst in the quieter haunts – the secluded coves, remote longshore villages, and small half-forgotten harbours – bait dealers are usually non-existent. Consequently there are occasions when every sea angler is obliged to fend for himself when requiring something to put on his hooks.

Bait can be gathered on practically any stretch of shoreline if one knows where to look for it. Rocks and rockpools produce mussels, prawns and soft crabs, with any number of other more or less anonymous creatures thrown in for good measure – weird little 'monsters' of the shallows, seldom mentioned in fishing books, but useful as baits nevertheless.

Even on a shingle beach it is not impossible to obtain a supply of bait; although this type of shoreline is certainly the least rewarding. In summer and early autumn the angler equipped with a shore-casting outfit and a set of mackerel feathers – or, better still, with a light spinning outfit – will often be able to provide himself with a supply of fresh mackerel for bait.

Another method which sometimes pays off is to allow the gulls to do all the work. As soon as you see several alight on the pebbles and start squabbling, hurry to the spot and the chances are that you will find a recently-stranded cuttlefish waiting to be popped into the bait-box. On long open stretches of beach the debris from recent seine-netting operations may also prove to be a source of free bait, the most common spoils being horse mackerel, cuttlefish, garfish and whitebait.

It is worth remembering that every sort of bait has a special appeal for some species of fish. For this reason, the angler who uses a wide variety of the baits listed below is far more likely to meet with success as an *all-round* sea angler than the person who is more conservative in this matter.

Incidentally, although the point has been mentioned in a previous chapter, it might be as well to stress once more that a wooden or plastic receptacle should be used when gathering any kind of sea bait. This is because the action of salt water on many metals has an injurious effect on live sea creatures, and taints the flesh of dead baits.

A. WORM BAITS

Lugworms. This bait owes its popularity to the fact that it appeals to a wide variety of bottom-feeding fish, and even to a a few mid-water species. The worms vary locally in size, colour and toughness – the most highly prized being the large black variety.

The lugworm obtains nourishment by burrowing in tidal stretches of sand or muddy sand, its presence being indicated by shallow depressions in the sand known as 'blowholes', and by spiral coils of sandy excrement called 'casts'.

On most lug grounds the worms are fairly easily obtained by digging in the vicinity of these tell-tale marks with a garden fork or spade. Where the worms are reasonably near the surface a fork is the better tool for the job because it is less likely to injure the worms.

There is also another large type of lugworm which burrows straight down to a depth of 2 feet or more into the sand. On some parts of the coast professional diggers use a special spade when digging for these deep-burrowing lug. It is similar to a farmer's trenching spade, with a long, narrow, tapering blade.

Worms damaged during the digging process should be kept apart from the sound ones, and when sufficient have been gathered a small quantity of damp sand should be placed in each partition of the bait-box to help keep the occupants alive. When fishing on a hot day the bait-box should be kept in a shady spot if possible, and on no account should the worms be subjected to direct sunshine or rain.

Lugworms can be kept alive for about three days if laid out between sheets of clean newspaper. Change the newspaper at the end of the first day.

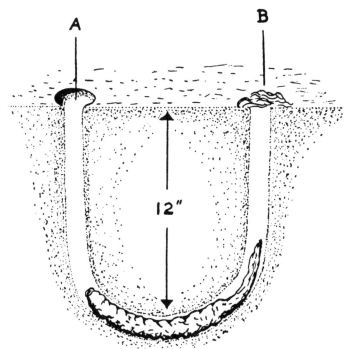

Fig. 19 The Lugworm "at home".
To dig it out, the spade or fork is thrust into the sand between and alongside the pit, A, and the cast, B. Normally it is necessary to go two spits deep, the first forkfuls being cast aside quickly, and the second attack made in a slightly slantwise direction to take the fork underneath the worm.

Black lugworms are best preserved by nipping off the head and squeezing out the innards by running the body through the fingers from tail to head. They can then be stored for several days in a refrigerator, or for several months if packed in sealed polythene bags and placed in the deep-freezer.

It should be stressed that only *black* lugworm can be stored in this way. The smaller, softer varieties of red or 'blow' lug do not take at all kindly to deep-freezing. As soon as they are thawed out they become a horrible gooey mess that is completely useless as a hook bait.

Ragworms. Several species of ragworm are used as salt-water baits, ranging from tiny red harbour ragworm measuring only 2-3 inches in length, to the large king ragworm which often measures about 8 inches – and occasionally attains double that length. All these worms possess a somewhat compressed, segmented body, with a fringe of centipede-like legs along either side. The largest species are most commonly obtained by digging with a fork on estuary shores which consist of mixed mud and gravel. The small harbour ragworm, on the other hand, is more likely to be encountered in the bottom mud of tidal harbours and estuary creeks.

Boulder-turning is another way of gathering sizeable, brightly-coloured ragworm, and on a suitable stretch of shore a good supply of bait can be obtained in a short space of time by this method. Flattish rocks resting on a close-packed mixture of mud and shingle are the ones which produce best results. Each boulder should be flung over as quickly as possible, so that any worms resting underneath may be grabbed before they have a chance to wriggle into the mud. Afterwards the

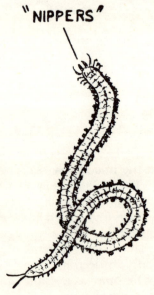

Fig. 20 Ragworm, showing the hooked nippers which have to be avoided when baitingup.

boulder should be replaced in its original bed.

As most novice bait-hunters discover sooner rather than later, the ragworm is armed with a pair of hooked nippers which are capable of inflicting a mild prick. To avoid this happening, the worm should be held firmly behind the head when baiting up.

To bait up with a large or medium-sized ragworm, the hook point should be inserted into the worm's mouth; after which the worm is threaded carefully around the bend of the hook and up the shank before bringing it out again well down the body to leave an inch or two of the tail hanging free.

In two ways ragworm are preferable to lugworm. They are cleaner to handle and easier to keep alive. When stored in a *clean* bait-box, among sacking which has been rinsed in sea-water, a supply of ragworm will remain active for a week or more. A regular check should be made on the contents of the box, however, and if any dead or ailing worms are noticed they should be removed at once.

B. MOLLUSC BAITS

Mussels. This familiar bluish-black shellfish, shaped somewhat like the kernel of a large Brazil nut, is a popular salt-water bait for many kinds of bottom-feeding fish, including cod, whiting, plaice and flounders. Mussels are easily gathered at low tide on those coasts where they are to be found clinging in large colonies to the base of harbour walls, pier stanchions, mooring hawsers and among the low-water rocks and large pebbles bordering sheltered sea lochs and tidal estuaries.

Mussel is a soft bait, with a tendency to fly off the hook when casting out from the shore. To overcome this problem it is essential to prepare the bait correctly before placing it on the hook.

Anyone armed with a stout knife can prise open these shellfish, but a certain degree of skill is also required if the meat inside is going to be fit for use after the job is finished.

A simple and efficient method is as follows. Hold the mussel in your left hand between forefinger and thumb, with that part of the shell which is normally anchored to the rocks or harbour piles facing towards you. Where the byssus, or 'anchor threads', protrude from the shell there is a slight gap

(A in the diagram, Fig. 21), and after scraping the growth away with the knife it is easy enough to insert the tip of the blade at this point.

Many sea anglers have their own favourite tool for opening mussels, and mine is an old table knife with the blade broken off to about half its original length. The tip of this stub blade is curved slightly (to fit the inside of the mussel shell), and sharpened to a chisel edge on a grindstone.

Having selected your weapon, first of all run the cutting edge of the blade down and around the blunt end of the shell (B), taking care to slant the blade upwards at the same time so that the cutting edge scrapes along the inside of the shell. Then reverse the blade and slide it in similar fashion towards the pointed end (C).

The knife should not be thrust in too deeply, except near the rounded extremity, where it is necessary for the blade to sever the adductor muscle (D) which keeps the shell closed tight. As soon as this has been cut the two halves of the shell will open easily, as though on a hinge, revealing the lobes of mussel flesh reposing in the lower half.

Close inspection will show the severed muscle (I'm sorry about all these mussels and muscles – they can't be avoided!) embedded in the mussel's flesh as a small white disc of gristle. Using the end of the knife-blade like a chisel, separate the disc of muscle from the lower half of the shell and then carefully scoop out the flesh in one piece.

Baiting up with mussel is largely a matter of threading the hook through the firmer sections of the shellfish's anatomy. It is important to use a fine-wire hook, and one should begin by inserting the point of the hook into the dark-coloured 'tongue' of the mussel – variously known on some parts of the coast as the 'beak', 'nose' or 'neb'. Bring the hook-point out through the thick hinged part joining the two fleshy lobes; then twist the hook and take it back through both lobes, and finally through the disc of tough muscle.

It is customary to use about three or four mussels on each hook, threaded one above the other on the hook shank. This results in a decent-sized mouthful for a hungry cod or bass, but for whiting and flatfish it is possible to use a slightly smaller offering.

One useful tip – shelling your mussels a few hours before

A well-stocked tackle box incorporating three cantilevered trays for hooks, swivels and other sundries.

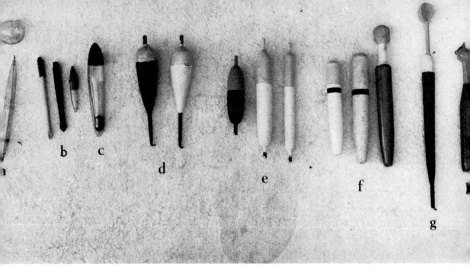

b   c

d

e

f

g

A selection of floats used for sea-angling: a—transparent plastic bubble floats fitted with water inlet plugs to allow adjustment of their buoyancy; b—small plastic floats for harbour mullet; c—self-cocking plastic float; d—cork-bodied sliding floats; e—expanded polystyrene sliders; f—home-made balsa wood sliders; g—home-made balsa slider with fluorescent antenna for maximum visibility in choppy water; h—self-cocking balsa "ninepin" float for surface-feeding mullet, garfish, mackerel etc.

Three useful items of equipment for the boat angler—a graph-type echo-sounder; a liquid-filled handbearing compass, and Admiralty chart.

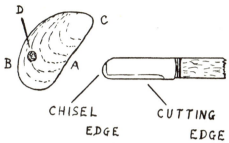

Fig. 21 Knife for opening mussels. (For explanation of symbols, see accompanying text.)

you actually need to use them, and exposing them to the wind and sun, will help to make the flesh firmer, and the baits easier to mount on a hook. Nevertheless, in rough sea conditions it may be advisable to tie the bait on with soft wool, and some anglers declare that red or orange-coloured wool used in this way adds interest to the bait.

Razorfish. These burrowing bivalves, with their long and slender shells shaped like an old-fashioned 'cut-throat' razor, make an excellent bait for bass, plaice and many other kinds of bottom-feeding sea fish. They are to be found along the lower spring tide limits of flat sandy beaches, where they live in vertical burrows which often descend for 2 feet or more below the surface.

When one of these burrows is approached at low tide, its occupant is likely to reveal its presence by sending up a spurt of water from a keyhole-shaped blowhole as it hurriedly retreats deeper into its lair.

Skilled bait-hunters are able to catch razorfish by thrusting a small spear-shaped implement down the shaft of the burrow. When the head of the spear encounters the shellfish it closes its shell hurriedly, trapping the head of the spear so that the bait can be drawn up to the surface.

An easier method, recommended for the novice, is to arm oneself with a packet of salt, a large plastic bottle full of sea water, and a spade. Treading softly, approach the keyhole-shaped entrance to the razorfish's burrow; tip in a small quantity of salt, and wash it down the hole with a few squirts of water. Very soon the razorfish will come to the surface.

With a quick slantwise thrust of the spade you can then cut off the retreat of your quarry, and pop it into the bait-box.

Clams also live in burrows, mostly in muddy sand near the mouth of an estuary. However, unlike razorfish they are found fairly near the surface – rarely deeper than 12 inches – and can be dug out with only a moderate expenditure of effort. Their position beneath the sand can be pinpointed by the *round* blowhole.

Clams make a first-class bait for bass. One favourite method of baiting up is to pull off the clam's siphon tube so that a quantity of the succulent flesh is left adhering to it. The siphon is then threaded up the shank of a fine-wire hook. The remainder of the clam meat can be chopped up and used to groundbait the swim when fishing an estuary channel.

Cockles. These familiar bivalve molluscs make an excellent bait for plaice, dabs, whiting, codling and wrasse. They bury themselves just below the surface in areas of sand or mixed sand and mud, and the bait-hunter is most likely to encounter them along the low-tide line in estuaries, or in sheltered sandy bays and inlets where there is not much wave action.

Although hidden below the surface, their presence is often betrayed to the practised eye by a slight humping of the sand, or by the two tiny blowholes made by the siphons through which the cockle breathes and feeds.

As a rule cockles are scratched up with the aid of a garden rake or draw hoe. To open the shells prior to baiting up, place the shellfish on a bait board or similar firm surface, and insert the tip of a stub-bladed knife between the two halves of the shell. Then work the blade downwards towards the hinged section of the shell. The mussel knife illustrated in Fig. 21 serves admirably for this purpose, and the chisel-end of the blade can then be used to scoop the flesh out of the shell.

Slipper Limpets normally live in shallow water beyond the low water mark, but on some parts of the coast it is not unusual for quantities of them to get washed ashore during onshore gales. The time to look for them is the morning after a strong blow. Pay special attention to the line of seaweed and other debris that forms the high water mark.

Slipper limpets are gregarious creatures, and more often than not you will find several clinging together. These clusters of slipper limpets are often referred to as 'chains'.

If stored in a clean hessian sack that is kept well soaked in sea water, your slipper limpets will remain alive for a week or more. Alternatively, if you wish to keep this bait for longer periods, the limpets can be shelled and placed in an airtight polythene bag for storage in a deep-freezer.

To remove these molluscs from their shells, you can again use the mussel skeining knife illustrated in Fig. 21. This is done by loosening the foot of the limpet from all adjoining surfaces of the shell. Then, lifting the foot with the knife blade, grip it with the fingers and pull it towards the rounded end of the shell.

Use a fine-wire hook, and mount the bait by threading the hook first of all through the softer parts before finally thrusting the point through the tough foot.

When fishing for smallish fish, such as flounders or whiting, your offering could consist of two or three slipper limpets on a long-shanked 2/0 Aberdeen hook. Larger fish, however, (notably cod and bass) are more likely to appreciate five or six on a size 5/0.

Squid and Cuttlefish. These highly specialized molluscs, together with the related octopus, belong to that class of marine creatures known as *Cephalopoda*. They are frequently caught in the nets of seiners and trawlers, and can often be purchased at the quayside when the boats return to harbour.

They make excellent baits – squid being the better of the two – and are particularly useful when shore fishing because the flesh is tough and stays on the hook well when casting.

Another important advantage of squid is that it stores well in a deep-freezer. Indeed, one of the most attractive baits of all is the small Californian squid, which is imported frozen into Britain – primarily for human consumption.

In some areas squid and cuttle can be caught by boat anglers when using a small live fish as bait. The squid do not become properly hooked, but sink their parrot-like beaks into the neck of the bait fish, rather like a ferret attacking a rabbit.

As the squid is reeled gently towards the surface a landing net must be slid quickly underneath it before it has a chance to release its grip. Net and squid should then be slapped around on the surface until the squid has discharged all its sepia. This is an unpleasant inky fluid that the squid uses as a sort of smokescreen in moments of danger or stress.

Squid can be presented on the hook in various ways. Small Californian squid are often mounted whole on a large hook, and provide an excellent bait for large bass, cod and conger. The head of a larger squid can be used in much the same way.

Squid tentacles, or sections thereof, are also a first-class offering for many smaller species – notably black bream.

The white flesh of the squid's body makes an attractive bait when cut into strips, and due to its pale colour and distinctive smell, which carries for long distances in underwater currents, is particularly useful when night fishing.

Common Limpets. On rocky coasts one does not have to search far for the ubiquitous limpet. Often despised as bait, the fact remains that in some localities it proves quite effective – particularly for sea bream and wrasse – and has the merit of being within reach as a rule at almost any state of the tide except high water.

To remove a limpet from a rock, take it by surprise, as it were, with a sharp sideways blow with a flat stone. Small limpets can be prised off the rocks with a strong knife blade, and these may be used whole upon the hook. In the case of larger ones, however, only the soft entrails which lie under the apex of the shell should be used, together with a small portion of the tough foot to help keep the bait on the hook.

Garden Snails. When nothing better is available, the ordinary garden snail can be used when fishing for pouting, wrasse and bream. Pouting are particularly fond of them, but for the other two species mentioned it sometimes helps to anoint the snails with pilchard oil.

C. CRUSTACEAN BAITS

Crabs. Many different species of crab are found in British waters, and the flesh of most of them is very attractive to fish. Unfortunately, because of its hard shell, a crab does not normally lend itself readily to mounting on a hook; whilst the flesh of a crushed crab is so flaky that it is fit only for use as groundbait.

However, during the course of its passage from infancy to old age a crab sheds its shell many times, growing a new and larger suit of armour on each occasion. The sea angler who searches assiduously at low water along a sheltered shoreline of mixed rock and weed is likely to discover a fair proportion of shore crabs which are actually engaged in this moulting process, and these are invaluable as hook bait. Usually they are to be found on the lower half of the littoral zone, hidden away in rocky crannies, under large clumps of trailing bladderwrack, or partly buried in soft mud.

A crab which is still wearing its old shell, but is preparing to shed it in the near future, is commonly referred to as a 'peeler'. The shell of a peeler usually has a dull, somewhat chalky appearance, and when disturbed the creature tends to remain cowering in its hiding place, instead of adopting an aggressive attitude, or scuttling rapidly away – as usually happens in the case of a normal hardbacked crab.

Incidentally, you will quite frequently come across a large crab carrying a somewhat smaller one beneath its abdomen. This is a preliminary to mating, and the large crab will always be a hardbacked male, and the other either a peeler or soft female.

When in doubt as to whether or not a crab is a peeler or hardback, the matter can be put to the test by pressing your thumb-nail against the side of the carapace. If the crab is a peeler there should be a slight movement or separation where the back of the carapace overlaps the lower half of the shell.

To use a peeler crab as bait, coax off the old shell to reveal the soft but firm body underneath, and kill the crab by piercing the abdomen with a small penknife blade. Then remove the claws. Whether or not you also remove the legs is largely a matter of personal opinion, but my own view is that a few legs waving around in the underwater currents helps to make the bait appear more lifelike to an interested fish.

Rather less frequently, the bait-hunter will also come upon crabs which have already shed their shells but have yet to acquire their new protective covering. These 'soft crabs', as they are called, may be used in the same manner as shelled peelers – which, of course, is precisely what they are.

Small or medium-sized crabs are best mounted whole on a round-bend hook, but large crabs can be cut in half before baiting up. To prevent the bait flicking off when casting, it should be attached to the hook with several turns of elasticated crimping thread.

Peeler and soft crabs are most common during late spring, but they remain reasonably abundant throughout the summer months and early autumn.

Hardbacked Crabs. As previously mentioned, hardbacked shore crabs are seldom used for general shore or boat fishing. However, they do have one important specialised use – and that is for wrasse fishing.

A large wrasse will quickly gobble up any small to medium-sized shore crab – and it doesn't matter at all whether the crab happens to be a softback or hardback!

Normally, when fishing from a rock position for wrasse, the bait only needs to be lobbed out about 5 to 10 yards, so baiting up is no great problem. One method is to thread the crab on to the hook shank and nylon dropper with the aid of a baiting needle.

Prawns. These small crustaceans are found among rock pools, and also in somewhat deeper water immediately off

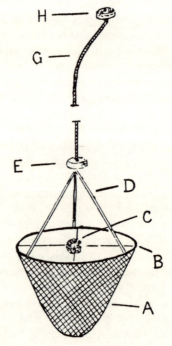

Fig. 22 Drop-net. (For explanation of symbols, see text.)

rocky coasts. As a livebait they are much esteemed by bass and pollack fishermen, as well as being useful for many other fish. Prawns also form an attractive bait when dead and – for preference – uncooked.

It is worth noting that the prawn is one of the few sea baits which can be caught on the fishing ground itself while angling operations are actually in progress. The tackle required for this job is a drop-net, like the one depicted in Fig. 22. Under normal conditions, off a suitable stretch of coast, one net will catch sufficient prawns to keep two or three dinghy anglers constantly supplied. Where tides are strong, however, it is better to net the prawns prior to the fishing trip, either in rock pools along the low water mark, or among seaweedy inshore reefs sheltered from wave action and currents.

A drop-net is very simple to make. The netting (A), which should have a $\frac{1}{4}$-inch mesh, is lashed to a metal hoop (B), or old bicycle wheel rim, so that it hangs down to form a deep, pouch-shaped bag.

Across the metal hoop two lengths of twine are stretched at right angles, and to these the bait (C) is tied.

The rope (G), with its cork floats (E and H), is attached to the metal hoop by a bridle consisting of three short lengths of codline (D), arranged so that the net hangs mouth upwards when lowered into the water.

Cork E helps to keep the bridle lines clear of the bait. Cork H supports the rope G, which should be considerably longer than the maximum depth of water, and it is not drawn to scale in the illustration. The corks are kept in place by stop knots, tied in the rope on either side of them.

Now for the method of baiting the net. Practically any 'over-ripe' animal matter will arouse a prawn's interest; fish offal, butcher's scraps, or – best of all – a piece of kipper. It is incorrect to tie the bait inside the bottom of the net, because many prawns will then feed happily through the mesh without entering the net.

When baited, the net is lowered into the water and allowed to remain on the bottom for a minute or two. If bottom fishing is being carried on from a boat at the same time, the bait in the net will also serve as groundbait.

Hauling in should be done as swiftly as possible, hand over hand without any fumbling. Those prawns which have been caught will be found leaping about in the bottom of the net – possibly with a lobster or edible crab for good measure. It is hardly necessary to mention that shaking hands with either of these last two creatures can be a painful business, so pick them up carefully by grasping them across the carapace, immediately behind the claws.

To present a live prawn to the fish in as natural a manner as possible, the hook should be passed through the second joint from the tail. Dead prawns may be placed on the hook head first, and the point brought out lower down the body, among the legs.

Hermit Crabs. Quite often in certain localities hermit crabs are brought to the surface in the drop-net when collecting prawns. (*q.v.*). Somewhat resembling a baby lobster, the hermit crab lives in untenanted whelk shells, moving into a larger residence from time to time to meet the requirements of its growing body. It can be evicted by cracking open (not smashing) the upper spiral whorls of the shell. This is best done by laying the shell on its side on the bait board, and then hitting it firmly with the *back* edge of a heavy-bladed knife.

When baiting up for medium-sized fish, such as flatfish and whiting, it is customary to use the tail section of the crab with just a small portion of its shell-covered thorax attached. This offering should be threaded on a round-bend fine-wire hook – the hook point being thrust first of all into the severed end.

For larger fish, including bass, cod and rays, you can use a whole hermit crab, with just the legs and claws removed.

Whelks make an excellent bait for cod, haddock, dogfish, sea bream and various other fish. They live on sandy areas of sea-bed some distance out to sea, so cannot normally be gathered by the sea angler himself. However, they can often be purchased quite cheaply from professional inshore fishermen, who often find them in their trawl-nets and crab-pots.

To extract a whelk from its shell, crack open the spiral whorls with a hammer, taking care not to damage the flesh inside. It is advisable to use a fine-wire Aberdeen hook – the hook point being first inserted at the upper (tapering) end of the shellfish, and then threaded down through the flesh until it emerges through the tough foot.

When baiting up for smaller species of fish, the whelk can be cut into portions.

Shrimps. When raw, and preferably alive, these tiny crustaceans make a useful bait for small flatfish. Peeled dead shrimps are also favoured by mullet. Shrimps may be netted in any suitable sandy pool, and should be placed in the bait-box with plenty of wet seaweed. Dip the box in the sea at frequent intervals.

D. FISH BAITS

Mackerel are present all around the British Isles from about late spring until early autumn, and they provide the sea angler with one of his most useful and readily obtainable baits. For really large fish, such as shark, tope and deep-sea conger, a whole medium-sized mackerel makes a very acceptable offering. For the general run of smaller fish, however, one normally uses strips of flesh cut from the side of a mackerel.

It always pays to use freshly-caught mackerel for bait, so it is fortunate that these fish can be readily caught by the angler himself. In the case of boat fishing, a spell of trolling or feathering on the way out to the fishing ground will usually supply everyone on board with a sufficiency of bait for the day. Results are not quite so certain for the shore angler, of course, but on a suitable stretch of coast there is usually a reasonable chance of obtaining an adequate supply of mackerel for bait by spinning with a small, shiny metal lure; or, alternatively, by working a small trace of mackerel feathers with a beach-casting outfit.

Incidentally, mackerel flesh is relished by other mackerel, and a small portion placed on the hook of spinner or feathers often increases the catch. For preference, an inch-long slice should be taken from the firm flesh just in front of the tail, so that the skin is half blue and half silver. This particular 'cut off the joint' is known as a 'lask', and so well does it remain on the hook that it is not unusual to take a dozen or more fish on a single strip of bait.

Pilchards used to be abundant in Cornish waters, but nowadays they are not so plentiful. This is a great pity because they provide an excellent bait for a wide variety of sea fish. In addition, the oil derived from pressed pilchards is often used, both inside and outside the West Country, to make other baits more attractive. Small bottles of the preserved oil are obtainable from most tackle dealers.

The fact that the pilchard is soft-fleshed makes it unsuitable for long-distance shore-casting.

Herrings. Another useful 'oily' fish bait which will have to be purchased as a rule from the fishmonger. Off certain parts of the coast, however, herrings can be caught for bait – if not for sport – by means of a many-hooked instrument known as a jigger. This is jerked up and down in the water until fish, coming close to satisfy their curiosity, are impaled on the barbs.

Sandeels. These small, slender-bodied fish make an excellent bait for bass, pollack, coalfish, cod, turbot, rays, flounders, plaice and many other species. Around many parts of the British Isles they are to be seen swimming in tight-packed shoals in sandy estuaries and harbours, but for much of the time they protect themselves from predators by burying themselves in the sandy sea-bed, or near the low water mark on beaches of coarse-grained sand or shell-grit.

The sandeels most commonly used as bait are about 5 or 6 inches long. A larger kind, known as the Greater Sandeel, or Cock Launce, grows to about double that size.

Sandeels are somewhat localized in their distribution, but in areas where they occur they can be scraped out of the sand near the low tide mark with a launce hook (see Fig. 23), or by using quick, scooping movements with a garden fork. When using the latter method, it is easier if two people work together, with one wielding the fork and the other grabbing the quicksilver sandeels before they have time to wriggle back into the sand again. This they are able to do with amazing swiftness.

Fig 23 Launce hook, used for scraping sandeels from damp sand near the low tide mark, or in the shallows. When doing this it is advisable to protect your "catching" hand with a glove, as venomous weever fish are also sometimes brought to the surface.

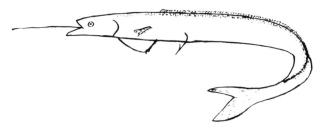

Fig. 24 Method of mounting a live Sandeel when drift-lining or trolling.

Sandeels are delicate creatures, and if required for livebaiting they should be transferred immediately into (i) clean sacking damped with sea water; (ii) a plastic bucket containing sea water, and preferably aerated with a small battery-operated aquarium air-pump; (iii) a small cool-box containing some ice cubes or a freezer sachet; (iv) a wooden courge floating in the sea itself.

Sandeels for float fishing may be hooked lightly through the back, just in front of the leading edge of the dorsal fin. For drift-lining or whiffing, the hook can be passed through the mouth, out through one of the gills, and then snicked lightly through the underside of the belly.

When using the large Greater Sandeel as bait, it is customary to slice a long, thin fillet of flesh from either side of the fish. They make a particularly good offering when fishing for turbot and rays.

Sprats. It is during the late autumn and winter months that these small silvery fish are offered for sale on the fishmonger's slab. They are an excellent bait for many of the sea-fish caught at that season, including cod, whiting, spur-dogfish and late bass. Being thin-skinned, sprats do not stay on the hook well when distance-casting, and if required for this purpose it is essential to use *fresh* sprats, and to attach each bait to the hook with a few turns of soft wool tied around the 'wrist' of the sprat's tail.

Garfish. Frequently caught during the summer months on light float tackle baited with tiny strips of mackerel, this strange-looking fish with a beaked mouth makes a reasonably good bait for skate, dogfish, conger, mackerel, etc.

Other Fish Baits. Several other small fish can prove very killing when used for specialized methods of sea fishing. Small *pouting, wrasse, pollack, poor-cod* and rock pool *butterfish,* measuring only 4 or 5 inches in length, are often taken very readily by large bass – especially when presented live on a flowing trace. The method of mounting these baits on the hook can be varied to suit the local conditions, but lip-hooking generally gives good results.

Small to medium-sized *pouting* are also taken well by conger; whilst in some areas tope seem to have a liking for *small black bream.*

4

Pier and Jetty Fishing

Most sea anglers first become acquainted with the pastime by dangling a line over the side of a pier, jetty or harbour wall. For the indifferent sailor, of course, the main attraction of pier fishing is that it offers to some extent the advantages of boat fishing, without the accompanying green complexion and various other discomforts. Also, for the raw novice who has yet to master the art of casting (see Chapter Five), a pier provides the means of getting a baited hook into deep water with the minimum of tangles and embarrassment.

Indeed, this inability to cast is probably the reason behind that angling mystery known as beginner's luck, which so often forms a subject for discussion among pier fishermen. Certainly, it is a fact that the 'expert' who casts his tackle 100 yards or more from the very end of the pier, so that it shall lie in even deeper water, is rarely the angler who obtains the biggest catch. This is because fish in the vicinity of a pier or jetty are nearly always to be found lurking within the protective shadow cast by the structure, where they prey upon the small marine creatures which seek shelter among the piles and masonry.

Sometimes beside a pier, and almost always near a jetty or harbour wall, there are spots which are specially favoured by certain kinds of fish. Usually these 'lies', as they are called, are patches of fairly still water on the fringe of a tidal eddy; for it is into such places that the currents waft drifting scraps of food, or feebly-swimming small fry. These specially rewarding angling spots are apt to shift with the fluctuations of the tides, which on most parts of the coast follow a fairly simple rhythm, flowing for several hours in one direction, and then ebbing for an equivalent length of time in a reverse direction after a brief intervening spell of slack water.

No hard-and-fast rules can be laid down on this very important sea-angling subject, however, as every stretch of coastline possesses its own tidal peculiarities. It is a simple enough matter, of course, to make oneself conversant with the times of high and low water, but this data *by itself* is of little use to the visiting pier angler, and it is always advisable to obtain more detailed information from a knowledgeable source, such as the local tackle dealer, harbour master, or fellow anglers possessing a more intimate knowledge of the district. At the same time, enquiries should be made as to the nature of the sea-bed, and careful note made of rocky ground which may yield a wider variety of species, and of any extra snaggy patches where terminal tackle is likely to be lost.

Most kinds of sea fish, at one time or another, have been taken on rod and line from the piers around the British Isles, but those generally caught during the summer months are dabs, plaice flounders and dogfish on paternoster or leger tackle fished on the sea-bed, and mackerel, bass, garfish and small pollack on float or driftline tackle fished in mid-water. Towards the end of the year codling and whiting also begin to provide sport for the all-the-year-round enthusiasts. In addition, many species of fish common to rocky localities are found in the neighbourhood of stone harbour walls; those most commonly caught being conger, pouting, mullet, wrasse and pollack. Detailed methods of angling for all these fish are given in a later chapter of this book.

A stroll along a pier or harbour wall patronized by sea anglers can be quite an education, and it is easy to tell the experienced fishermen from the beginners; the local 'regulars' from the holiday-season 'dabblers'.

Rod technique is perhaps the biggest give-away. As we have already mentioned, casting is not really necessary when fishing from a pier, but quite often it may be considered desirable. Obviously, when a pier is crowded with holidaymakers and other anglers, a good deal of care is necessary when casting, and the 'up-and-over' method is safer and preferable in every way to the side-swing method.

Similarly, a sloppily held rod, or one thrown down in boredom against a stone bollard or steel girder, is a fairly reliable indication that the owner has little faith in his own fishing ability, and not a great deal of regard for his tackle. A successful angler, on the other hand, is usually quietly confident and alert.

Few fishermen consciously think of their rod as a tool. Yet that is precisely what it is; and, as is the case with most tools, there is a right way to handle it – and any number of wrong ways!

Whether fishing from the beach, pier, rocks, harbour wall, or boat, a rod should be held at an angle well above the horizontal. A drooping rod, its tip pointing downwards towards the water, does not allow a bite to be felt so delicately, and is excusable only when float tackle is being allowed to drift away on tide, ·wind or current; or when retrieving a spinning lure.

A rod rest may be used for certain kinds of leger fishing without too much loss of efficiency, but when float fishing, tight-lining in mid-water, or drift-lining, it is better to maintain contact with the rod all the time.

Possibly the greatest test of good rod technique comes immediately after a fish has mouthed the bait. By means of the vibrations running through the rod and his finger-tips, the angler must guess at the nature of the fish that has paid him a visit, and reach a split-second decision on his next move. The hook must be driven home – that much he knows. But shall the strike be quick or delayed? Gentle or hard? Or would it perhaps be best to make no strike at all, allowing the fish – he hopes – to hook itself?

For the experienced angler the answer comes instinctively, but the novice needs some sort of rough-and-ready guide. It is, of course, dangerous to generalize when discussing any angling subject, but as a rule a fish that sucks and pulls cautiously at the bait should be given plenty of scope before any attempt is made to drive the hook home; whereas a fish that snatches suddenly and fiercely may be treated to a strike that is short and sharp.

In most kinds of sea fishing, when a hooked fish is powerful enough to make a run for it, you will be wise to put on pressure without actually stopping it in the early stages of the battle. Otherwise the fish may react by shaking its head, like a dog tugging at a leash, and in the process the hook is likely to be torn free. However, special problems are likely to arise when a fish has been hooked from a pier. Flatfish do not cause much trouble as a rule, but a lively bass, mullet or mackerel is always liable to head in among the girders. When this happens, the chances are that both fish and terminal tackle will be lost.

To reduce this hazard to a minimum, some pier anglers use a heavy rod and line, so that the moment a fish is hooked it can be hoisted out of the water. Regarded purely as a means of catching fish, this method may be efficient enough, but it is crane-driving rather than angling.

Even if the fish is kept clear of the piles, there still remains the difficulty of reeling it up to the deck of the pier, which may be 20 feet or more above the level of the water. An insecurely hooked fish is likely to fall back into the sea during this process, because its weight naturally increases as it is drawn out of the water. Sometimes it is possible to guide the fish to a flight of steps leading down to the water, so that by descending and reeling in at the same time, it becomes a fairly straightforward matter of netting or gaffing the fish in the orthodox manner. More often than not, however, the rods and lines of other anglers will prevent such tactics being put into effect, and if a really large fish has been hooked it will then be necessary to use a hooped drop-net, as illustrated in Fig. 22.

Next, a word or two about groundbaiting. This is always useful when pier fishing, and entails very little additional effort. A weighted net bag containing fish offal and crushed crabs is lowered into the water on the end of a line so that it lies at the same depth as the baited hooks, and 2 or 3 yards away from them. Every so often the net is jogged up and down in order to allow some of the bait to float clear of the meshes, care being taken to see that the net is so positioned in the flow of tide that the scent of the groundbait and released food particles drift past your fishing tackle. When fishing from a crowded pier this latter precaution is particularly important, because a carelessly positioned groundbait-container could actually attract fish away from your own hooks to those of a neighbouring angler.

However, there is little to be said in favour of fishing from the 'popular' kind of pier, where during the holiday months it is not unusual for hundreds of rods to be in use, spaced at intervals of only 1 or 2 yards. Such conditions may offer excellent social possibilities, but the fact remains that as a rule there simply are not enough fish to go round.

It is better by far, when confronted by this sort of thing, to turn one's attention to the smaller jetties, harbour walls and breakwaters; or to avoid the crowds by fishing at night. Most sea-fish are mainly nocturnal feeders anyway, and nearly always bite better after sundown. In some localities, moreover, the pier-head illuminations appear to attract the fish; whilst the period around full moon also seems to bring some of the larger species from fairly deep water close inshore.

Finally, while on the subject of night fishing, it is worth mentioning that many fishing harbours and rocky estuaries are inhabited by big conger weighing up to 40 lb. or more, which grow fat on the fish guts and similar scraps thrown overboard from commercial fishing-boats when they return to port.

These shallow-water conger are mainly nocturnal in their feeding habits, emerging from large sea-eroded crevices in the harbour wall, or from similar lairs, as darkness falls. A night-fishing session in quest of these congers, using strong leger tackle baited with a large offering of squid or fresh mackerel, is likely to produce some very exciting sport.

The best time to try for these big sea-eels is on a warm, sultry night in summer or early autumn, but good results can also be had quite often when conditions are far from ideal.

A large and angry conger is a formidable opponent, so don't forget to go equipped with a reliable lantern (electric, gas or paraffin), a strong gaff, and – last but not least – a large sack to accommodate the catch!

5

Shore Fishing

There are not many parts of our coastline where fishing from the open shore cannot be practised successfully throughout much of the year. Yet, owing to an incorrect or over-impetuous approach, many sea anglers who try their hand at this branch of the pastime find themselves consistently out of luck.

One very important point which is frequently overlooked is the need to carry out a preliminary survey of any hitherto unfished shore before actually wetting the tackle. Fish naturally congregate in those areas where there is an abundance of food, and for this reason the rod-and-line sport tends to vary considerably from one part of a beach to another. On most stretches of shingle or sand there are usually a few very localized spots which provide good results; whilst elsewhere, possibly only 100 yards away, the fishing may be mediocre, or even a complete waste of time.

Obviously, therefore, the would-be shore angler must first of all study the feeding habits of the fish he is going to try for. Where the shore consists of a flat expanse of sand or mud, many species work their way in with the flooding tide in order to prey upon the sandeels, shrimps, worms and other small marine creatures which inhabit this type of coastline. To discover the richest feeding grounds it is necessary to visit the shore at low tide, when it is a simple enough matter to note those places where the small marine life of the littoral zone is most abundant.

Kelp

Areas of kelp or rock are also sources of food for many kinds of mollusc- and crustacean-feeding fish, and a line cast out at a point where a beach of sand or shingle adjoins a patch of broken ground will generally produce good results. Here again, though, low-water prospecting is essential; and for preference this should be carried out during a low spring tide.

If the shoreline is backed by cliffs it is possible, when the sea is clear and the tide is low, to gain a gull's-eye view from the cliff-top of the sea-bed formation – the rocky areas showing up clearly as dark patches against the lighter tawny hue of snag-free sand. Don't try to memorise all the likely stances; instead, take a pencil and paper with you and draw a rough sketch map, marking on it the position of the underwater rocks in relation to various outstanding permanent features on the shore, such as landslips, longshore trees and shrubs, capstans, cliff-top fences, and so on. At the same time, remember that you may wish to fish after dark, so wherever possible choose landmarks which will be visible from the beach on a moonlit night, or will be silhouetted against the cliff-top skyline.

Shingle beaches usually shelve much more steeply than the sandy variety, and in consequence when fishing the former it is seldom necessary to cast out very far in order to get the baited tackle into reasonably deep water. A shingle beach therefore offers the best possibilities for the novice shore angler who is not yet very expert at casting. For the same reason, a shingle beach is also the best bet for any angler whose tackle is rather limited, and who only possesses a general-purpose rod not specifically designed for long-distance casting.

Sandy stretches of shore, on the other hand, usually require the use of a purpose-designed shore-casting rod – the most popular type being about 11 to 12 feet long, in two sections (see Chapter One). As mentioned previously, the reel must be of a size, weight and type to match the rod.

The newcomer to shore-casting would probably be well-advised to choose a fixed-spool reel, because this type enables the inexperienced to achieve good casting distances with a minimum risk of tangles and wasted fishing time. For average shore conditions requiring the use of 3 to 4 oz. of lead, I would recommend an 'intermediate'-sized reel – that is to say, one with a spool capacity of approximately 200-250 yards of 25 lb. breaking-strain nylon monofilament line.

A reel of this size is perfectly adequate for nearly all kinds of shore-casting, and is much pleasanter to handle than the very large surf-casting fixed-spool reels.

On the other hand, if a multiplier reel is your choice, it should preferably have a narrow, medium-capacity spool.

Also, the spool should be constructed of glass-reinforced plastic, carbon-fibre, or some other very strong and light material that is capable of withstanding the crushing and distorting effects of nylon line. Reels fitted with a heavy metal line spool are NOT recommended for shore-casting, because the weight of the spool creates a flywheel effect that is liable to cause over-runs and line tangles.

When loading your reel with line it is worth bearing in mind that – other factors being equal – casting distance is increased as the line diameter is reduced. Nevertheless, the novice shore angler would probably be well advised to use a fairly heavy line – say about 27 to 30 lb. breaking-strain – until he attains a reasonable degree of proficiency.

There are two reasons for this. First of all, if the terminal tackle becomes fouled by a rock, bunch of seaweed, or some other sea-bed obstruction, it may be possible to free it by brute force if the line has a reasonably high breaking-strain. In this event, of course, the pull should be exerted directly on to the line; not through the flexed rod, which is liable to be strained if maltreated in this way.

If the tackle appears reluctant to come free, it is best not to pull it too hard from the original casting position, because this

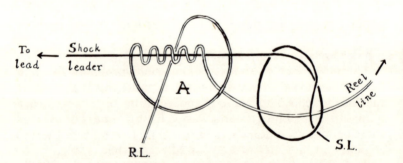

Fig. 25 Method of attaching a shock leader to the end of a reel line of lower breaking strain. To form the knot, first tie the end of the shock leader (S.L.) about 8 inches up the reel line, and pull very tight. Then twist the end of the reel line (R.L.) four times around the shock leader, and pass the end through the loop A, as shown. Wet the loose coils of nylon in your mouth; then pull them tight. Trim off surplus line, leaving a ¼-inch 'tag-end' protruding at S.L.

will only aggravate the trouble by wedging the lead or hooks more securely. Instead, walk along the beach reeling off line as you go, until the line is slanting out from the shore at an angle of about 45 degrees. A determined pull will then probably drag the fouled tackle sideways until it is clear of the obstruction.

The second reason why the novice shore angler should use a reasonably strong line is that when making a cast a tremendous momentary strain is placed on the line. Smooth casting, in which all jerky movements have been eliminated, can do a lot to ease this strain; but beginners are seldom smooth casters, and if too light a line is used at the outset the bottom tackle is liable to 'flick off' during the casting operation and be lost in the sea. Similar trouble will also be experienced if the dangling lead is allowed to rest on the beach during the backswing of the cast; for when the forward swing is made, the rod will already be travelling at speed before the line is suddenly snatched tight.

From the foregoing facts it will be seen that the shore angler is confronted with something of a dilemma. By reducing the diameter (i.e. breaking-strain) of his line he will automatically increase his distance casting potential ... but at the same time he will also increase the risk of his terminal tackle snapping off under the strain of casting.

However, there is one way around this problem – and that is by attaching a 'shock leader' of stronger line to the end of the main reel line.

For example, supposing you were planning to fish from a sandy surf beach with a rod designed to cast a 4-oz. lead. You could load your reel spool with 22-lb. breaking-strain nylon monofilament, and then shock-knot about 20 feet of 35 to 40-lb. breaking-strain nylon monofilament to the end of the 22-lb. line. This 20-foot shock leader is just long enough to stretch the full length of the rod and leave several turns around the reel spool prior to casting.

In this way the shock leader is able to absorb the fierce momentary stress of casting, but has virtually no adverse effect on your casting distance because the reel line itself is of a considerably lower diameter.

Incidentally, as you become more expert at surf fishing, and playing your hooked fish in through the breakers, you can

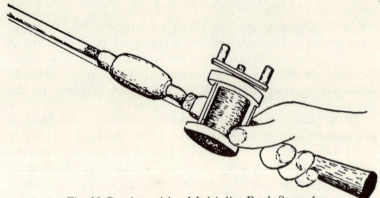

Fig. 26 Casting with a Multiplier Reel: Stage 1.

Whether using a single-handed rod with offset handle (as illustrated here), or a double-handed rod, the right hand adopts this position, with the thumb acting as a check to the spool. In the case of a single-handed rod, the forefinger encircles the trigger, and the rod is held so that the reel handles tilt upwards.

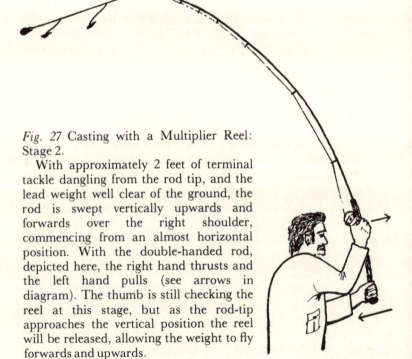

Fig. 27 Casting with a Multiplier Reel: Stage 2.

With approximately 2 feet of terminal tackle dangling from the rod tip, and the lead weight well clear of the ground, the rod is swept vertically upwards and forwards over the right shoulder, commencing from an almost horizontal position. With the double-handed rod, depicted here, the right hand thrusts and the left hand pulls (see arrows in diagram). The thumb is still checking the reel at this stage, but as the rod-tip approaches the vertical position the reel will be released, allowing the weight to fly forwards and upwards.

safely graduate to a lighter reel line than the 22-lb. breaking-strain suggested above. On a sandy, snag-free beach a reel line of 15 to 17 lb. breaking-strain is a perfectly practical proposition, provided it is used in conjunction with a suitable shock leader.

Of course, when fishing over rough ground it is necessary to use a stronger line in order to cope with the snags that are bound to occur from time to time.

Another teething problem which confronts the novice shore-caster when using a multiplier reel is the persistently recurring over-run, resulting in that extremely exasperating and time-wasting type of line tangle known as a 'bird's-nest'.

The cast is made, and everything appears to be under control – then suddenly, either towards the middle of the cast or at the very end, the reel begins to throw off large coils of loose line, which in a mere split second become hopelessly twisted together.

The reason for this sort of thing happening lies almost

Fig. 28 Casting with a Multiplier Reel: Stage 3.
The 'follow through', with the right arm fully extended, and the weighted tackle in flight. The thumb is gently controlling the spool to prevent an over-run.

invariably in faulty reel control; with jerky casting and the elasticity of a new line sometimes acting as contributory causes.

Before trying to cure the bird's-nesting habit, it is necessary to understand what happens to the weighted tackle after it leaves the end of the rod. It begins by travelling fast along the course of an arc, slowing down temporarily as it reaches the upper limits of its trajectory, and then gaining momentum again as gravity speeds it on its downward path to the sea. Upon entering the sea, the speed of the tackle is checked for a second time by the resistance of the water.

On both occasions when the speed of the tackle diminishes there is a tendency for the freely-spinning reel to throw out more line than the moving lead can cope with, and friction must be applied to the reel spool in order to counteract this tendency. The first slowing-down process, when the tackle is actually in flight, is a gradual one, and a very light thumb pressure on the reel spool will be sufficient to prevent over-running at this stage. The second check to the tackle, when it enters the sea, is much more abrupt, and the reel must be braked hard just as the lead is about to hit the water.

Night fishing is a stringent test of the shore angler's skill; for in the dark it is necessary to judge the position of a flying lead by instinct and experience. It is all too easy to collect a bird's-nest at night, and an exasperating and time-wasting job trying to untangle it.

A straightforward method of sorting out a bad tangle round the reel is to unfasten the terminal trace from the reel line; draw the line back through the rod rings, and remove the reel from the rod. It should now be possible to strip all the loose and bunched line from the reel by turning the spool with one hand, and easing away the line with the other. Any attempt to remove the line from the reel by pulling on it will only tighten the over-run coils and make matters worse.

Failing this simple solution, the loose end of line can be wound on a net-braiding needle. This inexpensive and useful item of equipment is a convenient shape for passing through any tangled loops as the winding proceeds. Finally, the untangled line is run off the netting needle on to the reel again.

Of course, when a fixed-spool is being used this sort of trouble cannot occur, and this is one reason why I believe this

Fig. 29 Netting Needle, or Shuttle.

type of reel to be the most satisfactory choice for a *novice* shore angler. With a fixed-spool reel it is possible for a beginner to cast moderately long distances after only a little practice, and the fast rate of retrieve also enables the reel to be used for heavy spinning, feathering for mackerel from rocky headlands and steep-to beaches, etc. There are literally dozens of medium- and large-capacity shore-casting fixed-spool reels in a wide range of price ranges, and nowadays most of them possess a high degree of resistance to salt-water corrosion.

The type of ground tackle used by shore fishermen around the British Isles varies considerably from district to district,

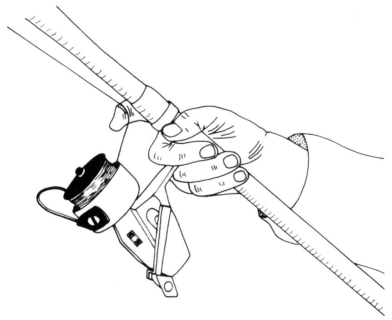

Fig. 30 Method of Checking a Fixed-spool reel Prior to Casting.

depending on the local sea conditions and nature of the sea-bed.

The permutations of rod design, reel type and capacity, line strength, type of trace, size and type of lead, etc., are almost limitless, but the following brief suggestions may help newcomers to shore fishing to choose a suitable outfit:

1. **Medium Surf-casting.** The majority of open-coast fishing spots fall into this category. I would recommend a hollow glass rod about 11 to 11½ feet in length, designed to cast a 4-oz lead, or thereabouts. Beginners will find a slow to medium taper rod easiest to cast with, and this type of rod is also best for casting 'soft' baits such as peeler crab, sandeels, etc. The reel can be either a fixed-spool or multiplier of suitable size and line capacity (see notes in Chapter One), and line strength can range from about 15 to 25 lb. breaking-strain, coupled with a 35-lb. breaking-strain shock leader to absorb the momentary stress of casting.

An outfit like this can be used in the vast majority of shore fishing situations, ranging from steeply shelving shingle beaches to surf-pounded, ocean-facing storm beaches. The main variations in fishing these widely differing types of shoreline will lie in the casting distance required to contact the fish; your choice of terminal trace, and the type of lead needed to cope with the local sea and sea-bed conditions.

Heavy surf usually calls for long casting and a simple non-tangle trace such as a single-hook running paternoster. The lead, of course, must be of a type that will hold the bottom well in the turbulent water, and two popular choices with modern surf fishermen are the sand wedge, and the patent 'Breakaway' surf bomb with wire anchor spikes which trip automatically when one strikes at a fish (see Fig. 9).

2. **Heavy Surf-casting.** On certain parts of the coast where shore anglers have to contend with tackle-snagging rocks and kelp-beds, there is some demand for a heavier outfit, in which the rod – although basically similar to that described in section 1 – is designed to cast leads of about 6 oz. Line strength is usually about 40-45-lb. breaking strain, and this is best used with a revolving drum reel – normally a multiplier, although the old-fashioned Scarborough type is still favoured along parts of the north-east coast.

3. **Light Bottom Fishing.** In sheltered estuaries, or even

from steeply shelving open-coast beaches when conditions are reasonably calm, it is possible to use a 9-foot medium spinning rod when legering or paternostering for bass and flatfish. The reel can be either a medium-sized spinning fixed-spool, or a small bait-casting multiplier. Line strength should be about 10 to 14-lb. breaking-strain, and the lead about 1 to $1\frac{1}{2}$ oz.

TRACES FOR SHORE-CASTING

Very often a trace which looks perfectly satisfactory on dry land will repeatedly end up on the sea-bed as an untidy, tangled heap. Sometimes the tangling occurs in mid-air while the tackle is being cast out; at other times it happens on the sea-bed as the bait and hook length are swirled to and fro by the underwater currents.

Many novice sea anglers try to cure this trouble by dreaming up highly complicated terminal rigs bristling with shiny wire booms and swivels. Unfortunately all this ironmongery tumbling around in the surf tends to frighten off all but the smallest and most reckless fish!

It is worth stressing, therefore, that far better results are likely to be obtained by curbing one's inventive enthusiasm, and keeping the terminal tackle as basic as possible.

For proof of this you need only look at the sort of bottom-fishing rigs used by those shore anglers who have learned the happy knack of bagging plenty of big fish. You will find that, almost without exception, they are content to use either a simple nylon paternoster or running leger.

You will find, too, that the experienced shore-caster seldom uses three hooks – the maximum permitted under the N.F.S.A. rules for sport fishing. Quite apart from increasing the risk of tangles, three baited hooks create so much extra wind-resistance that casting distance is reduced dramatically.

Also, when fishing over rough ground, three-hook tackle increases the risk of getting snagged up and losing one's all – including, possibly, a good fish.

Two hooks are perfectly adequate, and indeed there are many occasions when the specialist angler will do best by using a single-hook trace.

For trouble-free casting, and minimal risk of trace tangles, there is no better type of terminal rig than a light and inconspicuous nylon paternoster (see Fig. 1). In this set-up the lead hangs at the bottom of the main trace, so that when casting out the baited hooks and droppers stream neatly behind.

Provided you space out the hook droppers on the main trace so that there is no risk of the lower hook flying back and tangling with the dropper immediately above, you should not run up against any problems.

However, if the hook dropper shows a tendency to become twisted around the main trace, take a critical look at your method of baiting up. Very often a bait that hangs unevenly on the hook will spin round and round like a propeller as it rushes through the air during the cast.

It may also react in much the same way underwater when a strong tidal current is flowing. Either way a twisted and tangled trace is the inevitable result.

Fortunately this problem is easily cured. Simply thread the bait neatly and evenly on the hook, and all will be well.

When using a running leger, or its close relative the running paternoster (see Fig. 3), there is a slightly increased risk of trace tangles when casting, caused by the flowing hook length flying back and wrapping itself around the main trace or reel line.

However, there are a couple of simple dodges which go a long way towards ironing out these problems. First of all, it helps a lot if you brake the reel sharply a split second *before* the lead hits the water.

Then, as the lead enters the water, allow line to flow freely off the reel again until you feel the lead hit the bottom. Now lower the rod-tip and carefully reel in all slack line.

Finally, jerk the lead off the sea-bed with a backwards and upwards striking movement of the rod-tip. This will straighten out the terminal tackle, removing any coils and potential tangles from the flowing hook length.

Of course, difficult shore conditions are bound to occur sometimes, making it necessary to modify slightly the basic paternoster or leger rigs. Needless to say, if the turbulence of a heavy surf causes tangles to occur repeatedly in a boomless paternoster rig, a very simple remedy is to suspend the hook dropper from an elongated paternoster blood loop. This very useful loop knot juts out from the main trace at right angles to form an inconspicuous mini-boom (see Fig. 17).

If necessary, the loop can be stiffened by whipping it tightly for about nine-tenths of its length with nylon monofilament, which may then be made even more rigid with a coating of varnish or quick-drying waterproof glue. Of course, you must be careful to use a glue that does not react with nylon.

As an alternative to stiffening the loop with a whipping, you can cover it with a sleeve of transparent plastic tubing. The tubing from a disused ballpoint pen is ideal for this purpose.

Generally speaking, shop-bought booms are too large and clumsy to be used on shore-casting traces, but there is one notable exception that I can personally recommend. Made of plastic tubing, yet surprisingly strong and resilient, it is known as the 'Prospector' boom (see Fig. 2). One important advantage of this boom is that the length of out-jutting plastic tube can be cut to any length prior to assembly to suit the local fishing conditions. Of course, it is also ideal for most kinds of boat fishing.

GENERAL HINTS

If two or three hooks are used – and there are plenty of occasions when it is practicable to do so – it is a sound general practice to place on one hook an oily fish bait for its scent value, and on the other to offer a 'close-interest' bait, such as soft crab, prawn, ragworm, etc. As a general rule it is best to use baits which occur naturally in the locality – although I would hasten to add that many fish often give the lie to this rule. Among the fish regularly taken by shore anglers in the appropriate season may be listed; bass, pouting, pollack, wrasse, conger, flounders, dabs, plaice, lesser spotted dogfish, spur-dogfish, huss, mackerel, garfish, rays, cod and whiting.

When bottom fishing from a beach it is necessary to look to one's hooks at frequent intervals in order to make sure that they have not become blunted by continuous rubbing against the pebbles, or as a result of becoming caught up on some rocky snag. A hook can be resharpened on a fine carborundum slip, care being taken to rub it almost flat against the stone so that a very acute angle is formed at the hook-point. It is a mistake, though, to risk losing a good fish by sharpening a hook too many times. A hook costs very little, and there is no need to grieve when it becomes necessary to fit a new one.

For the sake of barefooted swimmers and sea-gulls, however, take care not to leave your old hooks lying around. And, incidentally, whilst touching on this subject, it might be as well to mention that considerable suffering can also be caused to birds by thoughtlessly discarding lengths of nylon line on the beach. On one occasion, on the day following a well-patronized sea-angling festival, I had to destroy no less than three gulls because their legs had been almost severed by strands of this very sharp material. In one case the nylon was attached to a baited hook, which the unfortunate bird had also swallowed.

6

Rock Fishing

To the would-be rock fisherman I would say: "First find your rock."

This may seem a rather obvious piece of advice, but the fact remains that in rock fishing much depends on the stance chosen. The angler who is over-eager to set up his rod and get to grips with the fish is apt to scramble unthinkingly on to the first wave-washed vantage point that presents itself; whereas a preliminary tour of inspection, made when unencumbered with tackle, almost always pays dividends.

Several good rock positions should be chosen so that, without wasting valuable fishing time later on, one knows immediately where to make for at various states of the tide. The fact that many rock-haunting fish like to lurk in comparatively sheltered water, just on the fringe of the tidal drift, should also be borne in mind.

Rock-fishing conditions vary considerably from coast to coast, and naturally you must take these variable factors into consideration when selecting your tackle and deciding on your strategy. As a general rule, however, you will be wise to use a fairly long rod – say a medium-powered beach-caster about 11 to $11\frac{1}{2}$ feet in length. The reason for this is that with a long rod it is possible to steer a hooked fish around rocky outcrops and trailing weed.

However, although a long and fairly powerful rod may be essential in some localities, and advantageous in others, there are quite a number of rock-fishing positions where a 9- or 10-foot two-handed spinning rod can be used to good effect.

More important, perhaps, is the fishing method and type of terminal tackle used. In many places, where the adjoining sea-bed is encumbered with rocks and kelp, bottom tackle is likely to become snagged and lost. It is then that float tackle often proves most useful. For this method of fishing a fixed-spool reel is generally preferred, mainly because it enables even light floats to be cast a good distance.

Before setting up your float tackle you should first of all decide how much lead will be needed to get the bait down to the required depth against the run of the tide. After this, a float should be selected which will cock up nicely under the weight of lead, without being so buoyant as to present too much resistance to a taking fish. Far too many sea anglers are inclined to put the cart before the horse – weighting their line to suit the float, and giving no thought at all to what goes on underneath the water.

If the depth of water to be fished is greater than the length of the rod, it will be necessary to use the sliding type of float, which automatically slips down the line as the tackle is drawn out of the water. It is prevented from sliding *upwards* by tying the nylon stop knot (se Fig. 12) to the line at the point where the float is required. This adjustable stop knot can be easily moved to any desired position, and is small enough to pass through the rod rings easily when casting or reeling in.

Some sliding floats are fitted with two small rings, or eyelets, through which the line is threaded. These are usually carrot-shaped, and in some cases may be equipped with an antenna tipped with small, brightly-painted marker fins. Floats of this type are very easy to see, and are especially suitable for use as roving floats which may be allowed to drift away for 50 yards or more on wind and tide.

For ease of casting, however, there is much to be said for the balsa cigar-shaped float. Easily made by the handyman angler, it has a hole drilled through the centre to take the line.

The 'bubble' type of float has made its appearance more recently than those already mentioned. Hollow, and made of transparent plastic, it is fitted with a valve so that the buoyancy of the float may be adjusted by letting in or ejecting water. It is particularly useful when fishing in sheltered water for mullet or bass.

The fairly robust kinds of float tackle normally used from exposed rocks may be weighted conveniently with a quick-change spiral lead, or one or two large drilled bullets. Light harbour and estuary floats, however, call for finer adjustment, and this is best done by threading a tiny drilled bullet just

Multiplying game reel.

Braided Terylene sea line.

Line winder.

Casting out into surf from a rock position. This method of bottom fishing is possible where a sandy area of sea-bed borders the rock, and it often produces catches of bass, flatfish, rays, etc.

The author with a good bass and a thornback ray taken while legering from a shingle beach. Very often beaches like this shelve steeply into deepish water, then level out on to a sandy sea-bed.

above the trace swivel, or by pinching on a few split shot.

The choice of hook used with float tackle will naturally depend on the size and kind of fish which frequent the locality. Mullet, which are often found around rocky coastlines, will need a small hook – something in the region of size 8 or 10. But for many other rock-visiting fish, such as bass, inshore pollack, mackerel and garfish, hooks in the size 2 to 1/0 range will generally prove most useful.

Suitable baits for all these fish will be found later in this book, and it is only necessary at this point to recommend in particular those which are natural to a rocky area, such as live prawns, ragworm, soft crabs, live sandeels and finger-sized pouting.

Groundbaiting can be very useful when rock fishing. Minced-up oily fish (mackerel, sprats, herring, pilchards, etc.), and crushed-up shore crabs and limpet flesh, can be cast into the swim a little at a time, or lowered over the edge of the rock position in a weighted net bag. Alternatively, the groundbait may be spread, a spoonful at a time, on a lip of the rock, where it will be gradually washed into the sea by the rising tide. This latter method is much favoured by mullet fishermen in the Channel Islands, where the groundbait, known as 'shervy', may include finely-minced horseflesh mixed with blood obtained from the local slaughter-house.

A problem arises in float fishing when the wind is blowing strongly onshore, for then one's float is apt to be returned by the sea almost as soon as it has been cast out. In some localities this puts paid to fishing altogether; but careful prospecting will often produce a rocky 'hook' or 'corner', from the end of which the wind can be used to advantage, and the line allowed to drift parallel with the shore.

Another method which I have used with success on exposed stretches of the Cornish coast, is to fill a bubble-float with sufficient water to render it only just buoyant. In this way there is hardly any part of the float showing above water to catch the wind, and the weight of the water ballast makes for long casts.

Whatever tactics are employed, it is important to prevent the line from becoming slack and sinking beneath the water in a great sagging loop. When this sort of thing happens it is impossible to strike effectively when a disappearing float

indicates an interested fish. Treating the last 40 yards or so of
your reel line with line floatant will help to overcome this
problem; but, even so, slow reeling in and repeated casting
will still be a necessity. Indeed, results are often improved by
keeping the bait on the move in this way.

Where a good depth of water comes right up to a rock
stance, spinning usually produces good results when there are
bass, pollack, garfish, mackerel or sea-trout around. The most
killing spinning lures are usually those which bear a
superficial resemblance to a sandeel, sprat, or some other
small bait fish. Among my favourite rock spinning lures are
shiny metal wobbling spoons such as the ABU 'Toby' or
Intrepid 'Flasha'; metal fish-shaped pirks like the ABU 'Krill',
and the very lifelike plastic sandeels. Some of these plastic
sandeels require a small up-trace Wye lead to provide casting
weight, but for rock and shore spinning I favour those which
have a tiny $\frac{1}{2}$-oz. barrel lead built into the belly.

In spinning, of course, one of the main objectives is to cast
the light bait as far as possible, and for this reason a lively rod
and a reel with very little inertia resistance are both essential.
The most popular choice among British sea anglers is a two-
handed 9-foot hollowglass spinning rod, matched with a
medium-capacity fixed-spool spinning reel loaded with 9 to
12-lb. breaking-strain nylon monofilament line.

In spinning especially it is important that the angler should
make himself as inconspicuous as possible; hurried
movements must be avoided, and full use made of cliffs, tall
rocks, and similar background cover, in order to avoid being
silhouetted against the skyline. If these precautions are
observed the fish will often take the bait when it has been
reeled in to within a few feet of the rock.

Earlier in this chapter it was stated that bottom tackle is

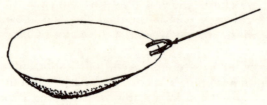

Fig. 31 Spoon-shaped Lead.

likely to be lost if used among rocks. As a generalization this is true enough. On certain parts of the coast, however, patches of clean ground lie within casting distance of the rocks, and in this type of situation it is possible to fish on the bottom, using a spoon-shaped lead (see Fig. 31).

Easily made at home by using an old dessert- or tablespoon as a mould, this type of lead has the important advantage of planing upwards through the water, over the top of sea-bed obstructions, when reeled in with a fast-retrieve reel.

We must also mention a method of rock fishing which, although not requiring much finesse, is widely practised from rocky scaurs and headlands bordering deep water. This is 'feathering' with a mackerel trace carrying three shiny tinned hooks adorned with brightly coloured feathers or tiny strips of plastic. After being cast well out, the lures are retrieved rapidly clear of the bottom with short, quick jerks.

A calm evening in summer or early autumn, when there is a thunderstorm brewing in the distance, is the time above all others to try one's luck with this kind of fishing. Under such conditions it is not unknown for fish to go suddenly crazy, snatching at the lures with every cast. Then a feathering trace, a lively rod and fixed-spool reel, will provide an evening of never-to-be-forgotten sport with mackerel, pollack, billet and the occasional garfish.

SAFETY HINTS

Rock fishing is potentially the most dangerous branch of sea angling, so always be on guard against taking any unnecessary risks.

NEVER fish from rocks on an exposed ocean-facing coastline in stormy conditions, or when big groundswells are rolling in. Even in apparently calm summer conditions, one must always beware of the occasional 'borer', or large freak wave which could easily wash you and your tackle off your vantage point. Sometimes these giant waves are the result of natural causes, but nowadays they are more likely to be produced by the wake of a huge supertanker – even though it may be many miles away and out of sight beyond the horizon.

Rock-fishing positions also vary widely in the sort of foothold they afford. Distrust those which are slippery, particularly if covered by a thin film of silkweed because this is really treacherous. The only reasonably safe way to fish in this sort of situation is to strap a set of rock spikes on to your boots. These are basically similar to the mountaineer's ice-climbing crampons, and provide a safe foothold by cutting through the surface film of weed and gripping the rock.

Always choose a rock that will allow you to land a hooked fish without having to take any foolish risks. Equip yourself with a long-handled gaff or landing net, and use it with caution. Experienced rock anglers nearly always fish with one or more companions, and go equipped with a safety rope so that the person gaffing a fish can be held securely by the others. On exposed coasts this is a very sensible precaution, because there are many precipitous rock positions where it would be quite impossible to scramble back on to the wave-washed rocks after falling into the sea.

Finally, before selecting a rock position, always acquaint yourself with the times and height of the local tides, and while fishing keep a wary eye on your line of retreat as soon as the tide starts rising.

7

Boat Fishing

Sea anglers have become increasingly boat-minded in recent years, and when one considers the many advantages to be derived from fishing afloat this fact is scarcely surprising. That the boat angler catches more fish than the person who operates from the shore or pier just cannot be denied; whilst, in addition, the fish nearly always run to a larger average size. Boat fishing also opens up prospects for trying out new angling methods and techniques.

One point which I would like to stress early in this chapter is that boat fishing need not be an expensive business. If several anglers join forces it should be possible for them to charter a boat for the day, and the services of a licensed boatman, for a fairly reasonable sum. Hiring a boat for inshore fishing on a 'skipper yourself' basis would naturally reduce costs even more; whilst for the angler who lives on or near the coast the cheapest proposition of all would be to buy a boat of one's own. A sound second-hand outboard-powered dinghy, suitable for two or three men, will often pay for itself in a couple of seasons, bearing in mind the present-day cost of fish.

Before taking charge of any kind of craft, however, the would-be boat angler *must* learn the elementary principles of seamanship. If you are a complete novice in this respect, the best way to gain the necessary experience would be to go out on several occasions with a competent boatman; preferably in the type of craft you hope eventually to own. Make your ambition clear to the boatman, and he will almost certainly give you a chance to familiarize yourself with the handling of the boat, and at the same time put you wise to the various local navigational hazards. On most stretches of coast these consist mainly of tidal currents, rocks, sand-bars, wind and waves.

It is reasonable to assume that every salt-water angler is acquainted with the basic causes and effects of ebbing and flowing tides. What is often overlooked is the relentless strength of the kind of tide-rip which is frequently to be found off rugged headlands, or swirling in and out of estuaries and through the entrances to Scottish sea-lochs. A small boat which gets caught up in this kind of water may well be carried on to a submerged sand-bar, smashed to matchwood on a rocky reef, or swept willy-nilly into an area of dangerously turbulent water. For example, when a heavy swell, rolling into an estuary-mouth, meets a tide-rip flowing in the opposite direction, the result is often a very ugly sea which could easily swamp a small undecked craft.

All this may sound rather alarming, and it is true that some exposed or tide-bedevilled stretches of coastline are best left entirely alone by the dinghy angler. However, around much of our coast the sea conditions are normally much more kindly, and a few simple, commonsense precautions will be sufficient to ensure against mishaps.

Fishing in or near an estuary mouth should be limited to those periods when the tide is flowing INTO the estuary. Well before the ebb begins to gather momentum, the anchor should be weighed and the boat headed for a less precarious position. Above all, one must avoid hanging on for 'just another few minutes' because the fish suddenly decide to come on the feed at slack water.

Bass fishing in an estuary is often best over the entrance bar, and provided that operations are confined to a rising tide there is little to fear under reasonable conditions. A falling tide, on the other hand, may mean trouble from breaking rollers as the water gets shallower. A breaking wave is a steep wave, and an unlucky one may cause a capsize. Even if there is no swell running, it is still necessary when fishing over a harbour bar to beware of the wash from large vessels.

In the open sea, too, there are tidal currents which result directly from the rise and fall of the ocean; although these are not generally so fierce as those encountered in constricted estuary channels. Nevertheless, they must be treated with respect, and their speed and times of ebbing and flowing carefully noted before setting off on a fishing trip. As already mentioned, fierce tide-rips are often encountered in the region of major headlands, and also over abruptly shelving reefs and sandbanks.

It is a common belief, even among quite experienced sea anglers, that these offshore currents slacken off when it is high or low water on the adjoining shore, in much the same way as do the tide-rips in estuaries. This, however, is far from being invariably the case. On many parts of the coast the tidal currents in the open sea 'over-run' the vertical tidal movements by as much as several hours, so that at high and low water they may be running at their maximum velocity. It is important, therefore, that local data should be obtained from a reliable source for estuarial tides and offshore tidal currents.

To warn the boat angler against going aground on a falling tide may seem unnecessary. Yet the tidal range varies so considerably around the British Isles that anglers visiting unfamiliar coasts are always encountering this sort of trouble. On the east coast of Ireland the tidal rise and fall is a mere 2 feet in some places, whereas in the upper reaches of the Bristol Channel it amounts to something like 50 feet. It is not to be wondered at, therefore, that miscalculations sometimes occur. Many muddy river estuaries, bays and creeks dry out amazingly fast, so that before a boat-load of unwary anglers are able to up-anchor and get under way they may find themselves stuck fast in the middle of a vast expanse of glutinous sludge. This may be an excellent opportunity to hold a sociable lugworm-digging party, but it is a poor alternative to a day's fishing!

Many mishaps among sea-going anglers are due to using inadequately equipped boats, so always check to see that your boat is seaworthy before taking it out. Make sure that there is a bucket or large bailing can aboard, and that the oars are in sound condition. If the boat is fitted with rowlocks, see to it that they are the right size for the oars, and tie the waist or shank of each rowlock to a convenient rib of the boat so that if one jumps out of its socket it cannot be lost overboard. Don't be careless about the oars just because the boat happens to be fitted with a motor; mechanical contrivances are always liable to break down when one is several miles down-tide and down-wind of base.

They are also liable to run out of fuel, so take a spare supply with you in an easy-to-lift can. If the can is of the kind which can be fitted with a spout-pourer it will simplify the business of filling a small outboard tank in a choppy sea. However, if a separate funnel is carried instead, be sure to hitch it to one of the boat ribs when it is not in use, so that it is kept well clear of any water or dirt in the bilges.

Likewise, carry some tools for the outboard motor in a small waterproof bag, along with a spare sparking plug, propeller shear spring, etc.

Some form of anchor must also be carried. For the angler this essential item of equipment serves a dual purpose. It prevents his craft from drifting while he is bottom fishing, and it also acts as a safeguard against the boat becoming unmanageable in winds, currents and tide-rips as a result of engine failure, or some other cause.

The type of anchoring device which can be used with safety will naturally depend on the size of the boat, and the local sea and tidal conditions. For a small open dinghy a simple killick, made by moulding a short length of chain into a heavy slab of concrete, will usually suffice. The killick should have a broad, flat base, because this shape offers the greatest frictional resistance when lying on the sea-bed, and also stows away

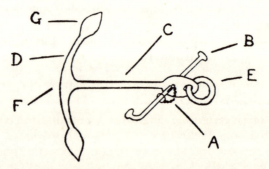

Fig. 32 A popular type of Small-boat Anchor.

When in use, the ring pin (A) keeps the stock (B) at right angles to the shank (C) and arms (D). Out of use, with the pin withdrawn, the stock folds flush with the shank for easy stowage. Other parts of the anchor mentioned in the text are the shackle or eye (E), crown (F), and fluke (G).

more snugly inside the boat when out of use.

When fishing in areas where tides run hard, or when using any craft larger than a small dinghy, you must go equipped with a fluked anchor. Any competent ship's chandler will advise you on the right size to suit your boat.

Weight for weight, a fluked anchor is far more efficient than a concrete killick, but you will find that the flukes bite into the sea-bed much more quickly and securely if you shackle in a fathom or two of chain between the anchor and the rope, or warp as it is often called.

When using an anchor over rough ground, it is essential to take precautions against the flukes becoming wedged among the rocks. This is done by 'tripping' the anchor before lowering it to the bottom. The chain (or rope) is attached first to the crown of the anchor, and then brought up the shank and tied to the eye with a short length of thin twine.

In the event of the anchor becoming fouled amongst the rocks, a sudden hefty pull on the warp will snap the light tripping twine, and the pull will then be transferred to the crown of the anchor – whereupon it should prove a fairly simple matter to coax the flukes away from the obstruction.

It should be noted that an anchor, especially a tripped one, must be allowed plenty of rope – say three or four times the depth of the water. Before attempting to break the tripping line, all this spare rope should be hauled in, so that the direction of pull is vertical.

With perseverance, an untripped anchor that has not become too badly fouled can often be freed by getting some way on the boat and pulling on the warp from several different directions, beginning with the point directly opposite that from which the anchored boat has hitherto been exerting its drag. Incidentally, when attempting to weigh a reluctant anchor it is always advisable to kneel down to the job. If you don't, and the anchor comes free suddenly, your shipmates will probably spend the next few minutes fishing for YOU!

One of the most important lessons which must be learned by the novice sailor is that the sea has to be respected at all times – even when it is as calm as the proverbial millpond. Whoever first coined the phrase about 'the hidden menace of the sea' certainly knew what he was talking about, for it is often when the inshore waters are blue and unrippled, and quietly heliographing beneath a blazing sun, that the local lifeboat has to go to the aid of some inexperienced boat-owner in distress.

A calm sea usually means that the wind is blowing offshore, and in localities where the beach is backed by high cliffs it only becomes apparent just how fiercely the wind is blowing after one has ventured some distance away from land. Then, in a matter of minutes, the glassy surface becomes rippled; the ripples grow into white-capped wavelets, and the wavelets heap themselves up into chop-licking white horses.

When things have reached this sorry state of affairs even the most unimaginative of novice skippers will realize that it is high time to put about and make for the shore. However, it is not the easiest thing to row into a choppy sea and make headway into the teeth of a strong wind. A faulty oar, a slinging rowlock, or some other small defect at such a time could, quite literally, prove fatal. So treat every boisterous offshore wind with respect, and refrain from venturing in a small boat far from the sheltering influence of land.

This brings me to the end of my cautionary remarks, and it is to be hoped that, in setting them down, I have not made boat angling seem an unduly hazardous pastime. I have merely tried to point out the dangers which are undoubtedly there for the reckless or unwary. Putting to sea in a boat, be it large or small, may be likened to crossing a busy road; it is safe enough if one takes adequate care, and virtual suicide when one acts blindly.

Already in this book, when dealing with shore angling, we have seen how fish tend to congregate in certain well-defined areas. The same thing applies farther out at sea, and the boat angler will have to learn how to locate these good fishing spots, or 'marks', by taking cross-bearings on prominent landmarks on the nearest stretch of shore. A good mark can often be discovered in the first instance by observing the activities of professional fishing-boats. The true angler, though, will always derive his greatest satisfaction from discovering his own marks, and a lot of help in this direction can be had by studying a large scale marine chart.

After a little practice in the art of reading it, a chart will provide the boat angler with a very accurate picture of the sea-bed over which he is sailing. He will, for example, be able to tell at a glance whether he is over sand or shingle, firm mud or ooze, weed or rock. Not only will this help him to decide what fish, if any, he is likely to find there, but it will also help him to decide in advance the baits that are likely to prove most acceptable, and the type of terminal tackle most suitable for the conditions.

Rocky headlands are good places to try for pollack and bass; whilst many flatfish like to lie in sandy hollows on the sea-bed, or near the edge of shelly banks, where they are sheltered from the full force of the tide. Also, in recent years a great deal of fishing has been carried on from Brixham and other south-coast resorts by parties of anglers fishing close to sunken wrecks in large specialist charter boats. Many of these craft are equipped with Decca navigational equipment, which is capable of pinpointing the position of a wreck to within a matter of yards – even though it may be lying upwards of 20 miles offshore, in over 30 fathoms of water.

Huge catches of giant conger (some in excess of 100 lb.), cod, ling, bream, and many other species of fish are taken from these deepwater wrecks. Needless to say, it is a rather expensive form of sea angling, and it could be argued that the impressive results are due more to the charter skipper's skill, and his sophisticated electronic equipment, than to any rod-and-line expertise on the part of his clients.

Small boat anglers who equip themselves with an Admiralty chart and grapnel (or, better still, an echo-sounder) can often try their hand at inshore wreck fishing on a smaller scale – and derive a lot more personal satisfaction in the process. Admiralty charts pinpoint the position of most inshore wrecks, and show the depth of water by means of sounding lines, which are similar to the contour lines on a land map. In addition, a marine chart features prominent longshore landmarks, such as church towers, lighthouses, flagmasts, headlands, etc., and by using these as sighting points it is usually a fairly simple matter to work out in advance a set of cross-bearings, and so navigate without delay close to the position of the sunken wreck. Final contact with the wreck is then made with the grapnel or echo-sounder.

Charts also show, by means of various symbols, the set of the flood- and ebb-tide streams in inshore waters, together with their speed and period of flow. This information will have a special significance for the angler who appreciates the marked effect that tides can have on the feeding habits and movements of fish. There is, in fact, still room for localized research on this subject, and the ordinary angler, with chart and notebook, could collect some very useful and interesting data over a period of years.

Clothing for the boat angler should be warm without being unduly bulky, and there is a lot to be said for the foam-padded waistcoat favoured by yachtsmen, which is not only cold-resisting but will also serve as a buoyancy jacket should the need ever arise. For wet weather, and when the spray is flying, I would recommend a two-piece suit consisting of foul-weather P.V.C. smock and over-trousers. Sou'-westers are obtainable in the same material.

Footwear is very much a matter of personal preference, although nailed shoes or boots, which would scratch paintwork or varnish, should definitely be ruled out. Canvas deck shoes may be comfortable in warm summer weather, but they are not particularly suitable for dealing with sharp-fanged shark, tope, conger and spur-dogfish.

A pair of calf-length wellington boots, worn *underneath* a pair of P.V.C. waterproof over-trousers, will keep the lower half of your body dry in all weathers. For safety's sake, choose a pair of rubber boots at least one size larger than your normal footwear, so that they are loose enough to be kicked off quickly in an emergency.

Long rubber thigh-boots are definitely NOT recommended when fishing in small boats. Admittedly, they look very sea-doggish and professional, but anyone unfortunate enough to fall overboard in them might just as well have a millstone tied round his neck.

Sea sickness is probably the main reason why so many salt-water anglers stick to the shore or pier, and refrain from sampling the superior sport obtainable from a boat. It is worth stressing, therefore, that this most unpleasant illness *can* be cured in the vast majority of cases. During the first few trips it is usually possible to ensure a reasonable degree of comfort by taking an Avomine tablet about an hour before putting to sea. It is also helpful if one's introduction to angling afloat is made in calm, mild weather, in a boat free from the smell of stale bait and a hot, oily engine.

Also, many people who are unaffected by the motion of a boat while it is under way begin to feel extremely uncomfortable as soon as the anchor is lowered over the fishing ground. The best solution in the latter event is to go in for one of the mobile forms of angling, such as trolling, drag-lining, or drifting with float tackle. Following half-a-dozen such trips made at fairly frequent intervals, it will usually be found possible to dispense with the Avomine tablets. After that, the cure will soon be complete – at any rate, so far as those conditions normally encountered by the pleasure angler are concerned.

8

Boat-fishing Techniques

The fishing methods available to the boat angler may conveniently be considered under two headings. First, those which are carried out while at anchor; and secondly, those which can only be practised when the boat is under way.

FISHING AT ANCHOR

The paternoster, in one form or another, is probably the tackle most generally employed from an anchored boat. Often this method is referred to as 'bottom fishing'; although strictly speaking the paternoster is seldom allowed to lie on the bottom beneath a slack line. The customary technique is to lower the tackle to the sea-bed, and then raise it a foot or two in order to draw it clear of seaweed and other obstructions. Sometimes, though, when after certain species of fish, it is necessary to place the hooks at a higher level.

As in most kinds of boat fishing, groundbaiting can make all the difference between success or failure. For this the 'chummy-bag' is normally used. It consists of a pouch of coarse sacking or small-meshed netting, which is weighted with a few pebbles and filled with crushed crabs or fish offal. Lowered overboard on a length of stout codline, or hitched to the anchor rope, it sends a scent trail drifting away on the tide, which sooner or later will attract hungry fish to the boat. If no sack or net bag is available, a large lidded tin with a number of holes punched in it will serve the purpose just as well.

For bottom fishing in its strictest sense, however, many anglers find that the running leger proves most effective. This is particularly noticeable when one is after fish which actually seek their food on the sea-bed, such as rays, turbot, plaice, flounders, conger, etc. Leger tackle is also the best choice when seeking shy-biting kinds of fish which are likely to be put off by the drag of a paternoster lead.

An argument which is sometimes offered against the leger is that where the sea-bed is covered with weed this tackle is liable to become fouled. The arrangement illustrated in Fig. 3 usually provides the answer to this difficulty by allowing the baited hook to stream out on the tide above the level of the weed. Instead of the pear-shaped lead, it is sometimes possible to use a midget chummy-bag weighted with some odds and ends of lead, and baited with oily fish scraps or cotton wool soaked in pilchard oil.

When trying for those fish which normally feed between mid-water and the surface, many boat anglers will decide to use float tackle. As this method has already been dealt with in detail in the chapter on Rock Fishing there is no need to dwell on it here, except to mention that the chummy-bag, if used, should be suspended at the same depth as the baited hook. The chief value of float tackle, from the boat angler's point of view, is that it can be used very effectively at slack water, when there is insufficient water movement to support a drift-line.

A general description of the drift-line, and some notes on the method of using it, have already been given in Chapter Two. It must be pointed out, though, that this form of fishing has long been a controversial subject among boat anglers. Dozens of minor variations are practised around the coasts of Britain, so that from estuary to estuary, and from headland to headland, opinions differ as to what constitutes a good drift-lining technique.

The fact is that tactics and tackle are bound to vary slightly in order to meet differing local conditions; the most important factors being the strength of the tide, the depth of the water, and the habits of the fish one is seeking. As the first two factors are certain to change during the course of a fishing trip, whilst the mood of the fish is likely to vary as well, it is obvious that the tackle must be modified at regular intervals. The substitution of heavier weights as the tidal flow increases, and of lighter weights as it decreases, is essential if the drifting bait is to be kept at the correct depth. Very often, however, when sport falls away, an alteration to the bait itself, or in the size of the hook, will produce a marked improvement. As a general rule, the nearer the bait is fished to the surface, the smaller and finer should be the hook.

Bass and pollack are two common quarries of the driftliner,

and for these fish live sandeels are the finest bait of all; whilst
live prawns can be very effective in districts where sandeels are
unobtainable. Among the dead baits, frozen and fresh
sandeels, and longish strips of fresh mackerel-flesh cut to
resemble a sandeel are both very good. In fast tides plastic
sandeels work well, and I have found that a tiny mackerel lask
attached to the hook of the eel improves matters – possibly by
giving the lure a fishy, lifelike smell.

Dead baits and lures should be kept on the move by sink-
and-draw methods, but whether or not this should be done
with live baits is a debatable point. My own system is to allow
the live bait to move around naturally on an unweighted line,
and to work it gently when using lead.

It will be appreciated that lead on the line makes it sag, and
for this reason a fairly pronounced strike is necessary when a
fish takes weighted tackle. An unweighted drift-line, on the
other hand, carries no slack, and a delicate strike is usually
advisable when using a non-stretch braided line. The
elasticity of nylon monofilament, however, necessitates a
strike varying in vigour with the amount of line between rod-
tip and fish.

Fishing for pollack and coalfish with the feathered lure
known as the cuddy fly may also be carried on from an
anchored boat by methods similar to those used when drift-
lining with other artificial baits. Although referred to as a 'fly',
this lure is really intended to represent a small fish, and
should therefore be worked beneath the water.

One rewarding method is to allow the fly to drift down-tide
until it is close to a submerged or partially submerged rock;
whereupon it is set moving in a series of short, fairly quick
jerks. Alternatively, if the rod and reel are capable of casting
such a light bait, the fly may be sent to a variety of likely
positions all round the boat, and then reeled in. This latter
process must remain largely a matter for personal experiment,
as on some days a slow, steady rate of recovery produces the
best results; whilst at other times an erratically moving fly
seems more inclined to arouse the interest of the fish.

In a few districts it is also possible to take bass with this
type of fishing. Usually, however, it will be found that a red- or
orange-dyed feather has a greater appeal to the bass than the
white feather of the orthodox cuddy fly.

It's never too early to begin shore-casting! Here the author's six-year-old son, Ian, is punching out a mackerel lure with a light 7-foot spinning rod. A few years later (*right*) he is catching bass like an old hand. The rod is a lively 9-foot hollow glass spinner, and the fixed-spool reel is loaded with 10-lb line. This type of bouldery shoreline is difficult to fish, but it certainly has great potential.

Inshore fishing from a small dinghy is capable of producing excellent fish like this specimen-sized thornback ray. It was taken by legering a mackerel strip bait on shelly ground bordering a patch of sea-bed rock.

A nice red bream comes aboard. When boating round-bodied fish like bream and bass it is advisable to use a landing net because their scales are liable to deflect the point of a gaff.

Threadline spinning from an anchored or slowly drifting dinghy with a silver-coloured wobbling spoon, such as the Abu 'Toby' illustrated in Fig. 10, can also yield good catches of bass, together with mackerel, pollack, coalfish and garfish. On some parts of the coast there are areas where bass shoal in large numbers at certain states of the tide, and in these favoured places it is often possible to enjoy wonderful sport with light spinning tackle.

One can catch mackerel, pollack, coalfish, etc. from a drifting boat by 'jigging' with a trace carrying a few feathered hooks. (See Fig. 76.) This can be a very killing method, and is useful for catching mackerel quickly as bait, or for the frying-pan. However, the novelty of catching large numbers of mackerel soon palls, and the sporting possibilities of this method are somewhat limited.

A more sophisticated method of jigging with a large, shiny metal pirk, weighing up to 7 oz. or more, is used on some parts of the coast (notably in the Firth of Clyde and other Scottish sea-lochs) to make large catches of big cod.

FISHING WHILE UNDER WAY

Trolling is the type of fishing most commonly employed from a moving boat; although, as in most other kinds of sea angling, the method covers a number of different techniques, requiring varying degrees of skill. The simple form consists of towing the familiar mackerel spinner behind a boat, on the type of tackle described in Chapter Two. Commonly used with a handline, it is an efficient method of obtaining bait on the way out to the fishing ground.

Success will depend mainly on two factors: knowing where the fish are likely to be found, and trolling the lure at the correct depth. Excitement and activity among gulls, terns, razorbills, guillemots, gannets and other sea birds will often reveal the whereabouts of a shoal, but as a rule the fishing depth will have to be determined by personal experiment, as mackerel tend to swim at various levels according to weather conditions, the time of day, and several other factors. When fishing from a power-driven craft it is a simple enough matter to adjust the depth of the spinner by altering the speed – as the boat moves faster, so the lure will rise higher in the water.

The mackerel is a fast-swimming fish, and it will eagerly

pursue a rapidly moving bait. Even so, there are limits to its capabilities, and rather than increase the speed of the boat too much it is better to fit a lighter weight. Conversely, if a spinner is worked at too low a speed it may give the fish time to make a leisurely inspection of the unnatural lure; in which case it is likely to become suspicious and sheer away.

When fishing from a sailing craft, the speed cannot, of course, be controlled so effectively, and a fairly large range of quick-change weights will be necessary if the lure is to be kept at the correct depth.

Trolling for mackerel is regarded by the majority of rod-and-reel anglers as unsporting; probably because they persist in using the cumbersome type of trolling tackle commonly used by the handliner. This means that a hooked fish not only has to fight a heavy weight, but also has to contend with the water resistance created by the moving boat.

Yet these disadvantages can be ruled out, and excellent sport obtained, if a light spinning rod is used, and the trace fitted with a streamlined 1 oz. lead. Alternatively, when trolling with this sort of light outfit, it is possible to use a self-weighted metal lure, such as a 1 oz. ABU 'Krill', with no additional up-trace lead. From a rowing-boat, which can be allowed to drift as soon as a fish is hooked, the sport will be even better, although the number of fish caught may not be so great.

We have devoted a good deal of attention to the mackerel because it is readily caught in large numbers all around the British coast during the summer months; whilst for its size it is probably our hardest-fighting fish. Several other very sporting fish may be caught in large numbers by trolling, however; the most notable being the bass and the pollack.

For bass, suitable lures are the plastic sandeel, rubber eels, and silvery, fish-shaped wobbling spoons. They should be trolled at a moderate speed near rocks, reefs, across a tide-swept estuary mouth, or some other known haunt of these fish.

Fig. 33 Plastic Sandeel.

Natural baits, however, are usually taken more readily – the finest of all being a medium-sized sandeel. A small fish mounted on a spinning flight, or a tiny eel, found under a longshore boulder, and threaded with a baiting needle for about a third of its length on to a long-shanked hook, are two other very killing baits.

As in the case of the mackerel, finding the depth at which bass are feeding is very much a matter of trial and error. They have a liking for water aerated by surf, and are often to be found lying close to wave-pounded rocks and tide-swept headlands. Usually, but not always, they will be found on the down-tide side, as this is where the bass are most likely to find the small fry on which they feed.

Pollack, which are almost invariably found in the vicinity of steep-to rocks, reefs and submerged wrecks, normally feed close to the bottom. When trolling for these fish, therefore, the trace will either have to carry a heavier lead, or the bait will have to be fished more slowly. Natural baits may consist of a sandeel, or a mackerel strip cut to resemble a sandeel. Among

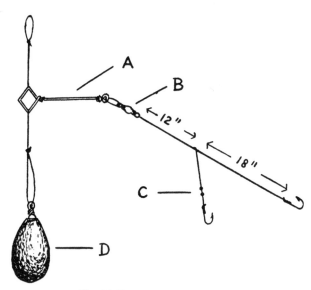

Fig. 34 Paternoster-trot.
A: brass wire boom; B: swivel link; C: split shot; D: swivelled "Arlesley Bomb".

the artificial baits the most killing without a doubt is a plastic sandeel. This should be presented on a 7 to 10-foot trace of about 17 to 20-lb. breaking-strain.

Finally, in this chapter on boat fishing methods, we come to the technique of drag-lining, in which the boat is allowed to drift freely with the wind and tide, dragging some form of bottom tackle along the sea-bed.

Obviously, this form of fishing is practicable only over snag-free areas of sand, shell-grit, gravel or mud; although local knowledge will sometimes permit its use close to the tail-end of a submerged reef. When fished near rocks in this manner, drag-line tackle may well prove the undoing of good-sized cod, pollack and ling. As a rule, however, it is flatfish and various other bottom-feeding fish of the sand and mud banks which are taken by this method.

One advantage of drag-lining is that boat, tackle and tidal current are all usually travelling more or less at the same speed, so that only a very small amount of lead is needed to keep the baited trace on the sea-bed. As for the choice of terminal trace, this depends very much on the type of fish one is seeking. For whiting a paternoster rig is best; although strictly speaking it is not used in the true drag-line style, as the lead is held just clear of the bottom so that the line hangs vertically. My own preference for drag-lining proper lies with the paternoster-trot or the free-running leger – the first-named for the smaller types of flatfish and codling; the latter when after large cod, rays, and turbot.

Dusk is a good time to try for rays, and it is worth bearing in mind that these fish have a liking for patches of shell-grit or gravel in the vicinity of rough ground. Night fishing for rays is also rewarding, but the fact that rocks are often not far distant makes drag-lining in complete darkness a risky business for the tackle, if not for the boat itself.

Another point worth remembering when drag-lining is that many fish swim into the tide as they feed. Consequently, there is a better chance of making contact with these fish when a breeze is blowing in such a direction that the boat is driven obliquely across the tidal current. On a still evening, when only the merest breath of air is stirring, a bit of canvas and a lashed tiller can sometimes be used with good effect by the sailing-dinghy owner.

Given suitable conditions of sea-bed, weather and tide, drag-lining will often produce better results than the more usual methods of static fishing. The slight disturbance of the mud or sand made by the trailing lead probably attracts the attention of the fish some distance away; whilst the fact that the bait is moving prompts them to snatch at it more eagerly than if it were lying motionless.

9

Sea Fish Worth Catching – and How to Catch Them

So far in this book we have discussed sea-fishing tackle and baits, and described the various ways in which they may be used. Except for a few brief passing references, however, little has so far been written about the fish themselves, and the object of this chapter is to give the sea angler a clear picture of the fish which may be caught on rod and line around the coasts of Britain.

Listed in alphabetical order for easy reference, the details given include a concise description of each species, together with notes on the areas in which it is found; the kind of coastline, water or sea-bed it favours most, and its feeding and migratory habits. In addition, details are given of those baits which have a special appeal for the fish under consideration, and the tackle and methods most likely to result in its capture.

ANGLER FISH

This remarkable creature is seldom mentioned in books on sea angling, probably because it is only caught by chance and skill does not enter into the picture. Despite this fact, however, the successful capture of an angler fish with rod and line has a certain prestige value, and its bizarre appearance is usually the cause of considerable interest among those present at the time.

The angler is a slow and awkward swimmer, so that in order to catch its food it is compelled, like its human namesake, to resort to low cunning. After choosing a likely 'beat', often on a patch of sea-bed where weed-covered rocks are interspersed with patches of muddy sand, it settles down patiently to a long spell of angling.

It is an adept at camouflage, and is capable of changing its colour to match its surroundings. Also, a fringe of weed-

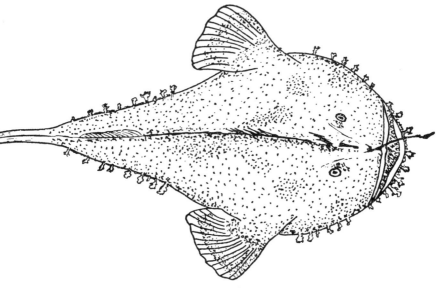

Fig. 35 Angler Fish.

shaped pieces of skin about its body and lower jaw helps to break up its outline, so that when lying motionless on the bottom it is almost invisible.

The 'tackle' used by this finny fisherman is light even by the most modern standards, and the manner in which it is used is very interesting. The first ray of the dorsal fin is over-developed to such an extent that it may best be described as a long, thin tentacle, sprouting from the front of the fish's head. This tentacle serves as a combined rod and line, and has at its end a tiny lure.

Salt-water fishermen could probably learn quite a lot about the use of artificial lures by visiting a marine aquarium and studying the technique of these fish. The bait is kept on the move in several different directions with a jerking motion designed to resemble the erratic swimming of some small sea creature.

To the eye of another fish this sort of movement must give the lure a much more lifelike appearance than the monotonous 'lure-flogging' adopted by many human anglers.

There is every indication that the angler is a discerning

fisherman, with a distinct preference for young pollack, pouting and whiting. The appearance of any of these fish will cause the lure to twitch to and fro in pleasurable anticipation, and if one of these small fish becomes attracted, it is cunningly guided by means of the lure to a position close to the anglers' enormous mouth.

The final scene is then played out before the watcher realizes what is happening. The jaws open and close with the speed of a camera shutter, and in one bewildering split second the unsuspecting victim is hooked, gaffed and utterly annihilated by a truly gruesome array of needle-sharp teeth.

More than one rod-and-line fisherman has learnt to his cost just how sharp the teeth of an angler fish can be, and should you happen to catch one, it would be as well to treat it with respect. These fish are capable of living for a long time out of water, lying motionless as though dead – until a hand or foot comes just a little too close to those gin-trap jaws!

BASS

These powerful, hard-fighting fish are dark grey on the back, shading to silver on the flanks and white on the belly. Bass found in British waters are at the northernmost limit of their distribution range, which extends south as far as the Mediterranean. Consequently, British anglers are most likely to encounter them around the south-eastern, southern and south-western coasts of England. They are also widely spread around most shores of Wales, and southern and western Ireland. The British rod-caught records for this species stand at 18 lb. 6 oz. (boat) and 18 lb. 2 oz. (shore), but the average fish usually weighs about 3 to 4 lb., and the capture of a 10 lb.

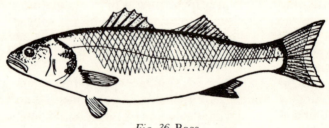

Fig. 36 Bass.

specimen may be regarded as a notable achievement. Good to eat, and providing excellent sport on reasonably light tackle, bass belong to the select company of sea fish chosen by anglers for specialist fishing.

Throughout summer and autumn bass are often to be found near surf-pounded rocks and submerged reefs a short distance offshore. Rugged headlands also have an attraction for them, and light spinning tackle worked from a suitable stance will sometimes provide good sport for the shore fisherman.

Bass have a roving nature, and their movements are governed to a very large degree by the ebb and flow of the tides. Thus, on a certain stretch of coastline, some of the shore marks may fish best during the early flood tide; others may yield their best results around half-flood or half-ebb; whilst some positions well up an estuary tideway may prove most profitable during the slack high-water period. Patches of surfy water sweeping over sand-bars and gravelly spits at the mouths of estuaries are also favourite feeding grounds for bass (especially during slack low water and the early flood), and some exceptionally good catches are made on occasions by anglers fishing these spots.

Feeding Habits. Bass are ever on the look-out for food, although the larger fish are often inclined to treat a baited hook with suspicion. Their natural diet consists largely of prawns, sandeels, shore crabs, swimming crabs, small edible crabs and small fish, including sprats, herring fry, and young wrasse, pouting, pollack, mullet, etc.

Shore Fishing. Surf-casting off a coarse sand or pea-gravel beach is probably the most popular method of shore fishing for bass. The terminal tackle should be as neat and inconspicuous as possible, and (depending on local conditions) the favourite rigs are: (i) a light monofilament paternoster (one or two hooks); (ii) a single-hook running paternoster; (iii) a two-hook Wessex leger; or (iv) a single-hook free-running leger with a flowing trace.

All these terminal rigs are described fully in Chapters Two and Five, together with hints on the most suitable leads to suit varying sea and shore conditions; the avoidance of trace tangles, etc.

Whatever type of terminal tackle is used when surf-casting, your main objective should be to cast the bait out to where the back-scour from the surf is uncovering the small marine creatures on which the bass feed. This type of fishing calls for firm baits which will stay on the hook well, such as squid, black lugworm, fresh mackerel strips and large ragworm. However, with careful baiting, one of the most killing baits of all is a medium-sized sandeel – despite the fact that these tiny, silvery fish are comparatively fragile creatures.

Where fairly deep water comes close in to a rocky headland, steeply shelving shingle beach, estuary mouth channel, or similar vantage point, it is often only necessary to cast a short distance in order to reach the fish. In such situations it is therefore possible to lob out larger and softer baits. Peeler crab, for example, is a particularly attractive bait for big bass, especially when fishing in a rocky area, or from an estuary shoreline.

From steep-to rocks, headlands and harbour breakwaters it is also possible to fish for bass with float tackle. For this type of fishing there is no better bait than a live medium-sized sandeel – unless it be (in rocky areas) a large live prawn.

Rocky or shingly shorelines (where the water is usually reasonably clear) are also capable of providing excellent sport with a light spinning outfit and suitable artificial lure. A medium-sized wobbling spoon is an excellent choice of lure, as it is easy to cast and will attract bass under most sea and shore conditions. A 1-oz. 'Toby' spoon is one of my favourites, because it is has a most tantalizing fluttering action in the water.

Boat Fishing. By using light tackle with a minimum of lead, the boat angler is able to enjoy to the full the sporting potential of the bass. One very rewarding method, which is particularly well suited to the inshore dinghy angler, is to anchor the boat a safe distance up-tide of a surf-washed rock or headland, and to send out a baited drift-line. Live sandeels and prawns are the best of all baits for this kind of fishing.

Another favourite method of mine is slow trolling with a medium-powered spinning rod and 12-lb. line around an estuary sand-bar, wave-washed rocks and islets, submerged reefs, rocky headlands, and similar hotspots. In this sort of trolling one can use either a fresh natural sandeel, or the artificial plastic variety, such as the well-known 'Red Gill'. It is, however, essential to use a long flowing trace, and to present the bait or lure at least 50 yards or more behind the boat.

Some other rewarding boat-fishing methods for bass include float fishing and legering in estuaries and shallow inlets, and spin-casting from a drifting dinghy in areas where bass are known to shoal regularly.

BLACK BREAM

Although comparatively small, with an average size of about $1\frac{1}{2}$ to $2\frac{1}{2}$ lb., black bream put up an excellent fight on light tackle, and are very popular with many south-coast boat anglers. They are somewhat localised in British waters, being mainly encountered off the coasts of Sussex (notably off the port of Littlehampton), Hampshire, Isle of Wight, Dorset, South Devon and the Channel Islands.

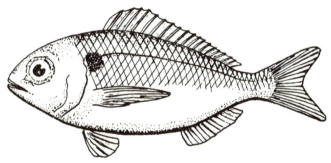

Fig. 37 Red Bream

Black bream are deep-bodied fish, and their coloration is very variable. However, adult fish are generally dark grey or bluish-grey along the back, shading to a dull silvery tint along the sides with stippled brownish longitudinal markings. Spawning males have a small band of bluish-grey between the eyes.

Season and Haunts. Black bream are mostly found near the bottom over areas of broken rock, bouldery clay, and in the vicinity of wrecks. They begin to appear over these marks round about May or June, depending on water depth and locality, and in some areas (particularly off West Dorset and South Devon) they remain until well into October.

The majority of black bream are caught by boat anglers, but on some parts of the coast they can be caught from piers and beaches. As a general rule, however, these shore-caught fish are rather small – one notable exception being the Channel Islands, where decent-sized black bream, weighing up to 3 lb. or more, are regularly taken from harbour breakwaters and selected rock fishing positions.

Feeding Habits. Diet includes shrimps, prawns, small molluscs, marine worms and various other small sea-bed creatures.

Shore Fishing Methods. As previously mentioned, specialist shore fishing for black bream is mainly confined to the Channel Islands and a few other localised areas. The methods used include:

(i) Light nylon monofilament paternoster or leger cast out from a pier-head or harbour breakwater butting on to fairly deep water, preferably on clear ground close alongside an area of weedy rocks.

(ii) Sliding float tackle adjusted to fish deep over an area of weedy rocks.

Boat-Fishing Methods. To enjoy the full sporting potential of the black bream, try drift-lining with a light spinning rod and 8 or 9 lb. breaking-strain nylon monofilament reel line. Use the minimum amount of lead needed to slant the line down to the sea-bed – a 1-oz. bomb being about right in average tidal conditions. Hooks should range from about size 2 to 8, depending on the bait used and the mood of the fish, and should be presented on a flowing 6-foot trace of slightly lower breaking-strain than the reel line.

In areas where tides are slack, the flowing trace can be attached to a single boom. This will help to prevent the trace tangling with the reel line when it is being lowered swiftly to the fishing depth.

The most rewarding fishing depth is usually about 3 or 4 feet off the bottom, but bream shoals do quite often feed at other depths (especially around slack water) so don't be afraid to experiment. If the fish are biting shyly, try reeling up very slowly, as this often helps to stimulate them into action.

Groundbaiting will almost certainly help to attract the fish and get them on feed, and this is best done by filling a weighted net bag or perforated metal canister with mashed-up mackerel flesh and guts, crushed shore crabs, etc. Alternatively, try soaking bran with some commercial grade cod liver oil.

The hook baits most appreciated by black bream are pieces of squid tentacle, fresh mackerel and herring strips, lugworm, ragworm, mussels, and small portions of sandeel.

RED BREAM

As its name implies, the red bream is a bright reddish-orange or crimson along the back, shading to silvery-red on the sides and below. A prominent distinguishing feature of adult fish is the dark patch situated on either side at the commencement of the lateral line. Young bream, which lack this mark, are commonly referred to as 'chad'.

At one time huge shoals of red bream visited our shores every summer, but from the early nineteen-twenties onwards their numbers began steadily to decline. In recent years, however, these fish have made something of a come-back, and some very good red bream are now being captured in West Country waters, especially in the vicinity of deepwater wrecks.

Red bream are a popular fish with many sea anglers. Although they do not put up quite such a spirited fight as the black bream, they certainly share the latter fish's excellent eating qualities, and are delicious when baked or grilled.

Fishing Methods. Red bream caught from the shore are usually small 'chad', and for this reason specialist fishing for this species is almost invariably carried on from a boat – the best-sized fish being found in water over 10 to 15 fathoms deep. Although plenty of bream will be caught during the daytime, they are primarily nocturnal feeders and bites usually become more numerous around sundown. If this period happens to coincide with slack water, so much the better, because light tackle may then be used.

As a rule bream are taken over broken ground or seaweedy patches, and in the vicinity of sunken wrecks. More often than not they will be found within a few feet of the sea-bed; failing this, the terminal tackle should be raised in stages through three or four fathoms. The terminal tackle, baits and groundbaiting techniques are basically similar to those recommended for black bream; although in actual practice the rod and line are likely to be slightly heavier in order to cope with the big pollack which are often encountered over deepwater red bream marks – especially off the coasts of Devon and Cornwall.

BRILL

This flatfish is related to the turbot, to which it bears a close resemblance. However, it is more oval in shape, and does not attain such a large size. It also lacks the blunt, bony tubercles of the turbot. The upper side is usually a mottled and speckled brown; although slight local variations in the background colour are quite common. Underneath, the fish is white.

Feeding Habits. The brill lives almost entirely upon small fish.

Fishing Methods. Normally an inhabitant of fairly deep water, the brill is usually taken by the boat angler over sandy or muddy ground a mile or more offshore. Occasionally, however, it comes inside the five-fathoms line, and may then be caught by anglers casting out from steep-to beaches or pier-

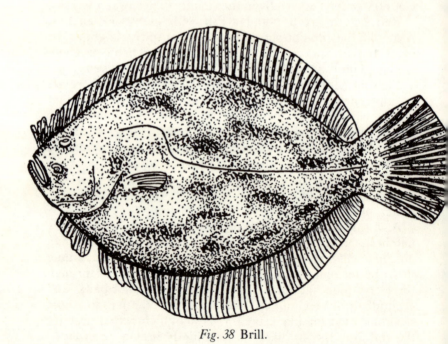

Fig. 38 Brill.

heads. Leger tackle carrying a fairly long trace and one or two long-shanked hooks usually produces best results.

Baits should consist of sandeels, mackerel strips, sprats, smelts, etc. The first-mentioned bait is undoubtedly best, but the others are effective provided they are used when absolutely fresh.

COALFISH

Known in Scotland as the saithe, the coalfish is black on the back, shading to bluish-green on the sides and silvery grey below. The lateral line is white and almost straight, and contrasts vividly with its dark background. Incidentally, this pale-coloured lateral line distinguishes the coalfish from its close relative, the pollack (*q.v.*), which has a dark, curved lateral line and a more protruding lower jaw.

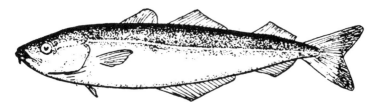

Fig. 39 Coalfish.

The coalfish is by nature an inhabitant of our more northerly waters; although it may be caught as far south as Cornwall, and in the vicinity of deepwater wrecks off the South Devon coast. The big fish found over these deep marks put up a superb fight on reasonably light tackle.

Feeding Habits. Fish, squid and crustaceans are all preyed upon by coalfish, which will travel long distances in pursuit of shoals of young herring. There is evidence also that these fish wreak considerable havoc on young salmon venturing into salt water for the first time.

Shore Fishing. It is mostly the younger and smaller fish – often referred to as 'billet' – which are taken by the shore angler. Where reasonably deep water surrounds a rocky headland or harbour wall, it is possible to use float tackle baited with a live prawn, ragworm, or a strip of mackerel or herring. Quite often, when the fish seem reluctant to bite, they can be persuaded to snatch at the baited hook by slowly retrieving the float.

Spinning with an artificial lure, such as a small silver-coloured spoon or plastic sandeel, may also be tried if conditions are suitable.

When billet are close in under a rocky scaur or harbour wall, large catches can also be made by retrieving a cuddy fly or feathered trace under the water with short, quick jerks.

Boat Fishing. Driftlining 'deep and steep' with a long flowing trace is the most rewarding method when fishing over deepwater marks, including sunken wrecks. Recommended baits include mackerel strip and squid; also a live sandeel or small 'joey' mackerel.

Alternative methods include jigging with a shiny metal pirk, feathered trace, or one or two plastic sandeels presented 'paternoster fashion' on 6-inch nylon snoods from a heavier nylon monofilament main trace. The latter method is particularly attractive to really big wreck coalfish in the 20-30 lb. range.

In areas where the smaller billet are to be found off rocky headlands, and over inshore reefs, one can also obtain good results by trolling with a plastic sandeel or shiny metal spoon, or by spinning with similar lures from a drifting boat.

COD

This popular food fish has a heavy cylindrical body, which tapers rapidly towards the unforked tail. In its large head the upper jaw is noticeably longer than the lower, and this results in a 'receding chin', from the underside of which there depends a long barbule. The colour of the cod varies considerably, but is usually greenish-grey or brownish, with or without marbling or spots. Some cod captured from areas of kelpy rock are a deep reddish-gold colour.

Size is another very variable factor. Deep-sea trawlers have taken cod weighing over a hundredweight, and one truly enormous specimen, caught on the other side of the Atlantic, actually tipped the scales at $211\frac{1}{2}$ lb. The rod-and-line angler, however, can count himself lucky when one of his fish tops the 15-lb. mark, and in fact most of those caught from the shore will be considerably smaller. Those under about 6 lb. are usually referred to as codling.

Cod visit our inshore waters towards the back-end of the year; the first arrivals being the codling in September. They are followed by larger fish until by December – weather permitting – anglers are making their biggest catches.

Feeding Habits. The cod's diet is probably more comprehensive than any other fish caught in British waters. Normally it swims close to the bottom where, if any remotely digestible marine creature happens to get in its way, it simply opens its mouth and swallows it. Sometimes, indeed, the items swallowed are downright indigestible, so that gutting a cod is always something of an adventure. Pine-cones, plastic drinking beakers, a bunch of keys, false teeth and a tin of corn plasters are just a few of the many intriguing objects which have been found inside these amazing fish!

Shore Fishing. During late autumn and winter, cod are caught in good numbers from steeply shelving beaches and rock positions around the north, east and south-east coasts of Britain. Elsewhere their arrival over inshore marks is more localised.

Beach-casting with a paternoster rig (5/0 hook on a 9-inch dropper) is a widely practised method of shore cod fishing. Fairly long casts of about a 100 yards or more may be necessary to reach the feeding zone, and this necessitates the use of a fairly powerful outfit. Typically this could consist of an $11\frac{1}{2}$ to 12-foot rod designed to cast a 5-oz lead, matched with a multiplier loaded with 25-lb. breaking-strain main line and a 40-lb. breaking-strain 'shock leader'. In rough seas or

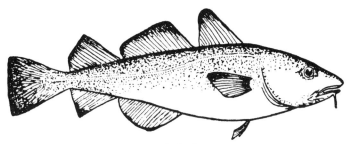

Fig. 40 Cod.

fast lateral currents it is best to use a spiked anchor lead – my own preference being for the 'Breakaway' type which automatically releases its grip on the bottom when striking at a fish.

On parts of the rocky north-east coast the local anglers have to cast out into snaggy rocks and kelp jungles, and then a much heavier reel line is necessary. The sinker is usually attached by a short length of weaker line so that it can be abandoned if it gets snagged up.

Baits include bunched lugworms, squid, mussels, slipper limpets, hermit crabs, ragworms and herring cuttings.

Boat Fishing. Paternoster or paternoster-trot are commonly used with the baits already recommended for shore fishing. When big fish are about, however, it is often a good plan to use a single large hook on a free-running leger. This can either be presented right on the bottom as a true leger, or a foot or so above the bottom in driftline fashion.

On some parts of the coast – notably over localised marks in a few favoured Scottish sea-lochs – excellent catches of big cod are made by jigging with a large shiny metal pirk weighing up to 7 oz. or more. The most famous of these cod marks is undoubtedly the Gantocks area, in the Firth of Clyde, but there are plenty of others.

When jigging for cod the lure should be worked fairly close to the bottom with a sink-and-draw action, and this can be done very effectively from a drifting boat. This method of fishing has captured some exceptionally large cod, and it originated in the fjords of Northern Norway.

CONGER

This large and extremely powerful sea-eel has featured prominently in countless 'tall' angler's tales; for there is

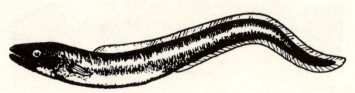

Fig. 41 Conger Eel.

something about its thick, slimy body and vicious, serpent-like head which tends to stir the imagination. Indeed, there is a sort of horrible fascination about fishing for big conger; which is probably the reason why in recent years rod-and-line fishermen in ever-increasing numbers have been trying their hand at this exciting pastime.

For many years the British rod-caught record for conger was held by that renowned angler of former days, H.A. Kelly, with an 84-lb. specimen captured off Dungeness in 1933. Although larger conger eels, some of them exceeding 100 lb., were taken fairly regularly by commercial fishermen, Mr Kelly's rod-caught record remained safe until 1970, when it was toppled by Colin Chapman with an 85-pounder while fishing out of the South Devon port of Brixham.

By that time many angling charter boats fishing in West-Country waters were equipped with sophisticated electronic navigation equipment which enabled them to pinpoint deepwater wrecks up to 30 miles or more offshore. These isolated wrecks, many of which had remained unfished for over half a century, were the haunt of countless huge conger, and during the 1970s the conger record changed hands several times. At the time of writing it is held by Mr R. Potter with a magnificent eel weighing 109 lb. 6 oz. He captured it in 1976 while fishing over a wreck south-east of the Eddystone. Make no mistake, however – there are undoubtedly plenty of bigger ones lurking down below, waiting to be caught!

The discouraging argument that fish nowadays rarely have a chance to attain their maximum size, owing to over-fishing, does not apply to the conger, because these big sea-eels spawn once, and once only, when they are fully grown. This occurs far from our shores, and the conger's reward for accomplishing this task is almost certain death. Obviously, therefore, the very fact that this species continues to flourish in great numbers is proof that millions of conger succeed in growing to their maximum size.

This maximum size varies considerably from fish to fish, but the average probably lies somewhere in the region of 30 to 40 lb. for females. The male fish are much smaller.

Just why a few conger seem to attain really gigantic proportions is a debatable point. It may be that these fish are sexually retarded. After all, if a normal conger grows until it reaches maturity, it is reasonable to suppose that an infertile female just keeps on growing.

Boat Fishing. The sheer strength and relentless pulling power of a big conger have to be experienced to be believed, and strong, reliable tackle is essential. For deepwater wreck and reef fishing I would suggest a short-butted glassfibre rod in the 50-lb. class, about $6\frac{1}{2}$ to 7 feet in length. A roller line-guide at the tip is a useful refinement.

The usual choice of reel is a heavy-duty multiplier, such as the Tatler 4 or Senator 6/0. This should be located with at least 250 yards of 50-lb. breaking-strain line. When fishing deep water most conger anglers prefer to use a nylon monofilament reel line because its smooth surface offers less resistance to tidal currents than braided line. Also, it is less likely to fray against the wreck.

The reel line carries a sliding Clements boom to which the lead is attached in leger fashion. The line is connected by a heavy-duty swivel to a 12-inch length of flexible stainless wire of at least 100 lb. breaking-strain. The hook needs to be strong and large – a forged 9/0 or 10/0 being about right in deepwater wrecking.

Of course, when fishing over shallower inshore conger marks, the tackle can be scaled down accordingly. However, even inshore conger can run pretty big – up to 40 lb. or more on occasions – so never under-estimate your adversary. Incidentally, *inshore* conger nearly always bite best towards late evening and after dark because they are primarily nocturnal feeders.

Conger will often pluck at a bait cautiously before finally deciding to accept it, and an over-impetuous strike will ruin any chance of taking the fish. As soon as the drag becomes really determined, a little firm resistance from the rod end will result in the startled fish doing all the striking that is necessary!

From thenceforth every effort should be made to heave the eel away from the sea-bed as quickly as possible. As the conger will be equally determined to gain the sanctuary of its lair, a tug-o'-war is the inevitable result.

Much of my own inshore conger fishing is done in an open dinghy, and in these circumstances I find it helps a lot to play out a big eel in mid-water. An over-lively conger, when brought to the surface, will often spin round and round at the end of the trace like a skipping-rope, and a single-handed struggle with rod, gaff and several feet of rapidly revolving eel can be a pretty nerve-racking business – especially when fishing at night.

A played-out conger is an easier target altogether; although even then care must be taken to send the gaff home near the head or tail – never in the middle of the body.

What you do next with your catch will probably depend on the size of your boat. Obviously, it is inadvisable to have a large and disgruntled conger slithering about the bottom boards of a small dinghy – especially if you happen to be wearing flimsy canvas yachting shoes! My own system is to drop the gaffed eel straight into a strong sack, unclipping the hook and short length of wire trace prior to closing the neck of the bag.

Incidentally, when opening the bag again at the end of the fishing trip, remember that conger eels live for many hours out of water. So beware of those which play possum. Many a finger has been bitten off by a 'dead' conger.

Shore Fishing. Conger are often hooked by shore anglers fishing after dark from rocky beaches and old stone harbour walls. Although the average size of shore-caught conger tends to be rather small, there are plenty of beach, harbour and estuary positions which regularly produce hefty eels weighing up to 40 lb. or more. The most suitable tackle for this sort of fishing is a strong leger trace with a 7-inch length of flexible stainless wire, or soft 'unbiteable' twine, next to the hook. This short hook link should be attached to the main flowing trace by a strong swivel-clip. This enables a freshly-caught conger to be detached from the terminal tackle without placing one's fingers too close to those vicious teeth. It only takes a few seconds to unclip the old hook and wire link from the swivel, and to fit a new one in its place.

Long casts are rarely needed when shore fishing for conger, and my choice of rod is usually an 11 or 11½-foot beach-caster. A *strong* multiplier reel should be used (NOT a fixed-spool), and the line should be at least 30 lb. breaking-strain.

Baits. Most fish baits will be taken; the most effective being oily varieties such as mackerel, herring, sprats and pilchard. Conger are also very partial to squid.

DAB

Averaging about 8 oz., the common dab is one of our smallest flatfish. As a sporting species, of course, it comes nowhere, but for its eating qualities it is well worth catching, and is much sought after by utilitarian anglers.

The colour of its upper side varies, but as a rule it is a lightish brown, either with or without darker spots. The underneath, or 'blind side', is white. In the lateral line there is a very abrupt curve just above the pectoral fin, and this distinguishes it from the Long Rough Dab, in which the lateral line is almost straight. The Smooth Dab is merely a local name for the Lemon Sole.

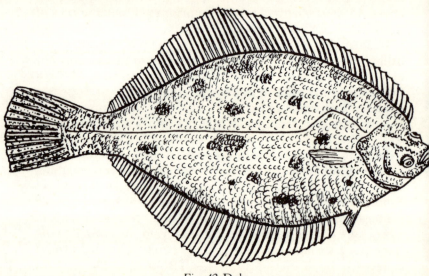

Fig. 42 Dab.

In common with all flatfish, the dab begins life with a round body and an eye on either side of its head. While still in its early infancy, however, it gradually takes to swimming at deeper and deeper levels, at the same time taking on a pronounced tilt to the left – or, to put it more nautically, with a heavy list to port. In this way the post-larval dab gradually becomes a true flatfish, swimming and resting on the sea-bed on its left side; whilst the pigmented upper side takes on a colour that matches almost exactly that of its surroundings. The underside (which hitherto was also pigmented) becomes white.

Most remarkable of all, however, is the fact that during this post-larval transformation from symmetrical fish to flatfish, the eye which would otherwise have finished up on the underside travels round the top of the skull until it ends up in a more useful position beside the other one.

Thus a dab is said to be 'right-eyed', in order to distinguish it from various other species of flatfish which instinctively choose to lie on their right side, and so finish up with eyes on the left side of the head.

Feeding Habits. The dab inhabits shallow, sandy bays, and feeds mainly on small sea-bed creatures such as hermit crabs, clams, sand-stars, lugworms, tube-worms and sandeels.

Fishing Methods. Whether fishing from boat or pier, the methods and tackle used to catch dabs are more or less identical. The fish are easily taken on a light leger or paternoster-trot carrying two or three size-8 hooks baited with lugworm, ragworm, peeled shrimp, mussel, soft crab, hermit crab or cockles.

DOGFISH

Several different species of dogfish are found in British waters. All are small members of the shark family, but have widely differing habits.

The Smooth Hound. There are, in fact, two species present in British waters – the Common Smooth Hound (*Mustelus mustelus*) and the Stellate Smooth Hound (*Mustelus asterias*). Both have a slender, tope-like body which may attain a length of 4 feet or more. In the case of *Mustelus mustelus* the body is usually a uniform grey on the back with lighter sides and whitish belly. Some fish also have some widely spaced black spots. In *Mustelus asterias*, the greyish colour on the back may not be so uniform, and there are white spots scattered over the back and sides.

Both species live close to the bottom in areas of sand, mud or muddy sand, and may be encountered in a wide variety of depths from close inshore to 50 fathoms or more. They will take soft crab and oily fish baits. Unlike the next two dogfish on our list, they give a reasonable account of themselves when hooked on light tackle. Use a flowing leger rig with a length of flexible stainless steel wire next to the hook.

The Greater Spotted Dogfish, or Bull Huss, is a bottom feeder and favours a rocky locality. It is frequently caught on hooks and baits intended for conger. Although most commonly taken by boat anglers, some are also caught when shore-casting from rocky stretches of coast.

With its blotchy leathery skin, the Bull Huss is rather an ugly brute. For all that, it makes good eating when skinned, divided into cutlets, and deep-fried in batter.

The Lesser Spotted Dogfish is found mainly on sand or muddy sand, and is often caught inshore during the summer months on fairly light leger tackle and smallish baits. I once caught a good specimen with half a whitebait! The most popular bait, however, is a slender strip of fresh-caught mackerel presented on a 2/0 or 3/0 hook.

The colour of this fish varies from greyish to yellowish-red, with darker blotches and small black spots. It cannot be called a fighter, but some have a disconcerting habit, when caught from a boat, of spinning round and round in the water, causing a badly tangled trace unless it is adequately swivelled.

It makes reasonably good eating, and can be prepared for the table in the same way as the Greater Spotted Dogfish, although some may consider the flavour somewhat inferior.

The Spur Dogfish. Unlike the bottom-dwelling dogfishes already described, the spur-dog may be encountered at all levels – particularly when in pursuit of shoals of pelagic fish. It is also more streamlined than the greater and lesser spotted dogfish, and its colour is dark grey or brownish on the back, with a few pale spots, and white underneath.

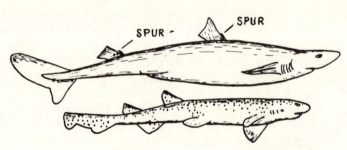

Fig. 43 Spur Dogfish (*top*) and Lesser Spotted Dogfish.

Off various parts of the coast, ranging from Scotland to Cornwall, the spur-dog hunts in large 'packs' with a wolf-like rapacity. It is almost certainly the most hated fish in British waters, for not only does it rob the nets of the commercial fishermen, but also causes untold damage to the nets whilst doing so.

No particular skill is required to catch the spur dogfish, for it is such a bold biter that it virtually hooks itself. Indeed, many professional long-liners are able to quote instances where these fish, already caught by one hook, have dragged the line as far as the next snood and hooked themselves again.

They can be caught with most baits, although they have a preference for strips of oily fish, such as mackerel, herring or pilchard.

A pack of dogfish round the boat will provide almost non-stop action, but their presence will scare off most other fish. Therefore the angler suffering from a 'surfeit of dogs' would be well advised to up-anchor and slip quietly away to another mark in order to add variety to his bag.

It is worth mentioning in conclusion that the spur-dog can be dangerous. As its name implies, it is armed with a shark spur or 'pike' in front of each dorsal fin, and with these it will lash out at its captor's arms and legs if given half a chance. Before attempting to remove the hook, therefore, it is advisable to pin down the tail firmly with a booted foot and stun the fish with a heavy blow on the head with a priest, or similar 'blunt instrument'. Even then, I would advise you to keep your foot on the tail while disgorging the hook, just to be on the safe side.

FLOUNDER

This flatfish is found all round the coasts of Britain where conditions are suitable, and good catches are made close inshore over flat expanses of sand or mud. For most of the year (from early summer to midwinter) the flounder is mainly found in tidal river estuaries. During late winter and early spring, however, the adult fish migrate out into the open sea to spawn.

The flounder has a smooth back, which varies a good deal in colour from district to district. Those taken on a sandy bottom are often dark brown, whilst mud-feeders are sometimes almost black. Some fish bear faint yellowish or pinkish spots, which fade soon after they have been caught. Normally, the eyes are on the right side of the head, but occasionally a 'reversed' specimen may be taken which has its eyes on the left.

Feeding Habits. Adult flounders feed near the bottom on a diet consisting largely of lug and various other marine worms, sand shrimps, sandeels and other small fish.

Shore Fishing. Good results are often obtained with a light paternoster-trot; or, alternatively, a Wessex leger with one long-shanked size 1 or 2 hook below the lead, and another above. Repeated casting and reeling in is more likely to arouse the interest of the fish than allowing the baits to lie motionless; whilst quite often this also avoids trouble from bait-robbing shore crabs.

In places where even the foregoing tactics are of no avail against the crabs, it may be better to use light float tackle set to fish only a few inches above the bottom. Yet another alternative is to use a single-hook leger rig, with a small cigar-shaped balsa float threaded about 4 to 9 inches up the flowing

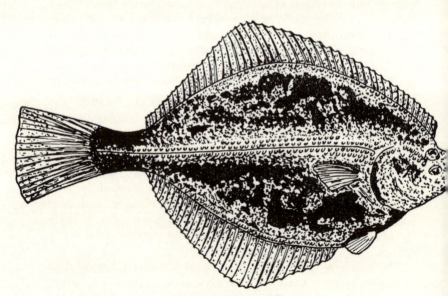

Fig. 44 Flounder.

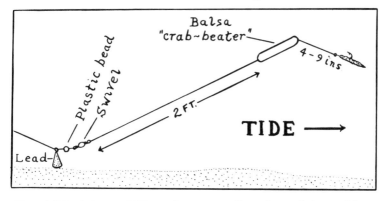

Fig. 45 "Crab-beater" Trace for estuary flounders, plaice and bass. It incorporates a small submerged balsa float to lift the baited hook a foot or so off the bottom.

trace to lift the baited hook clear of the bottom – and out of reach of the crabs! When a flounder takes the bait, the strike should be delayed for a second or two.

Baits recommended are lugworm, ragworm, peeler and soft crab, hermit-crab tails and live shrimps.

Boat Fishing. Tackle and baits as suggested above for shore fishing may be used from an anchored boat. In addition, there is the 'baited-spoon' method. In this a revolving plastic or shiny metal spoon, about 3 inches long, and carrying a single long-shanked hook, is baited with ragworm and trolled gently behind the boat, which should be rowed with the tide at about slow walking speed. This method of fishing can be very rewarding, but it is important to use the correct sort of spoon. Most coastal tackle-dealers stock a selection of flounder spoons, and my own preference when dinghy fishing lies with the plastic spoon, which seems to have a lighter and more attractive action. Metal spoons, on the other hand, are preferable when casting out from the end of an estuary jetty, or some similar shore vantage point.

When using a baited spoon it is important to present the worm so that it does not slide down the hook shank to form an untidy-looking lump in the bend of the hook. To prevent this happening one can use a sliced-shank hook; or, alternatively, a small short-shanked hook (about size 8 or 10) can be attached alongside the main long-shanked hook to hold the head of the worm in position.

GARFISH

Once seen, never forgotten – that is the garfish; for with its long beaked mouth and slender bluish-green and silver body, this 'midget swordfish' is quite unmistakable. Its remarkable appearance has, in fact, earned for it a wide variety of local names, such as Longnose, Needlefish, Snipe Eel, Spear Fish and Mackerel Guard. In some parts it is also known as Mouldybones, owing to the fact that its bones are a bright pea-green colour. This is probably the reason why, in Britain at any rate, it has never been a popular food fish, although it makes quite pleasant eating.

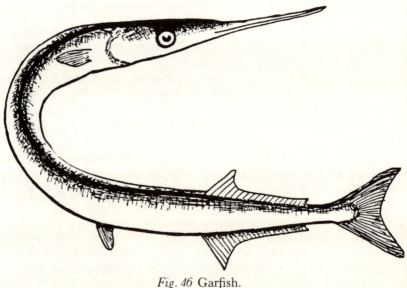

Fig. 46 Garfish.

Garfish, incidentally, are born acrobats, and on fine days when the sea is calm, individual fish will often be seen leaping over scraps of floating driftwood – apparently for the sheer joy of it.

Feeding Habits. For the most part garfish feed near the surface, and they have often been observed in pursuit of whitebait shoals, sandeels and other small fry.

Boat Fishing. Comparatively few boat anglers deliberately set out to fish for garfish. This is a pity, because a lot of fun can be had by doing so. A distant relative of the tropical flying fish, the garfish when hooked will put on a most remarkable acrobatic display, often leaping high into the air, and sometimes actually 'walking' along the surface of the water on its tail.

Many garfish taken on rod and line are caught while trolling for mackerel with a single-hook spinner, but if the boat is moving at any speed all the excitement will be taken out of the encounter. Also, many fish will be lost as a result of the hook failing to lodge firmly in the garfish's beaked mouth.

Using a sailing boat, I have often caught garfish, fairly hooked, on what might be called 'light-breeze' tackle. This consists of an unweighted nylon trace bearing a small tinned long-shank hook baited with a mackerel lask, and having a white plastic 'feather', cut from a discarded bathing cap or beach ball, whipped to the shank.

This tackle is suitable only for near-calm conditions, when there is just enough air movement to keep a little way on the boat. A motor boat is useless, and rowing does not seem to be so successful.

A more orthodox method of catching garfish is to anchor the boat a little way off a rocky headland, or some other known haunt of these fish. A few mackerel are then chopped up for use as groundbait, and a handful of the oily flesh dropped over the side of the boat at regular intervals every two or three minutes.

To appreciate the full sporting potential of these fish, your tackle should consist of a light spinning rod and reel, and a line of about 8 lb. breaking-strain. With this a size-6 hook, baited with a tiny strip of mackerel, is drifted about 20 to 30 yards astern of the boat on the tidal current. As a rule there's no need to put any lead at all on the line, because garfish normally feed very close to the surface.

If using a fixed-spool reel, the bale-arm should be left open so that a biting fish is able to strip line off the spool without feeling any resistance. After two or three seconds, however, the bale-arm should be tripped shut, and the hook driven home with a quick sideways strike of the rod.

An alternative method is to use light float tackle in place of the driftline. Both methods will catch a variety of other species in addition to garfish, including mackerel, bass and (in some areas) the occasional sea-trout.

The fight that a decent-sized garfish will put up has to be experienced to be believed. To have one on the end of your line, and a light spinning rod in your hands, is to know all the thrills of big-game fishing in miniature.

Shore Fishing. Garfish can be caught from a low-level pier or harbour breakwater by casting out light float tackle carrying a size-6 hook baited with mackerel or sandeel strip, and set to fish fairly near the surface. The swim should be groundbaited at frequent intervals with handfuls of chopped-up mackerel flesh. If the supply of mackerel runs short, freshly-caught garfish are equally effective, both as groundbait and hook-bait.

GURNARDS

Large specimens of this rather unusual-looking fish are always welcomed in the kitchen for baking. It may be easily recognized by its large armoured head and mouth, and its 'butterfly wing' pectoral fins which are sometimes very beautifully coloured on the inner surfaces. From the front of each of these fins there project three rays, which look rather like spindly legs. These, rather surprisingly, are equipped with taste-buds, and are used when probing the sea-bed in search of food.

Most sea anglers are content to divide the gurnards they catch into two groups, according to colour, and to refer to them as grey gurnards and red gurnards. However, six different species are found in British waters, and a good deal of confusion often arises in their identification. Those of interest to the rod-and-line angler are:

Grey Gurnard (the only grey species) – colour on the back and sides is usually purplish-grey or slate-grey with white spots, but variations occur and the general coloration may occasionally be purplish-red, or even quite red. The belly is white.

Red Gurnard – colour is usually a brilliant red which extends

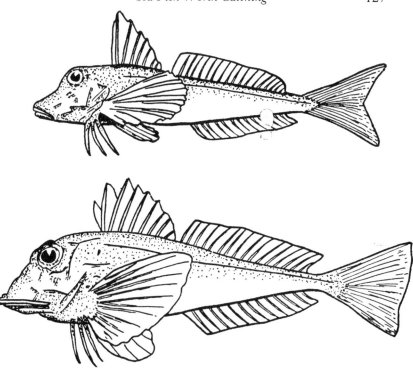

Fig. 47 Red Gurnard (*top*) and Piper.

to below the gill covers. The belly is white. The lateral line is crossed by deep vertical bony plates.

Tub Gurnard (also known as the **Yellow Gurnard** or **Sapphirine Gurnard**) – colour very variable, but usually red, reddish-brown, reddish-yellow, with greenish or golden tints. The coloration is never such a pure, rich red as in the Red Gurnard. Underside pale pink or white.

Piper – a deepwater species that is mostly encountered in depths of 25 fathoms or more. Colour is fairly dark red on the back, lighter on the sides and white underneath. It is equipped with a deeply forked snout which projects well in front of the mouth. There are also some long and formidably pointed spines situated on and immediately behind the gill covers.

Feeding Habits. Gurnards mostly frequent sandy areas of sea-bed, although they may occasionally stray among neighbouring reefs. With their wide, blunt snouts and delicately probing 'legs', they spend most of their time rooting about on the bottom for worms, shrimps and small crabs.

Shore Fishing. During the summer months gurnard come close inshore, and it is then that these fish may be caught from harbour walls or piers which provide access to fairly deep water. Almost any of the usual shore baits will arouse their interest, but they are particularly fond of sandeels, hermit-crab tails and live prawns.

Boat Fishing. The gurnard seldom engages the attention of the specialist fisherman, and most of those caught with rod and line are taken when bottom fishing for other species. Those who troll for mackerel from a sailing boat with a baited spinner also sometimes catch gurnard when the breeze slackens and the lure sinks close to the bottom.

Using a somewhat similar principle, gurnard fishing may also be carried out with leger tackle over sandy ground that is free from rocks or other snags. The boat is allowed to drift with the tide, so that the lead and baited hook drag along the bottom. Only a very light lead need be used, as both boat and water will be moving at the same speed.

Recommended baits are live sandeel, live prawn, ragworm, hermit crab, or a 3-inch strip of mackerel-flesh.

HADDOCK

This highly-prized food fish is a member of the cod family. Unlike the cod, however, it has a slightly forked tail, and its colour is deep greyish-brown or purple above, lighter on the sides and silvery underneath. The lateral line is black and well-defined, and there is a black blotch on either side above the pectoral fin.

Many years ago, before the advent of power trawling, the haddock was found in large numbers all round the coasts of Britain. Nowadays, however, the angler will catch very few of these fish in southern waters, and the best grounds lie off the coasts of Scotland.

Feeding Habits. Haddock are gregarious fish, and may be encountered in large shoals where the sea-bed is of soft sand. They feed on a diet consisting mainly of shrimps, small crabs, sand-stars, worms, razor clams and other molluscs.

Fishing Methods. Normally a boat is necessary when

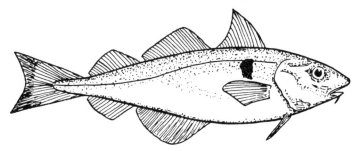

Fig. 48 Haddock.

fishing for haddock, as these fish only come close inshore where the coastline falls away very steeply. The shoals move all the time while they feed, so it may be necessary to try several marks before meeting with success. Either paternoster or leger tackle may be used, but it is essential to keep the baits lying on the bottom.

If the mark covers a wide area, and is free from sea-bed obstructions, good sport may often be had by using leger tackle from a drifting boat. This method also increases one's chances of striking a shoal.

Professional fishermen usually regard mussel as the best bait for haddock, but soft crab, mackerel strip, herring, sprat and bunched lugworms and ragworms are also good takers. Bickerdyke, who fished during the hey-day of the haddock, advocates a hook baited with squid and tipped with mussel.

HAKE

This member of the cod family was at one time very common in British waters, but like the haddock, mentioned previously, its numbers have been greatly reduced by over-fishing. Today, as far as most sea anglers are concerned, the hake might never have existed, and its virtual disappearance

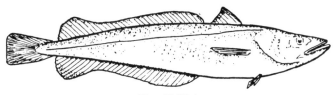

Fig. 49 Hake.

may be regarded as a warning that the bounty of the sea is not so limitless as many people are apt to suppose.

In appearance the fish is long and slender, with the rear dorsal and anal fins extending along more than half the length of the body. It is dark grey on the back, and silvery-white on the sides and belly. The mouth is very large and full of long, sharp teeth, but the lower jaw lacks the barbule possessed by many other members of the cod tribe. Mature fish attain a length of 4 feet.

Feeding Habits. The hake is a deepwater fish, and is commonly regarded as being a nocturnal feeder. It is also occasionally quoted as being a bottom feeder, but this is by no means entirely true, for during summer and autumn it obtains much of its food by preying upon shoals of mackerel, herrings and pilchards.

Fishing Methods. In summer and autumn, when hake move into reasonably shallow water, a few of these fish are still taken by boat anglers off the coasts of Cornwall, and around parts of Cork and Kerry, in south-west Ireland. Nowadays they are seldom fished for deliberately, although occasionally their very scarcity induces boat anglers to try for them. Nevertheless, most hake taken on rod and line come as a surprise catch when boat fishing over deepwater marks, at dusk or after dark.

Like conger, these fish will bite through a nylon trace, and it is necessary to use a few inches of wire next to the hook. Driftline or leger tackle, fished on or close to the bottom with a flowing trace, usually produces the best results. Recommended baits include large strips or fillets of mackerel, herring and pilchard, or a whole small 'joey' mackerel.

HALIBUT

This large and immensely powerful flatfish has its eyes on the right, and is usually a marbled olive-grey colour on the upper side. The underside is white. At the time of writing, the heaviest specimen caught on rod and line tipped the scales at 212 lb. 4 oz. (off Dunnet Head, 1975), but commercial fishermen have taken giants weighing up to a quarter of a ton.

Unfortunately this angler's dream fish – or nightmare! – is not often caught on rod and line in British waters, although it takes a suitably baited hook readily enough. Its normal haunts

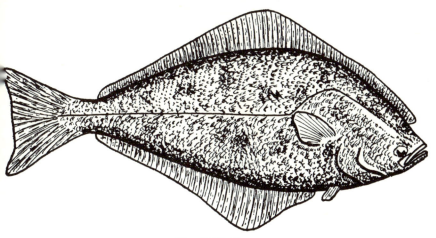

Fig. 50 Halibut.

are the chilly depths off the coasts of northernmost Scotland, Orkney, Shetland and Iceland, but very occasionally a few strays are caught further south – notably off the Atlantic coast of Ireland.

Feeding Habits. The halibut is a deepwater fish with a depth-range of about 50 to 700 fathoms. It has much the same tastes as its tinier flatfish cousins – only on a vastly bigger scale. Just as the dab, for instance, will happily feed on small shrimps, so the halibut will scrunch up lobsters, crabs and squids. Codling, whiting and many other types of bottom-feeding fish are also engulfed by the halibut's capacious mouth.

Fishing Methods. Specialist fishing for halibut is mainly carried on during the summer months in the Pentland Firth area, off the northern tip of Scotland, and around Orkney and Shetland. A powerful rod and reel is required, of the type recommended for big common skate, and the terminal tackle is usually a leger arrangement equipped with a swivelled 3-foot cable-laid wire trace and 8/0 or 9/0 forged steel hook. Because much of the fishing is carried on over snaggy ground that is liable to trap the lead, it is a wise precaution to suspend the lead from a running Clements boom by a 4-foot length of 'weak' (20-30 lb. breaking-strain) line.

The reel line should be at least 50 lb. breaking-strain, and 80 lb. breaking-strain would be a wise choice where conditions are rugged and really big fish expected. Best baits seem to be squid, large fillets of fresh mackerel, herring or coalfish, or small whole fish. If some movement can be given to the bait, so much the better.

JOHN DORY

This weird-looking fish is sometimes taken by chance on rod and line when drift-lining with a live sandeel or similar bait. It is not nearly so interested in a dead bait.

The John Dory is usually greyish-olive or brown in colour,

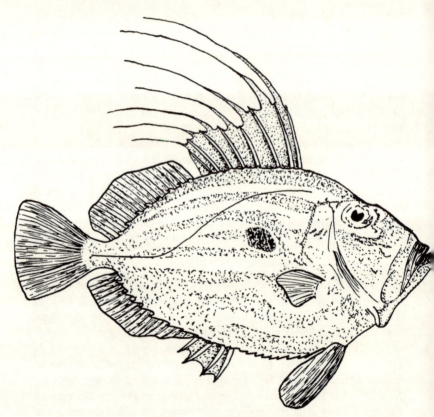

Fig. 51 John Dory.

with yellowish stripes and patches; whilst on either side of the body there is a central black spot. These spots are sometimes referred to as St Peter's Fingermarks; for according to tradition it was from the mouth of this fish that St Peter extracted tribute money.[1]

Certainly the mouth is a remarkable one. Fashioned like a bellows, it is protrusible to form a tube several inches long.

Unable to capture its food by speedy pursuit, this ungainly hunter drifts and sidles its way close to the chosen prey; then suddenly the cavernous mouth opens and unfolds, and the unsuspecting fish is literally 'sucked in'.

MACKEREL

This well-known fish has a beautifully coloured, streamlined body – greenish-blue on the back mottled with black vertical wavy bands, and brilliant silver around the lower sides and belly. There are also 'shot-silk' highlights of blue, gold and delicate shades of pink, but these quickly fade after the fish is dead.

Fig. 52 Mackerel.

Although large quantities of mackerel are taken commercially during the winter months off the coast of Cornwall, it is mainly during the warmer months of the year that these fish are of interest to the rod-and-line angler. With minor regional variations, the first mackerel shoals appear inshore during May or early June, and they remain within range of the shore and boat angler until September or early October.

---

[1] An identical story is told of the haddock, which carries similar marks. Of the two fish, however, only the John Dory is found around the shores of the Bible Lands. In any case, the incident in question is supposed to have taken place at Capernaum, on the inland Sea of Galilee.

Feeding Habits. Mackerel are very swift swimmers. Vast shoals of them pursue sandeels, young herrings and many other kinds of small fry.

Boat Fishing. In Chapter Eight we have already discussed the method of trolling for mackerel from a moving boat. There are, however, several other ways of mackerel fishing available to the angler afloat, and the most productive of these is 'feathering'.

Professional fishermen, intent upon obtaining large and profitable catches, often use as many as two dozen feathered lures on a single heavily-leaded trace. The angler using a fairly light rod, however, would be wise to restrict himself to six lures when seeking bait in a hurry; or to only three if sport is his main objective. To be honest, however, there is nothing very sporting in feathering for mackerel – partly because the fish virtually commit suicide, and partly because a heavy lead, weighing at least 1 lb., is needed to prevent the trace becoming tangled up by several hooked mackerel all trying to swim in different directions.

Nevertheless, mackerel fishing *can* be fun if you use the right tackle and tactics, and my own favourite is spinning with a light single-handed trout spinning rod, using a tiny $\frac{1}{2}$-oz. silvery spoon or metal fish-shaped 'Krill' lure.

The latter method is best carried on from a drifting dinghy, rather than from a larger boat equipped with masts and similar obstacles which will inhibit your casting.

On this type of lightweight tackle a mackerel is capable of giving a really good account of itself, and despite the fact that some fish will inevitably live to fight another day, it is nevertheless a very efficient method. Indeed, if the boat is located close to a surface-feeding shoal you may well finish up with more mackerel than other anglers who are jigging laboriously and boringly directly beneath the boats with a string of feathers.

Shore Fishing. All the methods recommended for use from an anchored boat may be employed from pier, harbour wall or rocks when local conditions are suitable. In addition, light float tackle, baited with whitebait, sandeel, mackerel or pilchard cuttings, is often used.

Light spinning with a small self-weighted silver-coloured lure is another very sporting method of catching mackerel, and

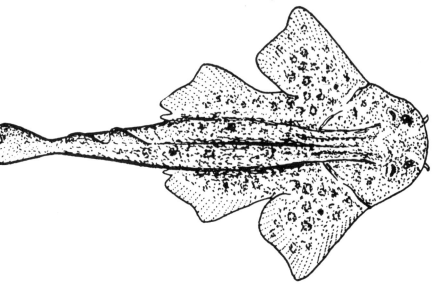

Fig. 53 Monkfish.

may be carried on from suitable steep-to shingle beaches and rocky headlands, harbour walls, piers, etc. This kind of fishing is most productive when a mackerel shoal is actually seen breaking the surface, or when a flock of sea-birds 'working' a particular area of water provides a clue to their presence.

MONKFISH

Known also as the angel-fish, the monkfish is a member of the shark family; although to the casual observer it usually appears to have a closer resemblance to the rays. It possesses a flattish body; broad, fleshy pectoral fins, or 'wings'; and, in its large squat head, a cavernous mouth filled with many ugly, inward-pointing teeth.

Attaining a considerable size, the record rod-caught monkfish for British waters is, at the time of writing, the 66-pounder taken at Shoreham in 1965. A 60-lb. male fish was also taken in 1954 at Highcliffe-on-Sea by a Mr J. Cooper.

An interesting feature of the monkfish is the fact that male and female fish mate in much the same way as land animals, and the young are born alive, and not hatched from eggs. It is a debatable point among some fishermen whether or not 'married couples' among monkfish continue to swim around together outside the mating season, but it is certainly true that during the summer months these fish are frequently caught in pairs. For example, immediately after Mr Cooper caught his near-record male fish, a friend in the same boat captured a female weighing 35 lb.

Feeding Habits. For most of the time the monkfish keeps close to the sea-bed, favouring areas of mixed mud and scattered rocks, where it feeds mainly on shore crabs, flatfish and other bottom fish.

Fishing Methods. The monkfish cannot truthfully be called a very sporting fish. Although some monkfish bore hard and put up a fairly good fight when they feel the hook, the majority are content to put up a rather passive resistance. It is even on record that an angler at Newquay, well into a 41-pounder, thought at first that he was 'playing' a large cardboard box!

On some parts of the coast monkfish venture close inshore during the summer and early autumn, and in these places they may be captured by anglers casting out from suitable rock positions or steeply shelving beaches; or when dinghy fishing over inshore marks.

The most suitable terminal tackle is a fairly strong single-hook leger, as used for large rays or medium-sized inshore conger. My own favourite bait is a large 'cutlet' of freshly-caught mackerel, or a mackerel head wrenched from the body so as to leave the guts trailing.

Incidentally, do not worry unduly if your bait is attacked by swarms of shore crabs. Monkfish are very partial to crabs, and any crawling over your bait will simply be an added attraction!

GREY MULLET

Three species of grey mullet are encountered around the British Isles – the Thick-Lipped Grey Mullet (*Chelon labrosus*); the Thin-Lipped Grey Mullet (*Liza ramada*), and the Golden Grey Mullet (*Liza aurata*). They are all very similar in their general appearance and feeding habits, but the thick-lipped variety is more widely distributed and attains a larger size.

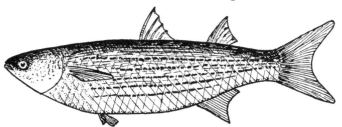

Fig. 54 Grey Mullet.

Although grey mullet may be encountered almost anywhere around the shores of Britain, they are generally most numerous in rocky areas, and in the estuaries, harbours and creeks of our southern and western coasts.

In appearance they are bluish-grey on the back, shading to silvery underneath, and marked with dark longitudinal lines along the sides. The Golden Grey mullet also has a conspicuous golden spot on each gill cover, and a smaller one on each cheek behind the eye. In all grey mullet the head is pointed, and the mouth small with very tiny teeth. The majority of fish caught will weigh about 2 to 3 lb., or possibly a little more in a good district.

Feeding Habits. Harbour and estuary mullet are commonly found in warm, shallow water, among rocks or piles covered with silk weed, or over a soft, muddy bottom. Their natural food consists of a mixed diet of small, soft-bodied water creatures, worms (both live and dead). They also swallow a good deal of silk weed, but whether the attraction lies in the weed itself, or in the microscopic animal life it contains, is uncertain. In many harbours the resident mullet shoals also become accustomed to feeding on galley scraps thrown overboard from ships.

Fishing Methods. Mullet fishing is mostly carried on from harbour walls and breakwaters, estuary shores and jetties, and from a few suitable piers. In certain areas they may also be caught by specialised rock fishing methods on the open coast. The fish are very wary, and usually view a manned dinghy with the utmost suspicion. On the other hand, an old weed-grown barge, moored in some quiet part of a harbour or estuary, is probably the best place of all to try for mullet. As a general rule, however, the angler will have to be content with a harbour wall, or the bank of a tidal estuary.

Early morning is the time to try, before people and boats are on the move. Fine tackle is essential, and the bait should be small and fairly soft. Bread baits (flake, paste or crust) are nearly always acceptable; whilst in fishing harbours, where the mullet are accustomed to feeding on discarded scraps of fish flesh and guts, a tiny strip of mackerel or pilchard makes an excellent hook offering.

The hook should be small and fine in the wire – sizes 8, 10 and 12 being about right for most baits. Light 'freshwater-type' float tackle presented on an inconspicuous line (about 5 to 7 lb. breaking-strain) is the most usual method of getting the bait to the fish. In sheltered harbours one can use a small quill float, but for more open water I prefer a small cork-bodied 'Avon'-type float.

Groundbaiting is essential when mullet fishing, and so far as possible the groundbait should resemble the bait being offered on the hook. In a harbour, where the mullet are already conditioned to feeding on bread and fish scraps, it is usually only necessary to groundbait your selected swim during the actual fishing session – just to draw them to the area and get them in a feeding mood.

In more open waters, however, the mullet will need to be coaxed away from their natural diet by generously pre-baiting the proposed fishing area over a period of several days before you go after them with rod and line. Soaked bread, mixed up with kitchen scraps to form a sort of thick porridge, is ideal for this preliminary groundbaiting. Later on, during the actual fishing session, you should use some form of bread bait on the hook, and at the same time groundbait the swim with small pieces of bread. However, never overdo this groundbaiting – 'little and often' is the best policy, so that the fish are kept interested without becoming glutted.

Although mullet may appear to be rather slow and lethargic fish to the casual observer, they undergo a complete and sudden character change as soon as they are hooked, and put up a tremendous fight on light tackle. The hooked fish should be gently led a few yards away from the fishing area, so as to avoid disturbing the remainder of the shoal.

When it has been played out, the mullet should be lifted from the water in a long-handled landing net – or in a hooped drop-net suspended on a rope if you happen to be fishing from a pier or harbour wall with no access to water level.

Other baits which have proved successful with mullet include small harbour ragworm, peeled shrimp, maggots, pork fat and banana pith.

PLAICE

One of our best-known flatfish, the plaice is usually brown or greenish-brown on the upper side, and marked with orange or red spots; underneath it is white. The eyes are on the right side, and behind these there is a ridge of bony knobs.

The plaice is found around most stretches of coast where the sea-bed is of sand, shell-grit, or – occasionally – mud.

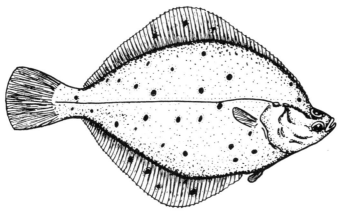

Fig. 55 Plaice.

Feeding Habits. Shellfish form the most important item in the diet of the plaice, those most commonly eaten being various kinds of small, thin-shelled burrowing bivalves, whilst the larger fish are known to consume numbers of razor and gaper clams. Marine worms, shrimps and small crabs are also eaten.

Shore Fishing. Although plaice are frequently caught by beach anglers casting out over areas of sand, the average size of these catches is usually rather small. However, during the summer months, when many plaice come into shallow water, some quite large specimens are taken from piers and in tidal estuaries.

Light leger tackle is useful for this kind of fishing, and if being used from an estuary shore, it should be cast well out. A sandy spit jutting out towards the deep-water channel where the river flows into the open sea makes an excellent stance as a rule.

Boat Fishing. When taken on a lively rod, a fair-sized plaice is capable of providing excellent sport. It is not always the deep offshore marks which produce the biggest plaice. Some really large specimens are regularly caught in sandy estuaries, and sea-lochs, within easy range of the dinghy angler.

Leger tackle with a long flowing trace, or a paternoster-trot carrying two or three long-shanked hooks, will usually produce the best results. When fishing a strange mark, experiment with various sizes of hook, or seek local advice on this point. The hooks can be baited with sandeel (an excellent bait in West Country waters, but not always productive elsewhere), razorfish (strongly recommended), mussel, ragworm, lugworm, soft crab or slipper limpet.

POLLACK

Also known as the lythe in Scotland, pollack are found in the vicinity of submerged reefs, sunken wrecks and rocky headlands. Although caught in varying numbers all round the

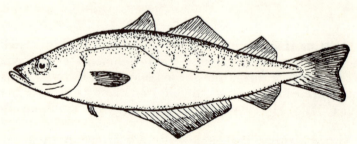

Fig. 56 Pollack.

British Isles, in a wide range of depths, the really big fish (weighing upwards of 18 lb.) are mostly encountered near deepwater wrecks and pinnacle-shaped rocks off our south-western and western coasts.

In many respects the pollack closely resembles the coalfish, and the two fish are, in fact, closely related. However, the pollack's greenish-bronze body, and the darker lateral line, are usually sufficient to distinguish this fish.

Feeding Habits. Pollack spend most of the day close to the rocky or wreck-strewn bottom, occasionally darting out to snap down some passing small fish or prawn. At night, however, and around dawn or dusk, pollack tend to hunt further afield, and are quite often found feeding higher in the water.

Shore Fishing. Where deep water surrounds a rocky headland, harbour wall, or lifeboat slipway it is usually possible to take pollack with float tackle baited with ragworm, using the cast-and-retrieve method. When one's rod and reel do not lend themselves to this kind of fishing, a static or drifting float may also bring results – a live prawn being an excellent bait for this purpose.

Spinning with a small silver spoon or plastic sandeel is also productive.

Boat Fishing. There are many boat fishing methods available to the pollack angler. In fairly shallow water the most enjoyable is probably drift-lining from an anchored boat, using a live prawn or sandeel as bait. A good substitute for a sandeel is a 4-to-6-inch strip of silvery skin cut from the side of a mackerel, but in this case the rod must be eased backwards and forwards to impart some movement to the bait.

Some lead will generally have to be used when drift-lining for pollack in order to get the bait down to the fish. Nevertheless, at dawn or dusk, when the fish often swim high in the water, it is a good idea to reduce the amount of lead.

Trolling for pollack often carried on from a moving motor-boat, using a plastic sandeel or the old-fashioned rubber eel, but although this is a killing method the sport cannot compare with that obtained by drift-lining at anchor.

Another method, which is often carried on from a drifting boat, is feathering. In Cornwall, and off the west coast of Ireland, pollack are sometimes caught on a commercial scale by this means, and the rod-and-line angler who adapts the tackle to suit his own needs frequently obtains large catches and hectic sport.

Finally, remember that a hooked pollack nearly always tries to head downwards to a place of refuge among the sea-bed rocks. So keep a tight rein on the fish during the early stages of the fight. Failure to win the opening round will probably mean that the fish – and your terminal tackle – will be lost.

POUTING

Generally regarded as 'the beginner's fish', the pouting is found all round the coasts of Britain where conditions are suitable. It is particularly abundant in southern and western waters, where it is known by a wide variety of local names: bib, blin, rock-cod and rock-whiting being a few of those in common use.

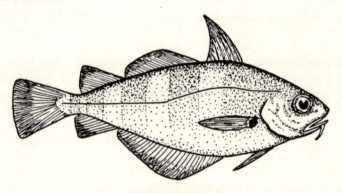

Fig. 57 Pouting.

A member of the cod family, the body of the pouting is somewhat compressed from side to side, and deep from back to belly. In colour it ranges from reddish-brown on the back to old gold underneath; whilst the majority of fish are marked on the sides with darker, rather broad vertical stripes. Other distinguishing features are the barbule beneath the lower jaw, and the black patch at the root of each pectoral fin. Pouting are not large fish, and in most districts a two-pounder would be regarded as a good specimen.

Feeding Habits. The pouting is a bottom feeder, and is

almost always found in the vicinity of rocky ground. In particular, it seems to favour places where the rocks are well covered by seaweed growths, and scattered among areas of sand, shell-grit, or – in some districts – mud. It enjoys a varied diet of small, thin-shelled molluscs, shore and swimming crabs, shrimps, marine worms, and small fish such as sandeels and gobies.

Fishing Methods. Because inshore pouting are rather small, there is little point in the harbour wall and beach fisherman deliberately trying to catch these fish. Nevertheless, if he is using bottom tackle he will probably find that plenty attach themselves to his hook, whether he wants them or not.

Good-sized pouting, as caught by the boat angler, are not to be despised, however. It is true that their sporting potential is strictly limited, and they make no exciting runs; nevertheless they are obliging fish, and often keep the reel turning on those days when the more sporting species will have nothing to do with one's temptingly baited hook.

Although pouting can be caught on most kinds of bottom tackle, including a two- or three-boom paternoster, the most satisfying method to use is deep drift-lining with a single-hook flowing trace, in the manner previously described for black bream. The hooks should be of the medium-shanked whiting variety, about half an inch across the gape.

Suitable baits are numerous and varied. Mussel, razor fish, mackerel strips, sandeels, ragworm, lugworm, prawns, shrimps, squid strips – even shelled garden snails are eagerly taken by these fish.

SHARK

Four species of big-game shark are found in British waters: the Blue Shark, the Porbeagle, the Mako and the Thresher.

The Blue Shark has a streamlined body, inky-blue on the back, lighter on the sides, and shading to white underneath. The five gill-slits are small, and the tail-fin is scimitar-shaped – the upper lobe being long and narrow, and rising well above the level of the back.

These fish are found off many parts of the coast, notably in the western reaches of the Channel, Cardigan Bay, Bristol Channel, and around the southern and western shores of Ireland. A record blue shark weighing 218 lb. was captured off

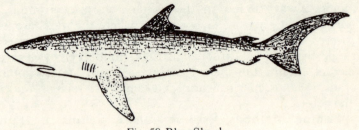

Fig. 58 Blue Shark.

Looe in 1959, but doubtless there are bigger fish waiting to be caught.

The Porbeagle Shark attains a greater size than the blue shark, and the body, which is thicker, is battleship grey or brownish on the back, shading to white underneath. The gill-slits are very large, and although the upper lobe of the tail fin is longer than the lower one, the tail as a whole has a more balanced appearance than the blue shark's.

The porbeagle is present off the southern and northern coasts of Cornwall and Devon; south of the Isle of Wight; in the vicinity of the Channel Islands, and may be encountered more occasionally elsewhere. At one time this shark was confused by British sea anglers with the Mako Shark (*q.v.*);

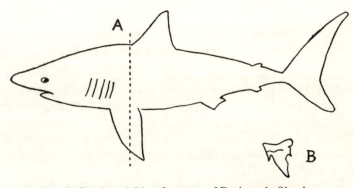

Fig. 59 Distinguishing features of Porbeagle Shark.
A: pectoral fin overlaps dorsal fin. B: tooth with small accessory cusps at the base. The teeth are more regularly arranged in the jaws than those of the Mako Shark.

there being a very close superficial resemblance between the two fish.

Two features help to distinguish the porbeagle from the mako. The leading edge of the porbeagle's dorsal fin overlaps the trailing edges of its pectoral fins; whereas the fins of the mako do not overlap. Also, teeth of the porbeagle have small accessory cusps at the base, which are absent in the case of the mako.

The Mako Shark. It was not until 1956 that British sea anglers realized that this species of shark inhabited the waters off our coasts in fair numbers. For many years they had been taken on rod and line, but almost invariably these captures were identified incorrectly as Porbeagle Shark (*q.v.*). The manner in which this misunderstanding eventually became straightened out is perhaps worth relating.

For several years the record porbeagle shark taken on rod and line in English waters was a 300-pounder caught by Mr John Eathorne, at Looe. Then, in 1955, Mr Eathorne lost his record to his wife, Mrs Hetty Eathorne, when she captured a 352-lb. fish.

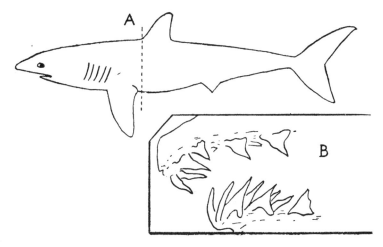

Fig. 60 Distinguishing features of Mako Shark.

A: pectoral fin does not overlap first dorsal fin. B: part of upper and lower jaws.

Note irregularly arranged teeth with no accessory cusp at base of teeth.

In due course the Shark Angling Club of Great Britain decided to claim Mrs Eathorne's shark as the largest porbeagle captured by a woman, and to substantiate this claim pictures of the fish and its teeth were submitted to officials of the International Game Fish Association, at New York. After a careful study of the pictures, the Americans declared that the British record porbeagle was, in fact, a mako!

So Mrs Eathorne relinquished her porbeagle record, and became instead the first holder of the British mako shark record.

The identity of the mako species at Looe was further confirmed by Dr G.A. Steven, Fisheries Naturalist at the Plymouth Marine Biological Laboratory, who also very kindly supplied details of the distinguishing features of the porbeagle and mako sharks for this book.

The Thresher Shark may be recognized without difficulty by its remarkable tail, the upper lobe of which is approximately the same length as the fish's body. It is found quite often around the south-western shores of England and Ireland. Like those sharks already described, it feeds largely on pelagic fish, such as mackerel, pilchards, herring, garfish and scad.

The thresher, however, captures its prey in a novel manner, by circling round a shoal and beating the water furiously with its tail. The small fish, bewildered and alarmed, congregate in a tight-packed bunch, through which the thresher then swims, engulfing dozens at every mouthful!

Tackle Requirements. Shark angling naturally calls for reliable, well-designed tackle, but just how heavy it should be depends partly on the user's skill and angling philosophy, and partly on the size and species of shark likely to be encountered. Plenty of blue shark – some of them weighing well over 100 lb. – have been captured on general purpose boat rods and medium-capacity multipliers loaded with 30-35 lb. breaking-strain line. Nevertheless, the angler who has ambitions to catch really big shark – especially the hard-fighting porbeagle, mako and thresher – will need to use special big-game tackle if he is to avoid disappointment, a burned-out reel clutch, and maybe injury to himself.

The logical approach to the problem is to decide first of all upon the line strength needed to beat the sharks one is likely to encounter, and then match the rod and reel to the line.

As a rough guide, I would suggest a line strength of 35 to 50 lb. breaking-strain for blue shark; 50 to 80 lb. for porbeagle, and 80 to 112 lb. for mako and thresher.

The rod should be of hollow glass and of one-piece design – that is to say, with a lively tip about 5 feet in length, and a separate 20-inch butt equipped with a screw-locking reel fitting. The rod rings must be sturdy and wear-resistant, and a roller end-ring is an advantage, especially in 50-lb. class rods and upwards.

The modern shark angler will almost certainly choose a multiplier reel, and this must be capable of holding approximately 400 yards of the chosen line. For blue shark fishing a medium-sized multiplier (4/0 to 6/0) will be perfectly adequate and most pleasant to handle; but for large porbeagle and the other more powerful species you will need a 9/0 reel.

A brief word about loading the reel with line. A nylon monofilament line is *not* recommended, because in shark fishing its tendency to stretch under strain can be a disadvantage when striking at a distance, as well as imposing a severe crushing strain on the reel spool when retrieving line. Braided nylon is satisfactory, but a line braided from Terylene Polyester yarn is, in the writer's opinion, best of all. It does not rot or stretch, and is soft, inert, and pleasant to use.

So much for rod, reel and line. Now to consider the terminal tackle. A good quality forged hook must be chosen, about 2 inches across the gape – the exact size depending on the type of bait to be used. As sharks have a habit of slashing at the line with their tails, and rolling themselves around it, the hook must be mounted on a rustless, cable-laid wire trace at least 16-20 feet long, and tested to 150 to 300 lb. breaking-strain, depending on the size of the sharks you are gunning for. Two or three really strong big-game swivels should be included at strategic points in the trace between the hook and the main line.

The angler who plays his fish standing up must wear a tarpon belt fitted with a padded cup to take the pressure of the rod-butt. Failure to observe this precaution will almost certainly result in severe bruising, and possibly in more serious injury. Shoulder or 'kidney' harness, designed to relieve the strain on the arms and back muscles, is also favoured by many anglers when playing large porbeagle and mako.

In a rough sea, however, there may be some danger in battling with a powerful shark while standing up, and a safer method is to sit in a coil of heavy rope, using the rope as a fulcrum for the rod-butt. Many boat-owners and charter skippers who specialize in big-game fishing fit their craft with revolving 'fighting chairs', which incorporate a gimballed fitting for the rod-butt.

Fishing Methods. There are no recognized marks for shark fishing in the strictest sense of the word, and the locality of the fishing ground will depend on the estimated movements of those shoals of smaller fish which form the shark's food. On reaching the scene of operations the boat is almost invariably allowed to drift, and a rubby-dubby bag made of fine-meshed netting, containing mashed-up mackerel, pilchards or some other oily fish, is lowered over the stern. The tiny particles of rubby-dubby drift away on the tide in a clearly defined trail, and any sharks which happen to swim across it will be tempted to follow it up to investigate. In doing so they will discover the angler's hook – and then the fun begins!

The hook is baited with a whole fresh mackerel or pilchard, and allowed to drift out behind the boat to a distance of about 30 to 40 yards, and a depth of some 15 to 30 feet. As a rule a large float is used and this often takes the form of an empty plastic detergent bottle. The reel line is threaded through a swivel lashed to the neck of the bottle, and stopped in position with a sliver of matchstick or rubber band.

The first indication of a bite is usually the disappearance of the float, accompanied by a sudden chattering of the reel check as line is stripped from the spool. The angler should allow the shark to run with the bait for a few seconds before striking the hook home with a really powerful backwards sweep of the rod-tip. At the same time any other anglers in the boat must immediately reel in their own lines. If this precaution is not taken it is quite likely that two or three anglers will all hook the same shark – a most frustrating experience for all concerned as it nearly always results in badly tangled lines and traces, and a lot of needlessly wasted fishing time.

When the shark has been thoroughly played out, the wire trace should be grabbed with a *gloved* hand, and the fish guided to a convenient position for gaffing. The gaff or gaffs (at least two should be carried) must be really strong, and should be sent home near the tail, and the tail lifted clear of the water as quickly as possible. A rope noose – prepared before the commencement of the fishing trip – can then be hitched around the root of the tail.

When it has been boated, a shark should be treated with respect – especially if it happens to be a mako, as this species has a reputation for lying as though dead, and then snapping suddenly with its formidable teeth at a carelessly placed hand or leg. Its tail, also, is capable of doing considerable damage.

At the first opportunity the fish should be despatched with some heavy blows from a lead-weighted 'priest' or heavy hammer on the snout, just in front of the eyes. Don't use the engine starting handle as a priest – I once saw one go flying over the side of the boat when being used for this purpose!

In the interests of conservation, avoid using a gaff on small sharks, so that they may be returned unharmed to the water to fight another day.

SKATE AND RAYS

Several members of the skate and ray family of fishes are caught on rod and line around our coasts. It is the larger species (some attaining a weight of 200 lb. or more) which are generally referred to as skate; the smaller species are usually referred to as rays. The rays are more numerous and widely distributed, and those frequently encountered are the thornback ray, small-eyed ray (also known as the painted ray), and blonde ray.

All have a flattened body lacking in true bones, their skeleton being composed entirely of cartilage and gristle. The pectoral fins are broad and fleshy, the tail is long, thin, and sometimes whip-like, and the mouth is situated underneath the body.

Feeding Habits. When hunting for food these fish seem to fly rather than swim through the water, using their pectoral

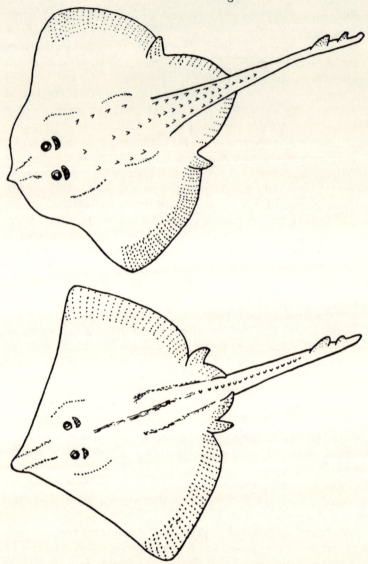

Fig. 61 Thornback Ray (*top*) and Common Skate.
Coloration and markings vary, but for general guidance see text. In each case the mouth is underneath the body, and so cannot be used for breathing purposes when the fish are lying on the sea bed. Instead, they are provided with spiracles, or 'breathing holes', situated directly behind the eyes.

fins in the manner of wings. From my boat, on a summer's day when the water was crystal clear, I once saw an inshore ray make a kill. It glided down upon a young lobster, smothering it like a blanket and preventing all hope of escape.

This must have been an unusual sight, because rays and skate feed mostly at night while in shallow water. Their diet varies according to local conditions, but normally includes small flatfish, gurnards, whiting, baby lobsters, swimming crabs and hermit crabs.

Shore Fishing. In some districts rays are caught in fair numbers by the pier and long-casting shore fisherman. Usually these are thornbacks, and (in the West Country) small-eyed rays. There are also places where, during the late summer and early autumn, large numbers of stingray may sometimes be taken from the open beaches. These latter fish should be treated with the utmost respect; for the venomous spine on the tail can pierce a thick rubber boot, inflicting a most unpleasant wound and causing temporary paralysis.

Before one of these fish can be regarded as safe, the venomous spine must be broken off with a pair of pliers or some other suitable weapon. This is best done by turning the ray over on its back and pinning it down with a boot, spiked rod rest or heavy gaff handle.

Plenty of rays have been captured by shore anglers on paternoster tackle, but for specialist fishing it is best to use a free-running leger trace carrying a single 4/0 hook. The most productive baits are a small whole sandeel, or a medium-sized tapering strip of fresh mackerel or herring.

Boat Fishing. The majority of rays taken by boat anglers will be thornbacks averaging about 7 to 13 lb. in weight, with a few larger individual fish. In certain areas, notably off the coasts of West Dorset, Devon and Cornwall, small-eyed rays also feature prominently in catches; whilst blonde rays, cuckoo rays, undulate rays and spotted rays are likely to show up in many areas on occasions.

A typical ray mark is an area of sand, sandy mud or shell-grit – often situated on the outer fringes of an area of sea-bed rocks.

Tackle for rays can be a light to medium-powered boat rod and reel, and a line of about 25 to 30 lb. breaking-strain. Terminal tackle should be a running leger with a few inches of heavier (50 lb. breaking-strain) nylon monofilament next to a single 4/0 hook. Recommended baits include strips of freshly caught mackerel; herring strips; whole small sandeels, or fillets cut from the side of a Greater Sandeel, and (mainly in estuaries) large prawns.

In a few localities boat anglers may also make contact with large Common Skate, which attain a weight of 200 lb. or more. Not nearly so common nowadays as their name would suggest, these huge fish are mainly located off the southern and western coasts of Ireland, northern Scotland, Orkney and Shetland.

There can be no such thing as fishing light for these fish, because very often a large specimen will cling to the sea-bed, using its huge flat body like a giant suction disc. It is a stratagem that has broken many a strong rod.

A powerful short-butted rod, a robust reel, and a 50 to 80 lb. breaking-strain line will form the basis of a serviceable outfit. To make up the terminal tackle, thread a running Clements boom on a 6-foot length of 80 lb. breaking-strain nylon monofilament, attach a strong big-game swivel at either end, and then attach a 12-inch length of cable-laid 120 lb. breaking-strain stainless wire to the lower swivel. To this wire link is attached an 8/0 or 10/0 forged hook. The top swivel of the trace is, of course, attached to the reel line, and a lead of suitable weight is clipped to the Clements boom. Two large gaffs with strong handles, and a padded tarpon belt to take the pressure of the rod butt, should also be included in the equipment.

Once a skate has been coaxed from the sea-bed, the angler's prime objects must be to play it against the tide and to keep its head up. To allow the fish to get its head down, even for a second, will mean that the angler will find himself battling not only with the power of the fish itself, but with the force of the flowing water pressing down against the tilted upper surface of its body.

The favourite bait is a whole fillet cut from the side of a freshly caught mackerel. A small 'joey' mackerel, placed whole upon the hook, is also excellent.

SOLE

This highly prized flatfish is taken by shore and boat

anglers during the summer months along parts of the Channel coastline (notably in the Solent area), and elsewhere in sheltered bays and sounds where the bottom is of soft, worm-inhabited mud. Being nocturnal feeders, sole are mostly caught after sundown and during the night.

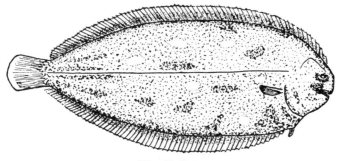

Fig. 62 Sole.

Light leger tackle produces good results when the hooks are baited with lugworm or ragworm.

TOPE

This small but typical member of the shark family possesses a slender body which may be anything up to 7 feet long. The average tope, however, is about half that length – the females, which give birth to living young, being heavier than the males. In colour the tope is grey or brown on the back, lighter on the sides, shading to white underneath.

Feeding Habits. The tope feeds near the bottom, mainly

Fig. 63 Tope.

on a fish diet. It is known to prey upon whiting shoals, and is also very fond of dabs and plaice.

Fishing Methods. Tope are widely 'distributed around Britain and Ireland, but their average size seems to vary considerably from district to district. Notable areas for big tope include the inshore waters around Pembrokeshire, North Cornwall, the Solent, Wash and Mull of Galloway. However, any angler who regularly fishes a sea-bed of sand, gravel, shell-grit or muddy sand should certainly try for this fish – if only to discover whether or not it is present.

Although tope may be caught off localized stretches of shore during summer and autumn, on the majority of coasts a boat is needed if one wishes to get to grips with these fish in reasonable numbers. A medium-sized dinghy will be quite large enough, and it is not necessary to try very far out. From late spring to early autumn, good-sized tope can be found in many places only a short distance beyond the five-fathoms line.

The fighting qualities of tope vary considerably from fish to fish. A good one will run far and fast, curvet and bore, using every ounce of strength in its body.

The fishing is usually carried on from an anchored boat, although on snag-free grounds drifting methods are sometimes used. Some enthusiasts try for tope on very light tackle, but the average angler would be well advised to use a medium-powered 7-foot boat-rod, and a multiplier reel carrying about 200 to 250 yards of 25 to 30 lb. breaking-strain nylon monofilament line.

Tope are normally fished for on the bottom, and the business end of the tackle consists of a running lead (clipped to a Clements boom), a swivel larger than the wire eye on the Clements boom, and a 7-foot trace of flexible cable-laid stainless wire. For shore fishing the trace is usually reduced to about 4 feet for ease of casting.

Fish baits are used – the most popular being fresh-caught mackerel and bream, and fresh or frozen herring. Hook sizes range from about 5/0 to 7/0, depending on whether strips, fillets or whole fish are used as bait. The hook is attached to a 12-inch wire snood, which in turn is clipped to the swivel-link fitted to the end of the trace.

The baited tackle is lowered over the stern of the boat and

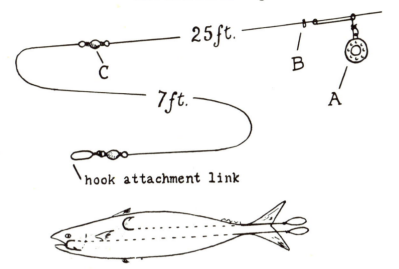

Fig. 64 Tope Tackle.

A: sliding lead on reel line. B: stop. C: swivel connecting to wire trace (with eye larger than wire loop on boom). Two hooks are often used when baiting with a whole fish (as shown), but a single hook is used when baiting with strips or fillets.

allowed to drift away on the tide for about 25 feet – the sliding lead being retained in the hand. A short stub of rubber cut from an elastic band is then clove-hitched on to the line to prevent the lead sliding down towards the trace; after which the lead is also consigned to the deep. In this way one obtains the advantages of a quick-release lead, whilst at the same time avoiding any drag on the line when a tope mouths the bait. When reeling in, the stub of rubber band bends double under pressure from the ring at the rod-tip, and the lead slides down the line out of the way.

Instead of the rubber stop, some anglers prefer to use a piece of bristle from a stiff broom, or a sliver of matchstick.

On tope grounds where crabs are a nuisance, a float is sometimes used to keep the bait just clear of the bottom.

As tope are seldom used as a table fish, the majority of sea anglers nowadays prefer to return their fish alive to the water after capture. For this reason they should not be hauled into the boat with a gaff. Instead, after being completely played out, the tope should be grabbed by placing one hand around the 'wrist' of the tail. In the case of a big tope, the other hand can then be used to grip the dorsal fin. It is then a fairly simple matter to heave the fish into the boat.

TURBOT

This is one of the larger species of flatfish, having been taken on rod and line to a weight of 31 lb. 4 oz. The average fish, however, probably tips the scales at something like a third of this weight, although size tends to vary from district to district. Once quite numerous over marks in the English Channel, off the coasts of Devon and Cornwall, and off south and west Ireland, it has become much scarcer in recent years due to over-fishing by trawlers.

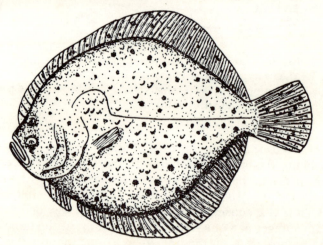

Fig. 65 Turbot.

The body of the turbot is thick and scaleless, and is covered on the left, or eyed, side with small bony lumps. The colour of this upper side tends to vary in order to match the fish's surroundings, but generally it is a mottled and speckled brown. Normally the underside is white, but turbot are very occasionally taken in which the right eye has failed to complete its journey round to the left side of the head, and these fish are often pigmented on both sides.

Feeding Habits. The turbot favours areas of sand or shell-grit, and – contrary to common belief – it is not unduly fussy about the depth of water. In summer and autumn good-sized fish may be taken over suitable ground anywhere between 5 and 50 fathoms, the shallow water marks usually being in the vicinity of river estuaries, or headlands adjoining areas of fast tides.

Small fish, such as sandeels, small whiting and poor cod, form the most important part of the turbot's diet, and these it will catch either by lying in ambush, or by vigorous pursuit.

Fishing Methods. The large flat body of a big turbot puts a considerable strain on one's tackle when one of these fish is being played in a fast run of tide, and this fact should be borne in mind when making up the tackle.

A running leger with a long flowing trace is the best choice, and as the turbot has a surprisingly large mouth the hook should be capable of accommodating a large bait. I normally use a large strip of freshly-caught mackerel, tapered to resemble a sandeel. Even better is a whole fillet sliced from the side of a Greater Sandeel.

Two main techniques are used when fishing for turbot, depending on the local sea conditions.

In areas where a fierce tide rips over a bank of sand or shell-grit, the boat is anchored up-tide of the bank, and the baited tackle streamed down so that it finishes up in the eddying water just below the down-tide edge of the bank. This is where the turbot are most likely to be feeding on the sandeels being washed out of the sandbank by the current.

The second method is used in areas where the tidal flow is of only moderate strength. The boat is allowed to drift over the turbot ground, with the baited trace dragging along the bottom.

As soon as a bite is felt, the angler allows line to flow freely off the reel for a few seconds. This gives the turbot time to swallow the bait; after which the reel is flicked into gear and the hook driven home with a determined (but not over-vigorous) strike. The turbot has a comparatively fragile membrane around each side of its mouth, from which the hook can easily be torn, so it must be played carefully until it is alongside the boat. To avoid the fish making a final panic-stricken flurry alongside the boat, it should be gaffed or netted while still a foot or two below the surface. My own preference is to use a *large* landing-net in preference to a gaff, as this avoids damaging the flesh of this valuable food fish.

WEEVER

Every sea angler should make himself thoroughly familiar with the two species of weever encountered in British waters. Not because these fish possess any special merit from the point of view of sport, but because they are both armed with venomous spines capable of causing intense pain and prolonged discomfort.

These spines are situated in the first dorsal fin and on the gill-covers, and a prick from them may be likened to the bite of an adder – both in its degree of seriousness and its effects.

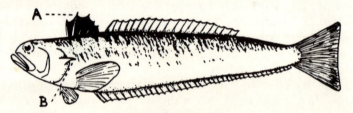

Fig. 66 Greater Weever.
Note venomous spines on first dorsal fin (A) and gill-cover (B).

The **Greater Weever** is an offshore variety which is caught as a rule by the boat angler fishing fairly deep water. It is mainly yellowish-brown in colour, with deeper oblique markings on the sides, and attains a length of up to 18 inches.

The **Lesser Weever** is a small fish, measuring at the most only about 5 to 7 inches from head to tail. This gives it a somewhat plumper appearance than the Greater Weever depicted in our drawing, but otherwise it has all the characteristics of its larger relative.

If either of the above fish is taken on the hook, it should be pinned down with a thick-soled boot or gaff handle, and stabbed in the head with a knife. Then, still keeping the fish pinned down, the mouth should be cut free of the hook; afterwards picking up the body by impaling it on the knife blade.

When fishing well offshore, the dead weever can be thrown

overboard. On or near the coast, however, the body must be disposed of with care, as the spines remain venomous long after death.

This member of the cod family is found all round the coasts of Britain, and a number of distinguishing features make it easy to recognize. It lacks the barbule which adorns the lower jaw of many of its relatives; its body is sandy or olive-coloured above, shading to mottled silver and gold on the flanks and white beneath. The lateral line is golden bronze. There is also a dark patch at the root of each pectoral fin, and the head is rather long and pointed.

The whiting is not a large fish, and most of those caught will be under 2 lb. The rod-and-line record stands at 6 lb. 4 oz. at the time of writing, the fish in question being caught off West Bay, Dorset. An earlier record fish of 6 lb. was taken off Shieldaig, on the west coast of Scotland, so it will be seen that the big ones are widely distributed.

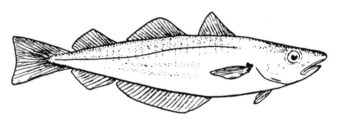

Fig. 67 Whiting.

Feeding Habits. The whiting is, quite literally, its own worst enemy, for it devours with relish large numbers of its own fry. Strangely enough, this ogre-like streak in the whiting's character helps to ensure its continued abundance, because every adult whiting caught by commercial and amateur fishermen increases the chances of survival of the rising generation.

Small herring, sprats, poor cod, sandeels, sand shrimps and pink shrimps are the other main items in the diet of the whiting; their importance varying with the seasonal movements of the fish.

Shore Fishing. Serious shore fishing for whiting begins in the late autumn, when the evenings begin to draw in and after there have been a few night frosts. It is then that the fish begin to venture close inshore – and, incidentally, it is then that they are in peak condition. These autumn fish may be caught from suitably situated piers and harbour breakwaters, and from steeply shelving beaches where there is an expanse of sandy or shell-gritty sea-bed within casting range. Night fishing almost invariably produces the best results.

A light nylon monofilament paternoster is usually employed, with hooks ranging between size 1 to size 4, according to the size and mood of the fish.

Boat Fishing. There can be no disputing the fact that it is the boat angler who catches the most whiting. The fish are likely to be found over sand or shell-grit, and it is customary to lower the lead to the sea-bed, and then draw it up again for a foot or two so that the baited hooks are just clear of the bottom.

Usually the boat is anchored, but where the sea-bed is level and free from obstructions the chances of striking a shoal may be increased by allowing the boat to drift. A perforated groundbait-container filled with minced-up sprats, and lowered to the fishing depth, helps to keep the fish tailing the boat once they have been found. Anchoring a drifting boat at this stage can be a mistake, as the arrival of the anchor on the sea-bed may immediately scare away the fish.

Drift-lining with fine tackle is useful when the water is clear and the fish are shy, but at other times a paternoster arrangement carrying two or three inconspicuous nylon or plastic booms is the most convenient to use. Speed in dealing with captured fish is essential if the interest of the shoal is to be maintained, and it will be found helpful if the bait supply is kept handy and ready to place on the hooks without any preliminary opening of shellfish or cutting up of fish strips. A reel with a rapid recovery rate will also save valuable time, especially when over deep water, and for this kind of fishing the multiplier type takes a lot of beating.

Whiting are often caught by boat anglers in their hundreds, but there is no risk of running out of bait because they will readily accept hooks baited with cuttings of their own kind.

Drift fishing around the Skelligs, on the Atlantic coast of Ireland. The sea-bed, nearly 30 fathoms below, is littered with similarly contoured rock pinnacles. They are the haunt of many big fish but drifting over such rugged ground calls for constant vigilance on the part of the angler. Only the boatman (*left foreground*) appears to be taking things easy. (*below*) The author with a good ling taken from the Skelligs. It fell for a large strip of freshly caught mackerel.

A played-out blue shark is heaved aboard. Note that the boatman is wearing gloves to protect himself against possible cuts from the wire trace.

A selection of shark fishing tackle and accessories: A—long-nosed disgorging forceps; B—spool of cable-laid stainless steel trace wire; C—box of brass ferrules for making loops in trace wire; D—combined wire-cutters and ferrule crimping pliers; E—17-foot shark trace with three heavy duty swivels and a detachable big game hook on an 18-inch wire link; F—wooden "priest" to quieten shark before removing the hook or unclipping the trace. (Note: the priest is usually loaded at its lower end with a core of lead, and the one shown here was made from an old oak ladder rung.)

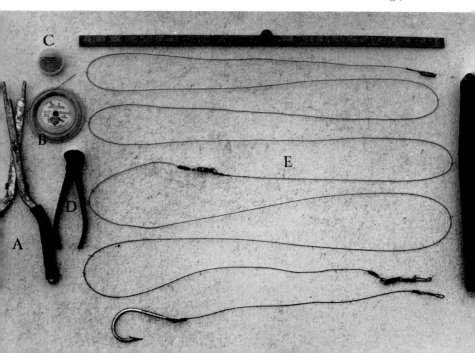

Other baits appreciated by them include mussel, sprats, ragworm, lugworm, hermit crab tails, and strips of herring or mackerel. They feed most eagerly at dusk or after dark on a frosty starlit night.

Three species of wrasse are likely to be caught by the angler fishing in British waters: the ballan wrasse, the cuckoo wrasse, and the corkwing. Their appearance is most distinctive, with large teeth and thick lips reminiscent of the traditional 'black-faced minstrel', and body colours which are nearly always conspicuous and often downright gaudy. Of the three species mentioned, the ballan wrasse is generally the largest, the corkwing the smallest, and the cuckoo the most colourful. In the latter case the adult male fish is a vivid orangey-gold, patched, lined and smeared with bright blue markings which also cover the head. The females are predominantly reddish-orange with a few dark blotches on the back.

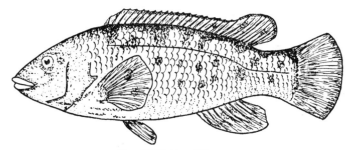

Fig. 68 Ballan Wrasse.

Feeding Habits. Wrasse live among weedy rocks, and many are found close inshore during the warmer months of the year. Their food consists of a wide variety of crustaceans, worms and molluscs natural to their habitat.

Fishing Methods. Fishing for specimen-sized ballan wrasse has become a favourite interest of many West Country shore anglers in recent years. These fish can be caught from harbour breakwaters, steep-to rocky beaches and rugged headlands, but the biggest specimens are usually taken when fishing from rock positions on the open coast.

As the sea-bed in these places is nearly always littered with numerous snaggy rocks, the terminal tackle must be kept as simple and inexpensive as possible. One useful arrangement is a single-hook nylon paternoster with the sinker attached by a short length of weaker line so that it can be broken free if it gets caught up among the rocks.

When rock fishing for wrasse the tackle only has to be cast out about 15 yards as a rule, so there's no need to use expensive shop-bought leads. An old nut or bolt, or a discarded sparking plug, hitched on to the length of weak line serves the purpose just as well, and costs nothing.

The single hook should be suspended on a 12-inch dropper of 15 lb. breaking-strain nylon from a 20 lb. breaking-strain main trace. The hook will vary from about size 1 to 2/0, depending on the type and size of bait being used. The baits most favoured by specialist wrasse anglers are smallish shore crabs (hardbacks are taken by ballan wrasse just as readily as peelers and softbacks), lugworm, ragworm and prawns. Other suitable baits include mussels, cockles and rock limpets.

As soon as a wrasse feels the hook it makes a tremendous power-dive for the nearest rock cover or kelp jungle, and if you allow it to succeed you will surely lose your fish and at least part of your terminal tackle. It is essential, therefore, to pile on the pressure immediately, and before long the fish will begin to tire. If only wrasse put up a more prolonged fight they would undoubtedly be classed among our most sporting species.

Don't forget to carry a long-handled landing net, or a drop-net, to lift the fish from the water after they have been played out.

Although I have on occasions eaten large ballan wrasse and found them quite palatable, the majority of anglers consider them a very second-rate food fish. There is therefore no justifiable reason for killing the fish, and the most satisfactory method of dealing with them is to place them alive into a nearby rock pool (where they can be photographed very attractively, if you so wish), and then release them into the open sea again at the end of your fishing session.

10

Night Fishing

Sea fishing is often at its best in the evening and after nightfall. Foremost among the reasons for this is the fact that many sea fish are nocturnal feeders, and during the hours of darkness they tend to venture closer inshore to hunt for the smaller creatures which inhabit shallow water. At night big fish are also more likely to smell or otherwise sense the angler's bait, without being put off at the same time by the sight of hooks and traces.

Any fishing expedition requires careful preparation if it is to be successful, and an after-dark trip is no exception. It is important to wear warm clothing; for it soon becomes chilly on an exposed beach or pier-head after the sun has gone down. Clothing, however, should not be too bulky, and in the case of waterproof jackets there should be plenty of room about the shoulders so that one's movements are not cramped when casting.

This question of casting is possibly the biggest problem facing the newcomer to night fishing. In the dark it is, of course, impossible to follow the flight of the lead out to sea, with the result that much valuable fishing time may be wasted by over-runs and 'bird's-nests'. Therefore, until a fair degree of proficiency has been acquired in the art of night casting, the angler using a revolving drum reel would be well-advised to play for safety by deliberately braking the reel a second or so before he thinks it is really necessary. Admittedly, this will reduce the length of his casts by several yards, but distance is not always an advantage when shore fishing at night. Bass, in particular, come so close in that 'expert' lead swingers often send their baited hooks far beyond the feeding zone of the fish into empty water.

Of course, on gently shelving shores, long-distance casting

is usually essential, and in these circumstances the beginner will find it best to start fishing in the evening, while there is still sufficient light to watch the flight of the lead. In this way his introduction to the difficulties of night casting will be a gradual one. Alternatively, he can use a fixed-spool reel and avoid all risk of over-runs.

The only special equipment required when angling after dark is some form of illumination. When fishing from a steeply shelving beach, where the angler is likely to remain in one spot for hours on end, the best choice is often the ever-popular paraffin pressure lantern. Although expensive to purchase in the first instance, this type of lantern is very robust (I've been using mine for over thirty years!), and it will emit an excellent light all through the night on one filling.

Lanterns powered by small butane gas cartridges are also favoured by some anglers, but they are more expensive to run than the paraffin variety, and the gas cartridges have a nasty habit of running out at the most inconvenient moments.

The night angler who fishes from a rock position or surf beach will obviously need a less cumbersome and more mobile type of light than a lantern, and the ideal means of illumination for this sort of fishing is an electric headband light. This is strapped to the angler's forehead, rather like a miner's light. Powered by a separate battery case, which can be clipped to a waistbelt or carried in a coat pocket, this type of light leaves the angler's hands free when casting or gaffing a fish, and the beam automatically follows the direction in which the angler is looking.

It should be mentioned, however, that the experienced night angler relies on his natural night vision as far as possible. Moonlight, or even starlight, will be all that is necessary for most of the time, and the electric headlamp should be used only when performing such tasks as baiting up or sorting out a tangle. Above all, never direct the beam of the torch into the eyes of other anglers.

It is easy to lose or damage items of tackle when fishing at night. The rod should never be left lying on the ground, where it may be smashed accidentally underfoot. Similarly, all smaller items of equipment – knife, spare leads, hooks, spools of nylon, and so on – should be replaced in the tackle-box immediately after use.

For beach fishing (as distinct from rock fishing) a tackle-box divided into several compartments, is preferable to a haversack, in which everything soon becomes hopelessly jumbled up. When rock fishing it is best to keep your tackle sundries down to the bare minimum, and if you do this it is often possible to carry everything in the large kangaroo pocket of a waterproof anorak.

Although it is true to say that sea fishing at night almost invariably produces better results than during the day, it is worth stressing that some nights are much better than others. A full moon, as well as providing welcome illumination for the angler, appears to tempt fish into shallow water, and makes them bite more boldly. The spring tides following the new moon also benefit the angler; whilst on the majority of coasts an incoming tide is better than an ebbing one. Bites come quickest as a rule during the two hours either side of high water, and then fall away as the ebb gathers momentum.

Light, apart from moonlight, is capable of influencing one's catch of fish. Bass and pollack, for instance, seem to hanker after the bright lights. In the Fal Estuary, in Cornwall, I have taken good fish by sending an unweighted driftline in under the lights of moored vessels and waterfront buildings. When the lights went out, however, spiral weights had to be added to the tackle because the fish then went down to deeper levels.

So far we have considered night fishing mainly from the point of view of the shore angler, but a full moon, coupled with a suitable tide and a reasonably calm sea, should tempt any experienced boat angler to try his luck afloat. There will be little need to go very far out because, as we have already said, the fish tend to come inshore after dark.

The fishing methods used will be the same as for daylight boat fishing; although artificial lures are naturally useless because these possess only a visual attraction for the fish. An exception may be made in the case of fluorescent lures for use at dusk, and phosphorescent lures which glow in the dark.

Usually, however, natural baits which attract well by scent will prove preferable in every way for night fishing.

A flashlamp or lantern must be carried by the dinghy angler at night – not only to simplify baiting-up operations, but to display temporarily upon the approach of other craft in accordance with the regulations laid down to prevent accidents at sea. This applies only to fairly small open boats – larger craft will have to carry navigation lights of approved pattern.

Tidiness is absolutely essential when angling at night in a small dinghy, and at all costs one must endeavour to keep the fishing tackle separate from the boat's gear. Hooks and line snarled up in the anchor cable can quickly produce chaotic conditions, and even endanger the safety of those on board.

Finally, a word about reefs and sand-bars, which on many parts of the coast are popular night fishing marks for the boat angler. Be particularly careful when approaching these hazards, for they are not easily seen at night, even in bright moonlight, and whether at anchor or under way it is necessary to bear in mind the fact that on a falling tide they will be getting closer to the surface all the while.

11

The Fish's World

The sea angler who wishes to become more than moderately successful in his pastime must be something of a marine biologist. This does not mean that he has to learn a lot of complicated statistics or tongue-twisting Latin names; for all practical purposes it will be sufficient if he understands something of those strange and fascinating influences which control the fish's movements, appetites, and habits.

"Imagine that you are in the fish's place," is a well-worn piece of advice which angling experts are in the habit of handing out to newcomers to the sport.

The maxim is sound enough, but it is by no means easy to follow. Fish live in a strange element; almost, one might say, in a different world. Consequently, the novice angler is bedevilled by many doubts. What exactly is the fish's watery sphere of existence like – to the fish? What – and to what extent – does a fish feel? Can it hear? Is it colour-blind?

With certain limitations, it is true to say that a fish has all the senses known to man. Most interesting of all, though, is the fact that it possesses at least one extra sense for which we have no name. The outward manifestation of this sixth sense is the lateral line, a feature common to the vast majority of fishes.

For centuries fishermen have pondered upon the significance of the lateral line, which in the normal round-bodied fish extends along either side from head to tail. In highly coloured species it often forms part of the camouflage scheme, but in others it consists of little more than a row of openings, or pores, set in the scales.

It was these pores which eventually helped to solve the mystery. On investigation by marine biologists they were found to connect with a thin, tube-like canal filled with mucus, situated just below the lateral line. This canal was in turn connected with three distinct groups of orifices or cavities in the head, whilst being also linked with a system of nerves.

That all this adds up to a special fishy sixth sense is practically certain, but it is so far removed from anything experienced by ourselves that we can do little more than guess at its precise nature. Most probably it is a sort of echo-sounding device, designed to warn the fish of obstacles in its path through the medium of water disturbances caused by its own movements. This would explain how a fish is able to swim and hunt among rocks during the hours of darkness.

It would also seem probable that this sixth sense is more highly developed in some sorts of fish than others, and this may account for the exceptional degree of caution displayed by certain species. For if the 'echo-sounding' theory is correct, it would appear to follow that such a delicate vibratory sense could also warn a fish of approaching danger by picking up the shock-waves made by a splashing oar, or similar unnatural water disturbance.

Since ancient times fishermen have remarked upon the almost uncanny way in which fish are able to sense a coming change in the weather. Now scientists have discovered that a storm raging out in mid-Atlantic causes an earth tremor on a beach in England a day or so before the heavy storm swell arrives. Fish, with their delicate sensory organs, would be able to detect this preliminary earth tremor, and so receive warning that rough weather was on its way. This would cause some fish to move out into the safety of deeper water; whilst others such as bass, might be tempted to move closer inshore.

It is the latter 'white water' fish which will interest the rod-and-line angler most at such times. A heavy swell breaking on the beach stirs up the sea bottom, and, emboldened by the murky water, the bass venture into the shallows to grow fat on the countless small sea-bed creatures unearthed by the pounding waves and swirling undercurrents.

The seasons in the sea tend to lag behind those on land. Thus an exceptionally hot summer normally results in unusually warm sea conditions during the autumn, and this may cause those migratory fish which are due to move away from our shores to be late in leaving. Similarly, a very severe winter generally results in unusually cold water around our coasts during the spring, and this may delay the seasonal arrival of mackerel and other fish by as much as several weeks.

Because a fish lacks any means of conserving or adjusting the warmth of its body, its blood temperature is, in effect, the temperature of the water which surrounds it. This means that it is very susceptible to changes in the underwater 'climate'.

As every sea angler knows, there is a tendency among many kinds of fish to seek deeper water during the winter months. This, of course, is because deep water is not affected by cold-weather conditions so much, or so suddenly, as the inshore shallows.

The bodies of some fish are more tolerant of changes of temperature, and these are the species which normally remain with us all the year round. Sometimes, however, in an exceptionally cold winter, even these hardy species may find conditions decidedly uncomfortable, and if they cannot get out into warmer water very quickly large numbers of them may perish. Harbour and river-mouth conger are occasionally taken off their guard in this way; particularly when a sudden severe spell arrives fairly early in the winter, causing icy river water to chill abruptly the still fairly warm sea water.

At certain places on the coast, where streams of warm water from factories and power-stations enter the sea, the very opposite of the foregoing state of affairs may arise, so that fish may actually converge upon the shallows to enjoy very localized summer conditions in mid-winter. In recent years, as new power-stations have been erected along the coast, numerous reports have come to hand of indifferent angling spots suddenly producing record catches of bass and mullet.

Of course, not all fish migrations lead away from our shores in winter. Cod begin to appear on the scene in autumn, but in this connection it is interesting to note that North Sea cod are unable to withstand cold conditions to anything like the same extent as their Arctic brothers. For instance, during the very severe winter of 1947, when pancake ice drifting out from the Dutch and German coasts brought the water temperature down almost to freezing point, the cod became covered with sores, similar to those caused by frost-bite, and eventually the fish died.

Water that is too warm can also prove fatal to a fish;

although the actual cause of death is sometimes quite different. As the body temperature rises to match the water temperature, the physical processes of the fish become speeded up to such an extent that it is unable to stand the strain. In other words, it lives so fast that it dies!

Fear and distress caused by over-warm water is probably the reason behind the mysterious disappearance of certain kinds of fish all along a stretch of coast during a spell of hot weather, and their return later with cooler conditions. This sort of thing usually occurs during a prolonged summer heat-wave, and it is at such times that a little knowledge of marine biology pays dividends. The fish are still there to be caught by the angler, but they have moved out to the deeper marks in order to find more equable conditions.

A thing which has puzzled many anglers at one time or another is the subtle difference which lies between salt-water and fresh-water fish. To transfer one of these kinds of fish from its own natural environment to that of the other is, in most cases, to condemn it to a speedy and terrible death.

The reason for this may be found in the phenomenon known as osmosis, a scientific term covering the percolation and inter-mixture of fluids separated by a porous membrane. When the porous membrane is of such a nature that it allows simple fluids to pass through, but obstructs the flow of dissolved solids, it is known as a semi-permeable membrane.

The mouth and gills of a fish incorporate semi-permeable membranes, and these are all that separate its blood from the water in which it lives. Now it is a law of osmosis that when two salt solutions of different strength (or concentration) are separated by such a membrane, fluid is drawn from the weaker solution to the stronger solution in an attempt to even matters up.

When we realize that a fish's blood is, in effect, a salt solution, it becomes obvious that osmosis is taking place in its body all the time. A fish swimming in the sea (sharks and rays excepted) is surrounded by a salt solution more concentrated than its blood, and in consequence fluid is drawn out through its semi-permeable membranes. A sea fish is able to make up for this loss of moisture by drinking, its body being specially adapted to extract the salt from the water and pass it back into the sea.

When a sea fish finds itself by mischance in fresh water the whole process of osmosis is reversed, so that the unfortunate creature may be likened to a submarine that has dived with its conning-tower hatch jammed open. Water floods in through its mouth and gill membranes, causing its blood-stream to become diluted, and overburdening the kidneys to such an extent that they break down under the strain. A grim end indeed.

The fate of an inland fish that finds itself in sea water is just as unpleasant, although the nature of its death is quite different. Normally absorbing water by osmosis, the fish suddenly begins to have its body-fluids drawn from it, so that its blood becomes thicker and ever more salty.

When we consider the difficulties involved, it seems remarkable that any fish could manage to exist both in fresh water and the sea. Yet, as we all know, salmon, trout, flounders, mullet, eels, bass, shad, and smelt all manage to do this, as well as a few other species of less interest to anglers.

This ability to thrive in two worlds is due partly to the fact that these fish are gifted with specially adapted bodies, and partly to an instinctive 'knack' in adjusting their habits to meet varying conditions.

Another aspect of marine biology which should concern

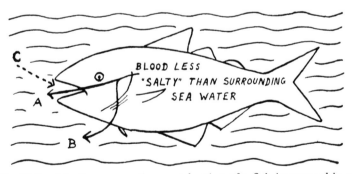

Fig. 69 In this diagrammatic reproduction of a fish immersed in sea water, fluid is being drawn out of the blood-stream (arrows A and B) by osmotic pressure – the tendency being for the blood to become as 'thick' as the surrounding water. A sea fish, however, is able to replace the lost moisture by drinking (dotted arrow C).

every sea angler is the growth rate of the commoner species of fish. If only more rod-and-line sportsmen realized how long it takes many fish to reach maturity, they would make sure that the small ones went back into the sea alive.

Flatfish in particular suffer severe losses at the hands of the 'baby-snatchers'. An angler may catch a two-year-old plaice, measuring about 8 inches from snout to tail, and ease his conscience as he slips it into his haversack with the thought that 'there is a meal in it' – and that it is at least as big as a fair-sized dab. Nevertheless, the fact remains that an 8-inch plaice is almost certainly an immature fish, while in some localities a female may have to attain a length of 12 inches or more before it can help to ensure, by spawning, the existence of future generations of its species.

One popular angler's fish with a very slow rate of growth is the bass. Females may be five, six, or even seven years old before they spawn, and may weigh only a little over the 1-lb. mark. Of course, weights and measurements vary considerably from district to district. It is fairly safe to say, however, that a really good fish of 10 lb. or more is likely to be about twenty years old.

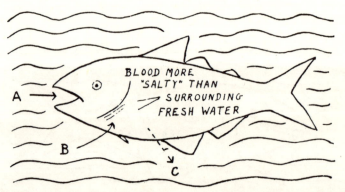

Fig. 70 In fresh water, which has a very low salt content, osmotic pressure forces water (arrows A and B) into a fish's blood-stream – the tendency being for the blood to become 'thinner'. Fresh-water fish, and a few species of sea fish, are able to counteract this tendency by disposing of the unwanted water through the kidneys (dotted arrow C).

In recent years it has become increasingly obvious that life in the sea is far from inexhaustible. Most anglers now realize that it is in the interests of their sport that small, immature fish should be returned to the water alive, and they abide by their own personal weight and size limits, or those laid down by angling clubs and authorities.

A minority, however – and quite a large minority at that – take the selfish view, and are in the habit of putting anything and everything in the bag. Such people, when reason will not prevail, should be shamed into mending their ways.

Small fish which are to be returned to the water should have the hook removed gently, so that the mouth, eyes, or jaw are not damaged. Also, because the slime on a fish's body is Nature's protection against various diseases and parasites, care should be taken to see that it is not removed by rough handling. If a landing-net is available, hold the fish inside the meshes; in this way a firm grip can be obtained with very little pressure of the fingers.

Some fish, when taken from fairly deep water, will be so damaged by the change in pressure that they will have little or no chance of survival, even if returned straight away. Wrasse and pouting in particular are subject to this sort of trouble, and when caught by the boat angler from fairly deep marks they are often hauled aboard with stomach and swim-bladder protruding from the mouth and eyes starting out of their sockets.

Fortunately, however, the majority of fish do not suffer to anything like the same extent, and will survive even after being taken from quite considerable depths. For instance, experiments have shown that young plaice put back into sea water stand an excellent chance of living, even after several hours of jostling and crushing in a trawl. In one test, when the fish were returned straight away, 71 per cent survived. When another batch was replaced after lying on deck for an hour, 36 per cent survived. No figures are available for fish caught on hook and line, but there can be little doubt that the survival rate would be even better, as many fish get trodden underfoot and injured when the contents of a trawl are being sorted.

Finally, lest any reader should think I have exaggerated the need for all fishermen, both professionals and amateurs, to help conserve our stocks of sea fish, I reproduce below some tabulated statistics showing how the North Sea plaice stocks have fluctuated in recent times.

It will be seen that after being reduced by many years of intensive trawling before the war, the plaice stocks replenished themselves when hostilities curtailed the activities of the professional fishermen. After the war, however, the resumption of trawling operations quickly brought about a decline in the numbers and size of the fish once more. For example, most of the fish caught during the twelve months following the spring of 1946 were between six and eight years old, and 15½ inches long. By 1949, however, most of the plaice being caught were four or five years old, and only about 12 inches long. Moreover, a great deal more time and money had to be spent in catching them.

NORTH SEA PLAICE CATCHES BY ENGLISH TRAWLERS

Year	Catch (cwt.)	Effort (hours fishing)	Catch per 100 hrs.
1936	310,958	1,674,924	18·6
1937	299,264	1,573,266	19·0
1938	244,674	1,359,102	18·0
1946	526,838	694,276	75·9
1947	433,187	791,936	54·7
1948	382,410	850,862	44·9
1949	304,661	875,406	34·8
1950	273,222	859,548	31·8
1951	278,505	872,395	31·9
1952	276,877	828,275	33·4
1953	304,255	811,841	37·5

Note.–The years 1945, 1946, and 1947 were particularly favourable for plaice spawning in the area covered by the above statistics. This caused a temporary 'bulge' in the population of the fishery, which in turn was reflected in a slight upwards trend in catches per 100 hours of fishing during the years 1952 and 1953.

The same story could be told for many other kinds of sea fish, and it is high time we heeded the warnings of the marine biologists and fisheries research officials. Fish must be caught, and larders must be filled. But, in the name of common sense, let those fish taken be mature specimens which have already spawned. In filling our larders, do not let us empty our seas.

12

Sea Angling Holidays

For the salt-water angler the great fascination of a seaside holiday lies in the opportunity it offers to fish from a different kind of coastline, to try out fresh tactics and tackle, and maybe go after some new species of fish. There is, in fact, something really stimulating about casting a baited hook into an unfamiliar tideway, especially when the water carries a reputation for harbouring potential record-breakers.

At the same time, though, it is necessary to realize that angling on an unfamiliar coast presents its own special difficulties, and it is no exaggeration to say that the majority of sea-fishing holidays are made or marred at the planning stage, long before the suitcases have been packed. Where to go, and when to go, are two very important decisions which should be made well in advance, and sorting over the various pros and cons makes a suitable fireside interest for those winter evenings when heavy seas make fishing impossible, and the rods are hung up in the tackle-cupboard.

Tastes differ widely among anglers, and in writing this chapter on holidays with rod and line it is possible only to make a variety of suggestions, leaving you to pick out those which appeal most. If you are a family man, for instance, there will be many likes and dislikes besides your own to be considered. Possibly your best opening gambit in this event would be to gather the entire household together and make a note of the various requirements.

You, personally, may hanker after a rugged bit of West Country coastline, where big pollack, bass and conger lurk. At the same time the wife may want to be fairly near some shops; while the youngsters will almost certainly demand a sandy beach, or an assortment of rock pools, swimming and snorkelling coves, cliff paths and smugglers' caves.

Once you have decided more or less upon the locality and type of place which will suit all concerned, I suggest you get out the back numbers of any fishing journals you subscribe to, and make a list of likely resorts which feature regularly in the 'big fish' news. It is also a good idea to buy or borrow from the local public library some guide-books which are lavishly illustrated with coastal photographs. Some of the 'Portrait Books' and 'The Regions of Britain' series – both published by Robert Hale – are well suited to this purpose. There are also some really excellent illustrated books written especially about Britain's regional coastlines and harbours.

After a few evenings spent in this sort of research it will be a simple matter to make a list of half a dozen coastal resorts, large or small, which are ideal not only for sea angling, but for all the other family interests. On request, the publicity departments of the larger resorts will supply information about sea fishing in the district; or, better still perhaps, they will put you in touch with the secretary of the local sea-angling club.

This brings us to the reason why, earlier on, I advocated planning a summer fishing holiday during the winter months, before the sea-fishing season begins to gather momentum. Club officials are very obliging, but they are only human. During the winter slack period they will be only too happy to send you useful information about the local marks, boat-hire facilities, bait supplies, tackle requirements, and so on. Later on, however, when they themselves are eager to spend all their spare time fishing, it need hardly be wondered at if their replies are not quite so detailed. So write early – and enclose a stamped, addressed envelope.

When making the final choice of an angling resort from the replies you receive, it might be as well to consider the possibilities of each place in all kinds of weather. For example, an open beach might give good sport during reasonably settled conditions, but a holiday which coincided with a prolonged onshore gale would be a dead loss. On the other hand, a river estuary, large harbour or sea-loch would provide sheltered tidal water fishing during unfavourable conditions; whilst in fine weather such places usually offer facilities for deep-sea boat fishing.

When you have settled the question of where the holiday is

A specimen 24½ lb turbot, taken while dinghy fishing out of Coverack, Cornwall, in the small dinghy pictured overleaf.

Two good bass for the author and his son. They were taken by shore spinning with artificial lures, and the largest weighed 10 lb 9½ oz.

A sailing/rowing/outboard-powered dinghy built by the author. Small trailable craft like this are ideal for inshore and estuary fishing.

A sheltered estuary camping spot visited by the author during a dinghy fishing cruise from Dorset to Helford River, in Cornwall.

to be spent, there still remains the problem of deciding when to go there. Often the possible dates are restricted by such considerations as business commitments, school holidays, and so on. Nevertheless, some sort of choice is usually available, and the final decision in this respect is likely, more than any other single factor, to decide the quality of your holiday angling.

Sea fishing, of course, will always be a chancy business, and few of us, I imagine, would want it otherwise – for therein lies the main appeal of our pastime. There are, though, certain basic principles which every salt-water angler recognizes, and it is simply asking for disappointing results to ignore them. For instance, it is a generally recognized fact that certain times, phases of the moon, and states of the tide often result in above-average catches.

The deep-sea angler should bear in mind that certain marks – notably deepwater wrecks and areas off tide-bedevilled headlands – can only be fished successfully around neap tides. Whereas many other boat marks in shallower or more sheltered waters yield their best catches of fish at spring tides.

Timing is just as important for the shore angler. Many species of fish are primarily nocturnal feeders, which means that round about dusk they are beginning to feel an urge to snap down any morsel of food which may present itself. At sunrise, too, many sea fish are filled with a similar desire to gorge themselves; whilst on many stretches of coast there is a marked tendency for the fish to take a bait eagerly during the early stages of the flood tide, or during the hour or two either side of high water. Obviously, therefore, if you can choose a holiday period when high water coincides with sundown (or dawn if you're an early riser) your chances of success should be particularly good.

In order to plan an angling holiday along these lines it is necessary to consult a nautical almanac. From this type of reference book it is possible to ascertain the rising and setting times of sun and moon, together with high and low tide data for places all round the coasts of Britain.

So far we have considered matters mainly from the point of view of the holiday angler who spends all his time at one place on the coast. However, many who possess a car or some other means of transport will probably prefer to move on every two or three days; thus obtaining both a change of scenery and a change of fishing. Camping or caravanning can be combined very pleasantly with this more mobile kind of holiday, whilst at the same time proving very useful on lonely coasts where casual overnight accommodation is often hard to find.

My personal experience of caravanning is limited, but tours with a tent I have enjoyed in plenty. At the time of writing they extend over a period of forty-odd years, and during that time I have come to regard fishing tackle as an almost essential part of my camping equipment.

Camping is just about the cheapest type of holiday you could possibly have. It is healthy and, above all, it gives complete freedom from all those petty restrictions normally associated with a seaside hotel or boarding-house. For instance, when holidaying with a tent it is possible to adjust your mealtimes to suit your own convenience. There is no need to pack up and trudge back to a landlady's boiled beef and carrots just when the fish are in an obliging mood.

Only when you have reached that state of semi-starvation when eating begins to seem even more important than fishing, will you need to think seriously about food. And, with the tent pitched nearby, your problem will soon be solved. The catch – possibly cooked in a portable fish-smoker – will go a long way towards satisfying your open-air appetite, and will be more delicious than any fish you could have bought off a fishmonger's slab.

This is no place to discuss the general techniques of camping; whole volumes have been written on the subject, and a selection of these works will be found in most public libraries. Nevertheless, it might be appropriate to discuss some of those points of particular interest to prospective camping-anglers.

It may only be a personal prejudice, but I always try to avoid the commercial camping sites. After all, one of the main advantages of using a tent is that it allows you to fish the lonely stretches of coast, where other forms of accommodation are unobtainable. Many ideal camping and fishing districts of this nature come to mind: out of the way coves and tidal creeks in the West Country; remote stretches of the Pembrokeshire coast; the mountain-fringed sea-lochs of the Scottish Highlands; and those wonderful bays in western

Ireland, around the shores of Cork, Kerry, Galway and Connemara.

For the motorist who also owns a small dinghy, the annual seaside holiday presents a golden opportunity to take his craft with him and go adventuring on 'foreign' waters. Boats exceeding about 11 feet in length will probably have to be towed on a trailer, but many small dinghies made of marine plywood, fibreglass, and other lightweight materials can be carried on the roof of an average-sized family car. The boat is usually loaded upside down on a 'ladder' type' roof-rack, and I have found that it is best to use braided synthetic rope when tying the boat to the roof-rack. Hemp rope tends to stretch and become slack during a long journey – especially if it happened to be damp when you started out, and then dries off later on.

Motoring with a boat is a type of holiday that has gained favour rapidly amongst the angling fraternity in recent years, and every season an increasing number of cars towing or carrying small craft are to be seen on the roads. To the owners of these mobile craft an unlimited variety of fishing waters present themselves, and if you have not already considered this type of holiday, it is high time you did so.

Obtaining a suitable boat trailer need not be a very expensive business. Second-hand trailers are to be picked up fairly reasonably at most small boat centres along the coast; whilst at some boat-yards it is possible to hire a trailer for the period of one's holiday.

The lightweight materials used in the construction of a typical car-top dinghy might at first seem a disadvantage when the boat is to be used from a rough shingle beach. In practice, however, a plywood boat need scarcely touch the pebbles. Two or three people can easily carry one straight from the car to the water's edge. Alternatively, it is possible to use a pair of pneumatic boat rollers, which make light work of shifting even a heavy old clinker-built boat. What's more, the air-filled rollers can be lashed inside the boat immediately prior to launching to provide valuable reserve buoyancy while at sea.

Sea anglers accustomed to doing their boat fishing from large charter craft are probably already shaking their heads, and declaring that a small outboard-powered dinghy is no fit craft for a salt-water fishing trip. Well, it certainly is not in a rough sea, or on an excessively exposed stretch of coast. But it must be remembered that the roving boat angler can pick his water to suit his craft and the prevailing weather conditions, and if a stretch of coast is chosen with an attractive selection of sheltered bays and estuaries it should be possible to get afloat on most days.

Of course, it would not be right to recommend the use of small craft without adding a cautionary note about tide-rips, offshore winds, and various other dangers which are waiting to ensnare the unwary amateur sea-dog. All these points have been dealt with in detail earlier in this book, in the chapter on Boat Fishing, and provided they are clearly understood, and the necessary precautions taken, a small dinghy for the sea angler and his family is a perfectly safe proposition.

Glossary of Sea Angling Guide-Books

Scotland for Sea Angling (The Scottish Tourist Board)
Angling Guide to Wales (Wales Tourist Guide)
Ireland – Sea Angling Guide (Irish Tourist Board)
England is mainly covered by a series of sea angling guides published by Ernest Benn, comprising:
Sea Fishing in Cornwall
Sea Fishing in Dorset
Sea Fishing in Hampshire and the Isle of Wight
Sea Fishing in Kent
Sea Fishing in North Devon and Somerset
Sea Fishing in South Devon
Sea Fishing in Sussex
Sea Fishing: The Wash to the Thames Estuary
Sea Fishing: The Humber to the Tweed
Sea Fishing in the North West

13

The Sea Angler's Workshop

The sea angler not only needs to know how to fish with his tackle to the best advantage; he must also know how to care for it when out of use. Modern rods and reels are expensive items which, if neglected, are liable to become unserviceable as a result of the corrosive and rot-producing properties of salt water. When properly cared for, on the other hand, they will provide a lifetime of pleasurable fishing.

The main object of this chapter is to offer guidance on problems concerning tackle maintenance and repair. A supplementary section also gives hints on making various items of tackle and gear, and, where applicable, describes how these things should be used.

SECTION I – TACKLE MAINTENANCE AND REPAIRS

Care of Tackle. Prevention is better than cure, and a great deal of trouble can be avoided by giving sea-fishing tackle a little attention before it is put away after use. Unfortunately, anglers are just as fallible as other mortals, and after several hours on the beach or at sea, maybe on a frosty night, it is tempting to say: "What's the sense of sorting out all this stuff now? I'll be using it again tomorrow."

Our climate being what it is, though, the chances are that the weather will decree otherwise, with heavy rain and persistent gales putting paid to sport – maybe for weeks on end. Meanwhile the tackle lies in a cupboard, out of sight and out of mind; the rod still in its salt-impregnated bag; a wet line on the reel; hooks rusting away with scraps of salty bait still adhering to them.

Salt, of course, is capable of absorbing moisture from the atmosphere, and for this reason fishing tackle which has come into contact with sea-water will remain perpetually damp if stored away without preliminary precautions. Before laying up rods, reels, lines, rod-bag, haversack, or tackle-box for any length of time, all these items should be thoroughly washed in fresh water to remove the salt, and the larger, more expensive hooks treated with a small brush dipped in fish oil. Rods should be hung up in the washed-and-dried bag, with the tapes loosely tied, and never on any account left propped against the corner of a room or cupboard.

There seems to be a widespread belief among sea anglers that nylon line is such long-suffering stuff that it can be abused almost indefinitely without ill effects. This is dangerous philosophy. Nylon-loaded reels should be washed periodically to remove sand and salt deposits, and the line tested for nicks and abrasions by running it through the fingers. The tail-end of the line is most susceptible to damage, and any part of it which fails to pass inspection should be cut off ruthlessly.

Nylon line which has been recently stretched in playing a large fish, or in freeing tackle from a sea-bed obstruction, should be re-wound loosely on the reel before putting it away, lest the tightening coils should cause the reel to warp or crack.

The best place to store nylon is in a drawer or dark cupboard; whilst one of the worst places is a window-sill open to strong sunlight. Although immune to attacks by insects, mildew, or rot, and resisting alkalis, oils and petrol, a nylon line will be ruined if allowed to come into contact with certain mineral acids, and some organic acids.

If there are experimentally minded children in the house, it is advisable to keep fishing tackle under lock and key. Reels especially seem to possess an irresistible fascination for small fingers, and secret fiddling with the drag adjustment must have been the cause of many mysterious bird's-nests 'collected' by exasperated angling family men.

A few words about rod ferrules might not be out of place. Grit and sand inside a ferrule will cause wear and jamming, so do use the rubber plugs provided by the rod-manufacturer. If, in spite of your precautions, sand does get inside, then make a point of removing it at the first opportunity.

Tight ferrules should never be forced; a dab of animal fat or pure lard will usually ease them, and improve the suction at the same time. Another point worth stressing is that when assembling or taking down a rod the ferrules should be gripped, and not the adjoining rod.

Renovating a Rod. However carefully it is used, a sea rod is bound to receive some sharp knocks now and then from barnacle-encrusted rocks, beach pebbles, pier girders and metal boat fittings. Sooner or later, therefore, the varnish becomes chipped and worn, so that it has to be renewed.

In order to provide a satisfactory key for new varnish, the old varnish should be roughened up with fine glasspaper, and all traces of the resulting dust wiped off with a soft, clean cloth. If any whippings are loose or frayed, or any rings broken or badly grooved, they should be renewed at this stage. It is important to use proper rot-proof whipping thread for this job.

It is also essential to use a good quality polyurethane varnish, which is not only waterproof but also sufficiently elastic to adapt itself to the flexing of the rod when casting or playing a fish.

There's no need to use a brush when applying the varnish to the rod – you'll find that your finger-tip does the job just as well, if not better. Allow the first coat plenty of time to harden off properly; then sand down lightly and apply a second coat. For best results the job should be carried out in a room that is free from draughts, damp, dust or artificial heating.

Preserving Nets. Landing-nets and drop-nets made of non-synthetic materials are susceptible to rot, and before being stored away for any length of time should be rinsed thoroughly in fresh water to remove all traces of salt. A landing-net can be dealt with easily enough in the bathroom, but a drop-net, with its many fathoms of seaweedy and slime-encrusted rope, may not be quite so easy to get past the wife.

An alternative, which will appeal to lazier mortals, is to hang the net out of doors for about a month until it has been washed clean by repeated storms of rain.

Various methods of preserving nets are used by professional fishermen, but for the rod-and-line angler the simplest and most efficient is the copper naphthenate preparation (Cuprinol) specially manufactured for preserving non-synthetic nets, and sold by most ship chandlers and ironmongers.

Landing-net frames and drop-net hoops which have become

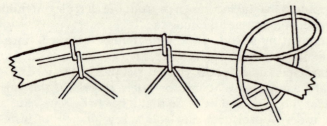

Fig. 71 Method of making the Marline Hitch, used when attaching netting to a drop-net hoop. In the case of small-meshed prawn netting, it is customary to hitch on every fifth mesh (and not adjoining meshes as shown here for simplicity). For added strength, tarred twine is often threaded through the outer meshes, and the ends joined to form a circle equal in size to the drop-net hoop. The marline hitches are then passed round both twine and netting. It is also advisable to knot every fifth marline hitch to avoid any risk of the line unravelling completely in the event of a breakage:

rusty will soon weaken those meshes which come into contact with them. In such cases it is advisable to remove the netting from the frame, and then clean off all traces of corrosion from the metal with emery paper. After wiping off the dust, treat the frame or hoop with cold galvani ,i g paint.

Whether the old netting is rcplaced on the frame, or whether new netting is bought for the job, must naturally be a matter for your personal judgement. When in doubt, however, it is best to err on the side of safety and buy new netting.

The same thing applies to the rope and bridles fitted to drop-nets. Test them thoroughly, and replace them if they show any signs of weakness.

Finally, a word about storing nets. A closed cupboard is not the best place for them, and it is much better to suspend them from the rafters of an airy attic or outhouse. On no account should they be left lying on the floor of a shed, where they may become rotted by damp, or chewed by rats.

Care of Reels. Many modern precision-built fishing reels are made of light alloys, and should receive the careful treatment to which they are entitled. Occasionally strip off the line and wash the spool and surrounding parts with warm soapy water. Dry and then lubricate all working parts with a good quality spindle oil.

On no account should a reel be stored in a damp fishing bag. Sea-water contains active chemicals which cause an electrolytic process to operate, and sooner or later damage will occur.

Sharpening Hooks. Needle-sharp hooks are essential for successful fishing. Although hooks are reasonably sharp when first purchased from the tackle dealer, tl / are not always so sharp as they should be, and a few seconds' work on them with a carborundum slip may well make all the difference between losing a shy-biting fish and catching it.

It should also be remembered that when fishing from a pebble beach, or among rocks, sharp hooks are liable to become blunted very quickly, and usually need sharpening it least once or twice during the course of a lengthy fishing session.

To sharpen a hook properly it is necessary to use the right sort of whetstone. It should be thin and of a handy size, so that it can be got inside the gape of small hooks, and it must have a very fine grain. Course-grained stones are much too drastic in their action, as also are files, and these should never be used except on gaffs and really large big-game hooks. Even these should be finished off with a fine-grained stone.

To produce a really keen point on a hook, the stone should be rubbed against the metal in an upwards direction from the point, at as acute an angle as possible. Care should be taken to keep this angle reasonably constant; although at the same time it is necessary to shift the position of the stone every few seconds so that the metal is removed evenly all around the point. An experienced angler should be able to turn a blunt hook into a real thumb-pricker with a mere dozen or so flicks of the stone. In this way a minimum of metal is removed from the hook, and it can be sharpened several times before being discarded.

At the other extreme, the careless or overzealous use of a stone can quickly reduce a hook-point to an inefficient stub, fit only to be thrown away.

SECTION 2 – TACKLE-MAKING

Making a Bait-Box. Although bait containers of one sort or another are obtainable at most tackle shops, the majority of handymen-anglers prefer to make their own, as they are then able to design something which will meet their own special requirements. Metal containers are not recommended, because these are liable to react with sea-water, thereby killing live baits and tainting dead baits. Wood is the most convenient material to use, and for lightness, strength and durability there is nothing to beat waterproof resin-bonded plywood.

A bait-box should be fairly shallow (about 4 inches deep) and fitted with a lid that is close-fitting enough to prevent the escape of worms and other small creatures. At the same time, however, it must not be completely airtight if you wish the bait to remain fresh for any length of time.

The length and breadth of the box may vary, but the minimum size recommended would be around 8 inches by 6 inches, as anything smaller is difficult to scrub out – and a bait-box must be kept scrupulously clean. My own favourite bait-box, illustrated below, is fitted with removable partitions so that three different kinds of bait can be carried and kept separate. It is made of 3/16-inch resin-bonded plywood, and is assembled with resin glue. The lid, which also serves as a cutting board, can be furnished with small brass flap-back hinges and a home-made copper 'hook and staple' fastening catch.

When the box is completed, the inside can with advantage be treated with a coating of pitch (NOT tar). This will prevent

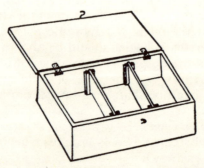

Fig. 72 Bait-box made of waterproof resin-bonded plywood, and fitted with slotted removable partitions. Brass flap-back hinges are recommended, and these should be screwed to blocks glued to the plywood. The lid is of solid $\frac{3}{8}$-in. wood, and when opened can be used as a cutting-board. Leather hinges are a cheap alternative.

the wood from soaking up smelly lugworm 'juice' and similar tainting substances, and thus make the bait-box much easier to keep clean.

Making Sea Leads. Sea-fishing leads are quite expensive to buy, and very easily lost, so it is well worth making up a supply from pieces of scrap lead.

Unless you possess more than average 'do-it-yourself' skill, and enjoy tinkering about for its own sake, I would advise you to steer clear of fancy designs which necessitate the making of troublesome two-piece moulds. These are usually made out of plaster of paris and, apart from being easily chipped or broken, they take a very long time to dry out. This last point is extremely important. The slightest trace of dampness will cause steam to be generated inside the mould as soon as the molten lead is introduced, whereupon molten lead will be ejected again with explosive force.

Professionally-made two-piece moulds, designed to produce sea-angling leads in a wide variety of designs and sizes, can be purchased very reasonably from specialist firms which advertise regularly in the angling magazines. These are a good buy for any angler (or group of anglers) wishing to make a large supply of special-purpose leads, such as streamlined surf-casting bombs, wired grip leads, etc.

However, it is also possible to make a selection of very useful shore and boat fishing leads by using a variety of easily available materials as casting moulds. Here are a few suggestions:

A. **Spoon-shaped Leads.** When shore-casting over snaggy inshore rocks, a spoon-shaped lead will be found extremely useful because when reeled in briskly this type planes upwards over the obstructions. It can be made by using an old tablespoon or dessertspoon as a mould. Before pouring in the molten lead, lay a loop of brass or stainless steel wire into the *pointed* end of the spoon to provide an attachment eye.

B. **Lead Pipe Offcuts.** These make useful leads for medium-distance shore-casting and inshore boat fishing. Begin by cutting the lead pipe into 2 to 3-inch sections, depending on the size of sinker required. Then fashion a wire attachment eye as described for the previous type of lead. Place the forked end of the wire into one end of the pipe and close the end of the pipe by squeezing it with a pair of pliers, leaving just the wire

eye protruding (see illustration). Place the closed-up end of
the pipe in an engineer's vice and tighten up hard. Now pour
molten lead into the open upper end of the pipe until it is brim
full.

When the lead has hardened, dip it in a bucket of water to
cool it, and then trim the eyed end of the lead with a few
strokes of a coarse file to give it a streamlined shape.

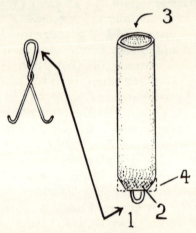

Fig. 73 Shore-casting Sinker, made from an off-cut of lead pipe.
Stage 1: Make wire eye and insert it in one end of pipe;
Stage 2: Close bottom half-inch of pipe by squeezing tightly in
vice;
Stage 3: Pour in molten lead;
Stage 4: Trim off corners to give lead a streamlined shape.

C. **Cone-shaped Lead.** A cone-shaped lead is the most
generally useful type for deep-sea bottom fishing, as its shape
minimizes the risk of it getting caught up amongst sea-bed
rocks and wreckage.

A one-piece mould to produce this type of lead can be made
quite simply out of a piece of aluminium sheeting, size
approximately 9 inches by 5 inches. Cut it to the shape shown
in Fig. 74, and bend it to form a cone, allowing about half an
inch overlap at the edges. Join these overlaps with three or
four rivets, taking care to keep the inside heads of the rivets as
flush as possible with the aluminium sheeting. There should
be a small open hole remaining at the tip of the cone.

To use the mould, thrust it point downwards into a bucket of DRY soft sand. Then push a hairpin-shaped piece of stainless steel wire down through the pointed end of the mould (see Fig. 74(2)) so that about half an inch of the loop is buried in the sand.

Now pour in the molten lead. By varying the amount of lead poured into the mould, you can make a selection of leads of varying size, ranging from about 4 ozs. to 1½ lb. or more.

Allow the lead to harden in the mould; then, with a pair of

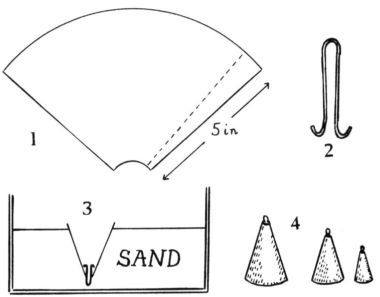

Fig. 74 Method of making Cone-shaped Leads.

Stage 1. From a sheet of aluminium, size 9 in x 5 in, cut a piece to the shape shown here, and bend it to form a cone. Dotted line indicates the area of overlap. Rivet securely using flat-headed copper tacks, and seal any gaps with fireproof cement or bread dough.

Stage 2. Bend a 2-3 in length of brass or stainless steel wire to form the lead eye.

Stage 3. Invert the metal cone in a bucket of DRY sand, and thrust the rounded end of the wire eye through the small aperture.

Stage 4. Pour in molten lead and allow to harden; then lift the mould out of the sand with pliers and tap out the lead. Cool the lead in a bucket of water.

tongs or pliers, lift the hot mould from the bucket of sand and tap it, wide side downwards, against the workbench. The lead will then drop out, and it can be dipped in water to speed up the cooling process.

Warning: Be very careful when handling molten lead, and for safety's sake wear a heavy apron and boots.

Make sure the utensil used for melting down the lead is made from heavy solid metal, with no soldered seams or other possible weaknesses. This includes the handle, which must be riveted on securely.

Make sure the utensil is resting firmly on top of the heating stove, and cannot topple over accidentally.

Clamp the mould firmly in a vice before pouring in the molten lead, and – as previously mentioned – make absolutely sure that the mould is quite dry.

Do the job well away from small, inquisitive children.

Making a Gaff. If you experience difficulty in buying a lash-on gaff head, it is possible to make a serviceable gaff from a large butcher's S-shaped meat-hook and a stout ash stick cut from a hedgerow. Leave the bark on the stick to provide a better grip.

About 3½ inches from one end of the stick, drill a hole that is slightly narrower than the thickness of the hook. Heat one end of the hook until it is red-hot; then thrust it into the hole in the stick, allowing it to burn its way through. Quickly, while the metal is still hot, hammer the lower bend of the S so that it is

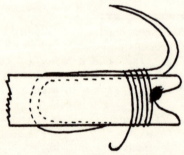

Fig. 75 The 'Meat-hook' Gaff, with the hook in the process of being lashed into position. The lashing should extend for about an inch beyond the full length of the hook.

embedded in the stick; then quench it in a bucket of water.

Lay on a strong whipping, or use two 'Jubilee' hose clips, to hold the hook securely in position. Then sharpen it to a needle point. The gaff is now ready for use.

Finally, remember that if your gaff is as sharp as it should be, it is a dangerous weapon. So guard the point of the gaff with a short piece of plastic tubing when it is out of use.

Making a Line-winder. Although the invention of rotproof synthetic fishing lines has reduced the need to strip lines regularly from the reel, a line-winder is still a useful thing to have in the workshop. For one thing, it makes it possible for a line to be wound off the reel and examined periodically for wear or damage; whilst it also simplifies the task of overhauling the reel itself, or replacing the line on the drum with one of a different type or breaking-strain.

An excellent line-winder can be made from a discarded electric flex spool, approximately 14 inches in diameter. Alternatively, cut out two discs of plywood of the same size.

Between the two flanges of the spool, about an inch from the rim, eight short lengths of broom handle should be fitted at equal distances. It is on to these, and not the hub of the spool, that the line will be wound.

Next, fit another short piece of broom-handle to one side of the spool to act as a winding handle; then pass a bolt through the hub and fix this with nuts and large washers to a sturdy 16-inch batten on the side opposite to the handle.

The winder is now virtually complete, but many anglers prefer to incorporate a reel-holder like the one shown in the photograph in Plate 5. This is made from a 2-foot length of broom-handle, screwed and glued to the supporting batten.

If desired, the complete linewinder can be mounted on a wooden stand, but this will make it a bulky item of equipment which will take up a lot of storage space. As good, if not better, results will be obtained if the stand is omitted, and the batten clamped upright in the workbench vice when the winder is being used.

Finally, it is strongly recommended that the winder be given a coat of hard gloss paint. This will prevent salt and moisture from damp lines soaking into the wood, and so retarding the drying process.

Making Feathered Lures. In an earlier chapter of this book we recommended the use of feathered lures for mackerel, pollack and other kinds of sea fish, and although these can be purchased at most tackle shops, there is always more satisfaction in catching fish with lures of one's own making.

First, of course, you will need a supply of feathers. Those incorporated in shop-bought traces often cover a remarkable range of hues; but white and red are the only colours you need bother about.

Hackle feathers from the domestic cockerel are very effective, but they are by no means essential. You can even use 'feather-shaped' strips of flimsy, brightly-coloured plastic. Some of the most killing lures I ever made were cut from a lightweight plastic raincoat discarded by my wife. Another useful material is orange-coloured baler twine, which should be unravelled into loose shreds. The possibilities for experimenting are endless.

The hooks for your lures should be tinned and fairly long in the shank. An assortment covering size 1, 2 and 3 is recommended.

Now for the method of tying the lures. First of all, with a razor blade, trim each feather as shown in Fig. 76(1), so that a little over half an inch of bare quill is exposed. Leave a slight 'stubble' on the quill, as this will provide a better grip for the whipping material.

Select a length of nylon monofilament snooding for the hook; slip it through the eye and tie the knot illustrated in Fig. 76(2), around the shank about half an inch below the eye. Immediately above it attach one end of the whipping material by means of a similar knot, encircling both hook-shank and snooding.

Ideally, whipping thread should be used for this purpose. If this is not available, however, strong waxed button thread will do very well. Pull the knot in the whipping material tight, hold it between finger and thumb, and make a few neat, tight coils around the hook-shank and nylon snooding.

After about half a dozen turns, lay two feathers along the hook so that the bared portion of each quill is lying along the upper portion of the hook-shank as far as the opening of the eye. Then continue the whipping around hook, nylon and quill until the eye is reached; finish off with a secure, non-slip

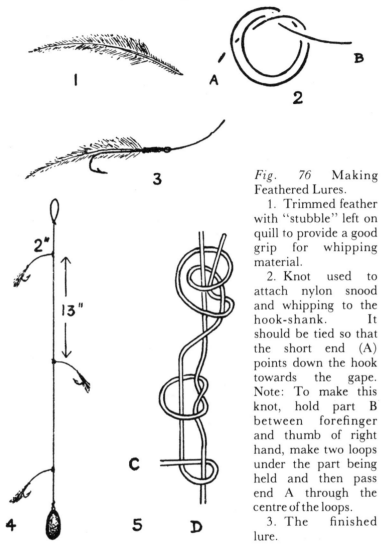

Fig. 76 Making Feathered Lures.

1. Trimmed feather with "stubble" left on quill to provide a good grip for whipping material.

2. Knot used to attach nylon snood and whipping to the hook-shank. It should be tied so that the short end (A) points down the hook towards the gape. Note: To make this knot, hold part B between forefinger and thumb of right hand, make two loops under the part being held and then pass end A through the centre of the loops.

3. The finished lure.

4. Feathered trace for use from boat or jetty, and suitable for a fairly light rod. A dozen or more lures could be used with a heavy weight and a stiff rod. The lures are worked in the water by raising and lowering the rod-tip.

5. Method of attaching lure snood (C) to the main trace (D). The snood should consist of stiff nylon monfil, so that it juts out nicely from the trace.

knot. Varnish the whipping and leave to dry.

Making a Lobster-pot. Among the thousands of sea anglers who own their own craft, comparatively few appreciate the advantages of adding variety to the catch and menu by setting one or two pots to catch lobsters and edible crabs. Yet dinghy angling and small scale potting go very well together on any suitable stretch of coast.

The system of working is very simple; the pots are emptied of their catch on the way out to the fishing ground, and then re-baited with unwanted spoils from the previous day's rod-and-line operations, such as wrasse, pouting, ray bodies, etc.

Lobster-pots vary in design from district to district, and I have tried most of them at one time or another. Those of cube-shaped construction are the most convenient to use from a

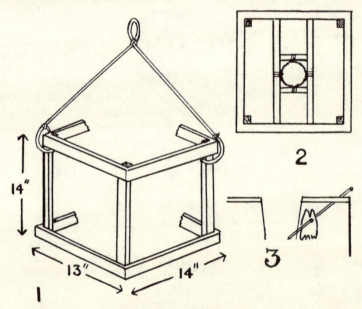

Fig. 77 Making a Lobster-pot.

1. Framework construction and rope bridle.

2. Top view of the pot, showing entrance fixed to the framework by lashings.

3. Method of baiting pot with skewer thrust through netting, bait, and wicker entrance. The high level of the bait entices the lobster to the top of the pot.

small dinghy because they can be stowed one on top of another.

The accompanying illustrations show how easily a pot of this type can be made from driftwood scraps. Galvanized nails should be used as a precaution against corrosion, and the netting (usually of courlene or some other synthetic material) should have a half-inch mesh so that prawns for live bait may be caught as well.

The bottom of the pot can be boarded over and weighted with pieces of scrap iron, lashed securely in place so that they cannot break adrift. Alternatively, concrete can be used to weight the bottom of the pot; in which case it is a good plan to scratch one's name in the concrete while it is still wet.

The rope bridle shown in the sketch is a personal preference; its main advantage being that if the rope frays through at one corner of the pot the opposite corner still holds firm. To the bridle loop there is attached a rope considerably longer than the maximum depth of water, and this should carry single corks at two-fathom intervals, and an empty gallon-sized plastic bottle at the end to act as a marker. This, too, could be marked with your initials to avoid confusion with other pots.

Bait in the pot is usually impaled on two skewers, thrust obliquely downwards through the top of the pot into the side of the entrance. The traditional type of skewer is made of straight-grained wood, but my own preference is for skewers made of stout galvanized wire, as these do not float out of the pot if the tuggings of a crab or lobster causes them to work loose.

The most productive areas to set your pots will usually be on broken ground (mixed sand and small rocks), or on sand in the close vicinity of individual larger rocks or rocky islets.

14

Buying a Boat

Boat-ownership has become so popular in recent years that the different types and classes of small craft now on the market can be numbered, quite literally, in their thousands. To the person with little or no previous experience of the subject, this wide variety of choice is confusing rather than helpful.

The first step to take, when trying to decide what kind of boat to buy, is to consider carefully the use to which your craft will be put, and the conditions it will be required to face. For instance, a deep-draught cruiser might well prove ideal when shark fishing many miles offshore, but when negotiating a shoal-ridden estuary, or the winding channel of a creek, it could be a constant source of worry.

If you are a complete novice, a small boat will almost certainly prove most suitable. It will be cheaper to buy, easier to handle – and both cheaper and easier to maintain. Most important of all, however, it will bring you into really close contact with the sea, so that you instinctively learn to respect the strength of tides, waves, and wind. Larger craft can follow later, after the experience and knowledge necessary for handling them have been acquired.

It is always a good plan, when seeking a boat for a particular purpose, to make a list of those features which you think it should possess in order to meet the special conditions. For instance, supposing you are looking for a 12-foot dinghy which could be launched by one or two people from an exposed beach. Your list of requirements might then read as follows:

1. High, clean-swept prow, so that the craft can be launched safely through surf.
2. High, raked transom to avoid swamping when beaching in a heavy ground-swell.

3. Wide beam, for stability.
4. Light construction, to facilitate hauling up a steeply shelving beach.
5. Must be easy to row, in case of engine trouble.
6. Hull and keel must be reinforced with bilge-rubbers and metal keel-band to avoid wear on pebble beach.
7. Small foredeck to protect gear from spray.
8. The boat must be large enough to stand up safely to local conditions, but small enough to be easy to maintain.
9. Built-in dagger-plate case for easy conversion to sail.

In much the same way, the 'ideal boat' for any type of coast can usually be arrived at by a careful study of local conditions, and by making inquiries from other boat anglers and small-craft enthusiasts with a long experience of the district.

Do not ask for just one person's advice; question as many people as possible, and compare their replies. On certain subjects there may be some difference of opinion, and you will then have to exercise your own judgement. On most points, however, a definite pattern of essential requirements will emerge, and these should be given priority on your list.

The choice between buying a new boat and a second-hand one is usually governed by the amount of ready cash available. By itself, of course, the word 'second-hand' means very little; it can be used to describe a boat that is almost as good as new, or a weed-grown hulk that is virtually falling to pieces.

Buying an *old* second-hand boat is always something of a gamble; especially when – as is usually the case – the timbers have been covered with several layers of new paint. The bottom boards should be removed, and the hull carefully inspected, both inside and out, for signs of previous damage or rot. Tell-tale signs are boards covered with copper or wooden patches, splits filled and camouflaged with stopper, landings warped or broken away from their rivets, and cracked or broken ribs.

In the case of a boat that has been lying at moorings, special attention should be given to the stem, close to the water-line, for signs of rot. A penknife blade, jabbed through the mask of new paint, will soon tell you whether the timber underneath is firm and sound, or soft and rotten.

Beach boats, and craft which have been lying for some time

on wet ground or mud, often become rotten around the bilge-planks, and a similar penknife test should be made on the underside of the hull.

In recent years some revolutionary changes have taken place in the boat-building trade, owing to the introduction of new construction methods and materials. From the dinghy angler's point of view, the most noteworthy of these new materials are undoubtedly glass-fibre and resin-bonded marine plywood. We will consider them in the order given.

Glass-fibre boats are constructed from a sort of cloth or 'felt', manufactured from threads of glass which have a thickness approximately one-tenth that of a human hair. Various firms have developed their own techniques, but basically the British system requires the construction first of all of a female mould of the boat, or boats, to be built.

The inside surface of this mould is first treated with a wax-like substance to facilitate the eventual removal of the completed boat. Then it is painted with a coat of resin, which, in due course, will form the outer skin of the boat.

On top of the resin a layer of glass cloth is laid and pressed into place, and this is followed by another coat of resin and a layer of glass 'felt', or mat as it is called in the trade. This process is repeated until a laminated glass hull has been built up to the required thickness and strength.

Glass fibre is very flexible stuff, so the hull has now to be reinforced with frames. These, too, are made of glass fibre, and are fixed to the inside of the hull with special adhesives. The most satisfactory method entails the use of hollow frames, which provide reserve buoyancy as well as making the boat more rigid.

A glass-fibre boat with built-in buoyancy has all the advantages of a wooden hull, whilst at the same time possessing none of the disadvantages.

Weight for weight, glass fibre is stronger than wood, and has no 'grain' to provide a line of weakness.

It is immune from attacks by wood-borers, such as the teredo, and the smooth, hard surface discourages barnacles and other marine growths. Those growths which do adhere are easily scraped off.

A glass-fibre hull cannot rot, warp, or absorb water, so that painting is quite unnecessary. During the manufacturing process the hull is impregnated throughout the laminate with the required colour, and this lasts the lifetime of the boat.

Finally, as the hull is moulded in a single piece, there are no joints or seams to open and leak. In the event of the hull being pierced in an accident, it can be repaired in a single day, so that the boat appears – and is – as good as new.

At the time of writing the initial cost of a glass-fibre craft is somewhat higher than one constructed of wood; yet, even so, the virtual absence of annual maintenance bills makes it a thoroughly sound economical proposition. Moreover, the very fact that a glass-fibre boat cannot deteriorate through rot or neglect ensures that it will always command a good price on the second-hand market, should the need ever arise to sell it.

Resin-bonded marine plywood has become firmly established as one of the most popular materials for small-craft construction, and there are several reasons for this.

First of all, despite its flimsy appearance, high grade marine plywood possesses a greater and more uniform strength than ordinary boat-building timbers. The fact that the grain is crossed in the adjoining veneers of the ply prevents any risk of splitting; whilst its ability to stand up to heavy impacts is quite remarkable. It has been proved, for example, that $\frac{1}{4}$-inch-thick plywood has a strength that is equal to timber planking of nearly double the thickness.

The resin glues which are used in the manufacture of high-grade marine plywoods are completely impervious to water and all climatic conditions. The result is a plywood that is proof against delamination, even after many hours of alternate immersion in boiling and cold water, or after years of exposure, unprotected by paint or varnish, to sea water, sunlight, frosts, and waves.

In plywood boat construction weight can be reduced to a remarkable degree, and this makes it particularly suitable for the angler who is seeking a dinghy which he can transport on the roof of his car, or haul single-handed up a steeply shelving beach. Of course, it is not recommended that a plywood dinghy should be dragged over sharp stones, but round water-worn pebbles are unlikely to do any harm provided that the bottom of the hull is protected with plenty of bilge rubbers, and kept adequately coated with a hard gloss paint.

BOAT-BUILDING FOR THE AMATEUR

Boat-building with the traditional materials – timber planking and copper rivets – has always been, and always will be, a job for the highly skilled craftsman. But the introduction of resin-bonded marine plywood opened up several completely new and simplified methods of small-craft construction, so that today perfectly satisfactory anglers' boats can be built at home by the amateur handyman, using a minimum of tools.

The significance of this, in terms of money saved, may be judged from the fact that in a professionally built boat the labour costs account for well over half the price of the finished product.

Many firms, realizing this, now specialize in the production of home boat-building kits, in which the plywood and other timber parts are prefabricated, ready for final shaping up and assembly in accordance with plans and instructions included with the materials. This system is strongly recommended; for not only does it dispose of much tedious marking out and hand-sawing, but it also avoids wastage of materials.

In many instances, in fact, it proves cheaper to obtain one of these prefabricated kits than it would to buy unprepared materials from a timber merchant. The reason for this apparent anomaly is that the relatively small cost of machining the kit parts is more than offset by savings gained from bulk purchases of timber direct from the importer, and marine plywood from the manufacturer.

Before ordering a kit, however, the would-be boat-builder should ask himself two questions: "Have I the necessary skill to do the job?" and "Have I the facilities?"

Let us consider first of all this question of skill. From my own experience, I would say that anyone can confidently set about the task of building a *properly designed* plywood boat, provided that he is (i) reasonably competent at handling ordinary woodworking tools; (ii) able to measure accurately, and (iii) willing to take his time over the job. In other words, care, common sense, patience, interest, and an average amount of manual dexterity will overcome all difficulties.

Secondly, the facilities required. I have heard of boats being built in back yards and gardens, but where resin glues are used, requiring careful temperature control, this is not to be recommended. A fair-sized workshop, garage, or unused room is almost an essential.

Apart from a work-bench and vice, the tools required are usually as follows: ruler, spirit level, square, plumb-line (made from a leger weight and fishing line), tenon saw, hacksaw, ½-inch and 1-inch chisels, mallet, smoothing plane, small block-plane, drill, rasp, screwdrivers (medium and small blades), hammer, spokeshave, and cramps. In the case of a sailing dinghy, a compass saw will also probably be needed in order to cut out the centre-board slot.

Cramps are the only things the average handyman will find himself short of. Large numbers are required for most kinds of boat-building, and they are expensive to buy. So while waiting

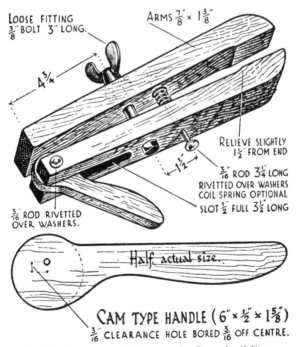

TIMBER STRAIGHT GRAINED OAK or ASH.

LOOSE FITTING
⅜" BOLT 3" LONG.

ARMS ⅞" × 1⅜"

4¾

RELIEVE SLIGHTLY
1½" FROM END

³⁄₁₆" ROD 3¼" LONG
RIVETTED OVER WASHERS
COIL SPRING OPTIONAL

SLOT ½" FULL 3½" LONG

³⁄₁₆" ROD RIVETTED
OVER WASHERS.

Half actual size.

CAM TYPE HANDLE (6" × ½" × 1⅝")
³⁄₁₆" CLEARANCE HOLE BORED ³⁄₈" OFF CENTRE.

Fig. 78 Home-made Cramps for Boat-building.

for the kit to be delivered it is usually a good idea to make about two dozen out of odd pieces of straight-grained oak or ash, some 3/16-inch metal rods, and a quantity of ⅜-inch nuts and bolts. (See illustration.)

Making the stocks is another job which will keep one busy while waiting for the boat materials to arrive. As a rule these consist of three parallel 3-inch by 2-inch timbers, set up on short legs. On top of these the boat is built upside down around moulds; the latter being loaned with the materials.

The stocks have to be set up dead level fore-and-aft and athwartships, and on an uneven floor this is no easy task. A final check should be made by stretching string across the stocks diagonally to make sure that all three timbers are the same height, and unwarped.

Care in setting up the stocks is the secret of successful home boat-building, and it is worth taking time and trouble over the job. When ordering a kit of materials, therefore, I would strongly advise the amateur builder to ask for details of the stocks in advance. He will then be able to erect them carefully at his leisure, untempted to skimp the job by a crateful of intriguing-looking boat-parts clamouring for his attention.

Incidentally, some designs require no stocks. This is naturally a saving in labour and materials; although the system calls for fairly even floor conditions.

Finally, a word about the designs available in kit form. These cover a wide variety of craft, ranging from tiny 7-foot pram dinghies to sizeable 20-foot cabin cruisers. Illustrated catalogues are available from the various kit-manufacturing firms, and if these are studied carefully it should be possible to choose a craft which approaches very closely to one's 'ideal boat'. In any case, when putting the finishing touches into any boat it is usually possible to make minor modifications to meet local conditions, or one's special angling requirements.

15

Boat Maintenance

Many boat-owning anglers lavish care on their rods, reels, lines, landing-nets, and gaffs, yet for some unaccountable reason neglect their hard-working craft to a degree that is often downright wicked. As a boat-lover it always grieves me to see one of these typical 'fisherman's tubs' – with its paintwork (if any!) peeling and blistered, its oars split and mended with lashings, its anchor rope and painter frayed and 'fox-brushed', and its upper strakes sun-warped and showing chinks of daylight between them.

Quite apart from the question of appearance, a boat that is neglected for season after season will before very long become dangerous to use, and the chances are that it will let its owner down at the very worst possible time. Obviously, a half-rotten board is most likely to spring its rivets when subject to the buffeting of a breaking sea, or a split oar to snap when one is pulling hard for shelter against a rising offshore wind.

The importance of carrying out a regular inspection and overhaul cannot be over-emphasized, therefore, and this chapter has been compiled with the object of helping the none-too-experienced boat-owner with those maintenance and repair problems which inevitably crop up from time to time.

Painting. A number of firms produce special marine coatings which possess outstanding resistance to the destructive properties of salt water, and the boat-owner would be well advised to use only these materials when painting his craft – especially as they cost little or no more than ordinary household paints. At the same time, however, it must be realized that the use of first-class materials will not, in itself, guarantee a first-class finish. Plenty of hard work and painstaking care will also be required.

If the hull is in bad condition it will be necessary to remove all traces of old paint or varnish, and this is best done by using a well-sharpened scraper and one of the paint-stripping compounds which are sold under a variety of trade names. Afterwards, any traces of the stripper left on the wood must be removed or neutralized in accordance with the instructions on the container; otherwise it will react on the new paint as well. Burning off with a blow-lamp is an alternative method of removing old paint, but it is not one to be undertaken lightly by the inexperienced amateur, owing to the risk of scorching the wood.

When the hull has been scraped off it should be sponged down with fresh water to remove all particles of dust, and then allowed to dry. It is, in fact, essential to make sure that the hull has dried right through, and not merely on the surface, as any moisture trapped inside the boards will inevitably try to escape, causing the new paint to peel off. For the same reason it is helpful if the scraped hull can be taken under cover, so that it is protected from the weather.

With the boat cleaned up and dry, all bare woodwork should be treated with priming paint of a type designed for use with the make of paint which is to be applied later on. The instructions issued by various paint manufacturers tend to differ slightly, but as a rule priming paint should be applied liberally in order to give it a chance to soak well into the wood; after which it should be brushed out thoroughly along the grain so that only a very thin film is left on the surface. Whether or not the priming coat is rubbed down with glass-paper after it has become dry and hard will depend on the type of paint used, and the manufacturer's instructions on this point should be followed carefully.

When the primer has dried, all cracks in the wood should be filled with a waterproof stopping compound. There are several on the market which are sufficiently elastic to adapt themselves to the swelling and shrinking of wooden planks, and the use of these is strongly recommended – particularly when dealing with clinker-built craft. Smooth down the stopping with glass-paper as soon as it has hardened sufficiently.

The next job is to apply the colour undercoating, and it is worth mentioning that two thin applications are better than one single thick one. The first coat should be rubbed down with fine waterproof glass-paper, wetting the paper in a bucket of water at very frequent intervals. This task should be performed thoroughly and vigorously, but at the same time care must be taken to avoid rubbing right through to the bare wood. Sponge off with a damp, clean cloth that is free from fluff; then allow the job to dry thoroughly, leaving the doors and windows open if the work is being carried out under cover. Apply a second undercoating and rub down again with waterproof paper, but do not use quite so much 'elbow-grease' this time. Clean up the hull again with a damp cloth, and allow to dry.

The hull is now ready to receive its final coat of paint, which will usually take the form of a high-gloss enamel. Care should be taken when applying it to avoid 'sagging', and this is best done by brushing the paint on in one direction; then crossing the brush-strokes and finally laying off in the original direction.

The brushes must, of course, be absolutely clean before starting the job, and a simple way of ensuring this is to wash them in hot water and a soapless detergent; afterwards rinsing thoroughly in fresh cold water. If possible, new brushes should not be used, as they are likely to be too long in the bristle. A well-worn brush will produce a much better finish.

When applying the finishing coat it is best to start work early in the morning on a warm, dry day. Above all, if working on or near the beach, avoid a sultry day when the shore flies are on the wing, because a freshly painted boat seems to have a magnetic attraction for them.

Varnishing. In many respects varnishing resembles painting, but at certain stages of the work there are important differences, and unless these are properly appreciated it is unlikely that a really first-class finish will be obtained. As varnishing is usually carried out on new, or fairly new craft, this is quite an important point.

First of all, the transparent nature of varnish makes careful preparation of the woodwork an absolute essential. All traces of grease, drips of marine glue, etc., must be removed; cracks must be sealed and the wood brought to a satin-smooth finish with glass-paper. Rub with the grain – first with fairly coarse paper; then with medium paper, and lastly with fine wet or dry (waterproof) paper. Use a cork glass-paper block, and before starting a new sheet remove any extra coarse grains of glass or grit by rubbing it lightly against another piece of glass-paper.

Remove all dust after rubbing down. Indoors, this is best done with a damp cloth, or by using the nozzle extension of a vacuum cleaner, if there is an electric power-point handy. Any 'whiskery' patches of wood should be treated with priming varnish. It will be found that after the primer has hardened the protruding whiskers can be rubbed off easily with fine glass-paper.

When dealing with small craft it is most important to use genuine marine varnish throughout, and once you have chosen a reliable brand it is advisable to stick to it year after year. This is because one brand of varnish does not always take kindly on top of another. If you always use the same kind of varnish, old work will merely need cleaning and lightly rubbing down before being treated to a couple of fresh protective coats. But if you use a different brand it will be necessary first of all, for safety's safe, to strip down to the bare wood.

Never prime new or stripped wood with a cheap grade of varnish, in the mistaken belief that what lies under the proper marine varnish does not really matter. Most manufacturers print their own special priming instructions on the tin, and these should be strictly adhered to. When it is hard, rub down this priming coat very thoroughly.

Always choose bright, dry weather for applying varnish, beginning work fairly early in the morning to give the work a chance to harden before nightfall. Fog, dew, sudden drops in temperature, and muggy conditions can prove fatal to a varnishing job; whilst hot sunshine falling directly on to the boat will cause bubbling. When the work is being done indoors, ventilate freely (but avoid draughts), and do not use artificial heat.

Put the varnish on with smooth, easy strokes of the brush. Above all, don't try to get the varnish into awkward corners by using a 'shaving-brush' technique; you will only create a froth. Instead, use a smaller brush. Give the outside of the boat three or four main coats, and the inside *at least* two; making sure that each coat is thoroughly dry before the next is applied.

To obtain a good key for each successive coat, it is advisable to rub down the undercoats lightly with glass-paper, taking care to remove all traces of dust.

Oars and Rowlocks. An oar can be lost overboard very easily, unless precautions are taken in advance. Anglers are particularly prone to this kind of mishap, because they are liable to have their attention distracted when they find themselves with a big fish, and if an oar slides out of the rowlock during the excitement it will probably go unnoticed.

An extra large wave may also lift an unattended oar out of its rowlock. If the boat is anchored, the oar may be carried away by the tide before it can be retrieved; or, if the boat is drifting, the wind will probably carry the boat away from the oar. Sculling with a single oar, by means of a sculling notch in the transom, is a possible way out of such a difficulty, but it is almost impossible to best a strong tide or wind by this method.

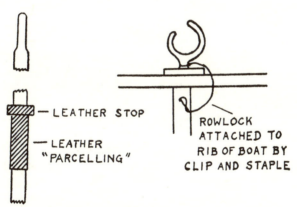

Fig. 79 Leathered Oar and Tethered Rowlock.

Perhaps the most satisfactory type of oar for sea work is that favoured by the professional fisherman – the shaft of the oar is fitted with a 'loom' through which is bored a hole which fits over a thole-pin projecting from the gunnel. Without swamping or capsizing the boat, it is almost impossible to lose this sort of oar.

Loomed oars, however, are too cumbersome for the small

light-weight dinghy. Instead, leathered oars should be used with rowlocks. To make these safe, the part of the oar bearing on the rowlock should be wrapped in leather thick enough to prevent the oar from jumping out of the rowlock aperture. Soak the leather in water before starting the job, and fix it with broad-headed copper tacks. An even thicker leather 'stop' should then be fitted (see illustration) so that the oar, when unattended, cannot slide downwards into the water.

However, even leathered oars, by themselves, are not entirely safe. There is still the chance of a heavy sea lifting an oar out of the boat, and taking the rowlock with it. To prevent this from happening, the rowlock must be made fast to the boat in some way.

The best method is to fasten a length of stout fishing-line about the neck of each rowlock, and then, at the other end of the line, attach a stainless steel wire clip, which can be fastened to a copper staple protruding from a nearby rib of the boat. This clip-fastener idea is a considerable improvement on the more usual method of tying and untying knots.

Patching a Boat. Accidents will happen, and sooner or later most boat-owners are called upon to make good a holed board. A rock may give 'old faithful' a nudge in the ribs when fishing close in to a reef, or an iron beach stanchion, unseen in the dark, may play a similar prank when one is hauling up after a spell of night fishing.

Normally, a carvel-built boat, with either a flat bottom or a hard chine, is the easiest type to repair. This is because one is then working on a broad and relatively uncurved surface. However, provided that the hole is not too big, and only one board is affected, a sound repair can be made without undue difficulty to any ordinary type of clinker-built craft.

First of all you will require two pieces of sound canvas, trimmed to a size large enough to cover the hole and leave a good margin. You will also need a sheet of fairly thick gauge copper, very slightly smaller than the pieces of canvas; a quantity of copper tacks, slightly longer than the thickness of the board to be repaired; and a block of hardwood (preferably oak or mahogany) trimmed, chamfered, and curved (if necessary) so that it will fit snugly over the inside of the hole.

Now to start work. First of all treat the two pieces of canvas to a liberal coating of tar or tar-varnish. Lay one piece over the outside of the hole and hold it in position, as taut as possible, with a single copper tack at each corner. Fix the other piece over the inside of the hole in the same way.

Next, punch tack-holes at about ½-inch intervals all round the edge of the copper sheet, shape it to fit the outer curve of the boat, and then tack it over the outside canvas patch. Trim away the protruding edges of canvas with a razor blade, and clench over the tack tips showing inside the boat.

The wooden block is fitted over the inside patch of tarred canvas in much the same way, except that brass screws are used for fixing. Screw-holes should be drilled to avoid splitting the wood, and the screws countersunk to give the job a neat, workmanlike appearance.

This method of patching is particularly suitable for sailing and rowing craft, as the copper patch does not increase the water-friction surface of the hull. Larger motor-powered boats are often patched with a wooden block outside as well as inside, but the general method of repair remains the same.

Buoyancy Tanks. It is a wise plan to fit any small sea-going boat with airtight buoyancy units, so that it cannot sink, even when filled to the gunnels with water and weighed down by a motor and passengers. When dealing with an angler's dinghy, though, there are special factors which have to be taken into consideration.

For instance, plastic buoyancy bags of the kind favoured by yachtsmen on account of their lightness are scarcely suitable for an angler's boat – they are too easily punctured by hooks and gaffs. As for the various kinds of corrosion-proof cylinders which are sometimes offered as an alternative, these are usually too bulky and too expensive to suit either a small dinghy or its owner.

However, it is simple enough to make a set of buoyancy tanks out of two, three, or four screw-capped plastic canisters. Widely used in industry, and non-returnable, they can usually be had for the asking in 5 and 25 litre sizes. Failing that, a beach-combing expedition will probably prove helpful, as most beaches are littered with a wide variety of plastic containers after every storm. Select the kind you need, taking care to choose only those which are perfectly sound.

It is a wise precaution to seal the screw caps with waterproof glue before fitting the containers into the boat, so that they cannot be removed by accident or meddling children. Also, it pays to give careful thought to the positioning of the canisters in the boat, especially where space is limited.

Transom and bow are both good places, but first make sure that foredeck and thwart are capable of withstanding the upwards strain which would be imposed on them in the event of the boat ever becoming swamped. In any case, the canisters must be lashed firmly in position to the boat stringers, and distributed evenly fore and aft to provide balanced buoyancy.

'Plastic Foam' Buoyancy. The plastic canister buoyancy units described above are efficient and inexpensive, but they have the undeniable disadvantage of taking up valuable stowage space.

Consequently, from the point of view of space economy, durability, and reliability, there is much to be said in favour of the modern types of puncture-proof and rot-proof 'plastic-foam' buoyancy materials. Blocks or panels can be shaped to fit snugly into the bottom of the hull, beneath the bottom boards, where they are fixed into place with a special adhesive to become an integral part of the boat.

As a result, the buoyancy material is positioned where it will be most effective should the boat ever become filled with water, and at the same time there is virtually no loss of stowage space.

'Laying Up' a Boat. The first task when laying up a boat is to remove the bottom boards and other loose gear, and give the hull a thorough scrubbing until all dirt, oil, weed, and marine encrustations have been disposed of. Then it should be careened on its side and sluiced thoroughly, inside and out, either with a hose or with buckets of *fresh* water.

The object of this is not only to rid the bilges of that stale 'baity' smell peculiar to anglers' boats, but also to swill away encrusted salt which would tend to keep the timbers perpetually damp throughout the winter months, with a consequent risk of rot.

A boat which has been used on a beach will have precious little paint left on and around its keel by the end of the season, and if nothing is done about this before it is laid up out of doors considerable damage may result. Unprotected by a skin of paint, the cracks between the strakes of a clinker-built boat become filled with rain water, and then, when a sharp frost occurs, this water turns to ice and forces the strakes apart. Sometimes even the ribs of a boat become cracked through strains imposed on them in this way.

The answer, of course, is to allow the hull to dry out thoroughly and then, after stopping all cracks with a preservative caulking compound, give it a coat of paint to keep out the rain. In the case of an old boat which is used from a beach, a coating of tar-varnish is probably better than paint below the water-line. Certainly it is a lot cheaper.

Ordinary coal-tar is also used sometimes for this purpose, but it is apt to become tacky in hot weather, causing extra friction between hull and pebbles.

In cases where the hull is sound, repainting is usually left over until the following spring. In any event, the harbour or estuary boat will have to wait until then for its anti-fouling treatment below the water-line, because this type of paint loses its special properties if allowed to remain for long out of the water.

Fairly large boats, fitted with a bung-hole, may be stored in the upright position, with the hull chocked up clear of the ground, and the keel sloping slightly so that the open hole is situated at the lowest point. This ensures complete drainage of rain water. On no account should the hull be left lying for the winter unsupported by chocks, for not only does this sort of treatment impose a strain on the timbers, but at the same time it allows some of the lower strakes to become waterlogged through constant contact with the damp ground.

Small lightweight dinghies rarely possess a drainage hole, and these should never be left in the upright position. Rain would quickly fill a boat laid up in this way, and the weight of all this water would then press outwards on timbers designed only to withstand an inwards pressure. Worse still, in cold weather this water would freeze and expand, and the boat might easily be damaged beyond repair.

The inverted position is the best one for a small dinghy being stored out of doors. Care must be taken, however, to allow the air to circulate freely under the boat, and this is done by propping up the gunnels to a height of several inches above ground level. Usually baulks of timber are used for this purpose, although personally I favour discarded motor tyres.

They are more resilient than wood, and, by adjusting themselves to the shape of the gunnels, provide a wider area of support.

Storage methods used under cover are usually similar to those described above. It is a mistake – and one commonly made – to prop a small dinghy on its side against a garage wall in an attempt to save space; for in this way the hull is liable to become warped and out of shape.

If space must be saved, it is a much better plan to cradle the dinghy and sling it to the roof-beams of the garage by means of ropes and pulleys. This is a method commonly adopted with car-top dinghies, as it facilitates loading and off-loading.

Care of Sails and Canvas. Sails which have come into contact with salt water should never be rolled up tightly, or packed away into a closed bag, for any length of time. Before storing away sails for the winter it is *absolutely essential* that they should be rinsed thoroughly in fresh water, and then dried.

. It is advisable, too, that the sails should be waterproofed. This can be done very quickly and easily with a preparation known as 'Nev', which also completely prevents rot and mildew, and does not alter the appearance or porosity of the cloth. The preparation is applied with an aerosol pack in accordance with instructions supplied by the manufacturers, and may also be used to waterproof clothing, rod bags, haversacks, etc.

Canvas boat-covers also need reproofing occasionally if they are not to become rotten, and a solution well suited for this purpose is sold under the name of 'Kanvo'. It is applied with a brush, and is available in various colours: green, buff, black, white, and tan.

Marine Glues. Although intended primarily for boat-building and boat repairs, the modern marine glues have many other uses for the sea angler who makes or mends his own tackle-boxes, bait courges, floats, rods, etc.

Completely waterproof, weatherproof, and rotproof, these remarkable synthetic resin adhesives will actually join two or more pieces of wood so that the joint is stronger than the wood itself. When tested to destruction, even after 1,000 hours immersion in boiling water, or years of alternative wetting and drying, it is the wood and not the glue which first breaks under the strain.

Quite understandably, a great deal of publicity has been given to the foregoing facts by the various manufacturers of resin marine glues, with the inevitable result that some users tend to regard these products as almost foolproof. It is a mistaken belief that is apt to produce faulty work; with the user blaming the glue, when in actual fact he should blame his own carelessness.

The first thing to appreciate is that there is no such thing as an all-round ideal synthetic resin glue. Practically every glue of this sort on the market possesses its own special qualities, which makes it particularly suitable for certain purposes – and, in varying degrees, less suitable for others.

One glue, for instance, may possess exceptional gap-filling properties; a second may be easier or quicker to apply; a third may give a longer 'shuffling' time during the assembly period; a fourth may produce better results on dense timbers, such as oak, or 'greasy' timbers, such as teak.

The angler who is planning an important job, like repairing an expensive rod or building a plywood boat, should therefore study the properties of the various glues, and keep faithfully to the maker's instructions after buying the one which best meets his requirements.

Temperature and pressure periods are two very important factors when applying resin glues, and the greatest care should be taken to see that the air temperature does not fall below the minimum figure specified. When working at night, or in the winter, in an unheated workshop, this is best arranged by raising the construction on trestles and placing an electric heater underneath, covering the whole with old blankets or a tarpaulin. Of course, when building a boat, the stocks would take the place of the trestles.

Constant supervision to avoid overheating is recommended; and naturally all wood shavings must be swept away beforehand, to avoid risk of fire.

Wooden surfaces which are to be glued should be absolutely clean and free of grease, and if planed smooth it is a good plan to roughen them slightly with a rasp, or by running a sharp-bladed knife many times across the grain.

Nearby wooden surfaces, which are likely to receive some of the surplus glue squeezed out of the joint, may be rubbed over with a candle stub in order to prevent the glue from adhering

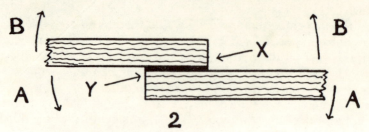

Fig. 80 Good and Bad Examples of Gluing.

1. When properly made with resin glue, a scarph joint is virtually indestructible. This is because the grain 'runs into' the glue, so that when the wood is under stress there is little or no tendency to split. (Note: the width of the bevels should be at least eight times the thickness of the wood.)

2. With certain kinds of wood a glued lap joint is comparatively weak when subjected to strains as depicted by the arrows AA or BB. This is because the grain runs parallel to the glued surfaces, creating a tendency for the wood to split in a lengthwise direction at X (in the case of arrows AA) or Y (arrows BB).

where it is not supposed to. This 'wrinkle' is well worth remembering when setting up moulds for boat-building; because it is a nuisance, to say the least, to discover that one's boat has become stuck to the mould when the time comes to lift it from the stocks!

The person using resin glue should never allow himself to be lulled into a false sense of security by the fact that this product is stronger than the wood itself. Adhesion by glue is only between surface and surface, and it only needs the surface layer of one piece of wood to splinter away for the assembly to fail.

Consequently, the weakest joints in many kinds of wood are those in which the grain runs parallel to the glued surface, because wood always splits or peels along the grain. This very important point is often overlooked by the amateur handyman, and the accompanying diagrams should help to illustrate it more clearly.

Outboard Motors. Doubtless most dinghy fishermen have said some harsh things about outboard motors in their time, for there can be no denying that when an outboard is in a temperamental mood it can be as stubborn as a mud-hugging skate. Nevertheless, the fact remains that these small portable power units can widen tremendously a sea angler's field of operations, and when properly maintained – which is all too seldom the case – they will give almost trouble-free service.

From the dinghy-owner's point of view there is a great deal to be said in favour of the outboard motor. It is less costly than an inboard engine of similar power output, and it does not take up valuable space inside the craft. Moreover, unlike an inboard engine, fitting costs next to nothing, and the additional weight can always be discarded when one is dragging the boat up a steeply shelving beach, or transporting it on or behind a car.

Buying an outboard motor has its own special problems and, for the uninitiated, matters are often complicated rather than simplified by the wide range of engines on the market. It is of prime importance, of course, to choose a model that is the right size and power for the boat.

So far as size is concerned, the most important factor will be the length of the shaft. If too long, the boat will be carrying an unnecessary weight, whilst draft and water friction will be increased. On the other hand, if the shaft is too short, the driving power of the screw will be greatly reduced through being 'baffled' by the keel or transom.

No advantage results from using an outboard engine that is more powerful than is absolutely necessary. If this is done, one of two things will result. Either the boat will be over-driven and her trim and seaworthy qualities spoiled, or the engine will have to be throttled right down, which sooner or later will probably result in plug trouble. Both tempers and spanners are apt to get lost when changing plugs in a choppy sea.

Fitting an outboard is usually a very simple matter, but even so it pays to give careful thought to the task. Bear in mind the fact that when the screw is thrusting at the end of its shaft the strain on the transom will be very great, and that this strain is trying to snap the wood in its weakest direction – that is to say, along the grain.

Therefore, if you think a reinforcing board of hardwood is necessary – and it usually is – be sure to fit it so that the run of the grain is vertical. In this position the wood is better able to resist the stresses put upon it by the engine. It is a fact worth emphasizing that many new dinghies are permanently damaged at the very outset, simply because their owners failed to take this precaution when first fitting an outboard motor.

Although the ordinary transom-stern type of dinghy offers no special problems, many anglers possess craft which have to be specially adapted before an outboard power unit can be fitted. Consider, for example, the lerret, or double-ender, commonly used for beach work. With 'bows' at either end, this craft is particularly well suited for landing on surf-swept shingle, but the absence of a transom presents something of a problem when one wishes to fit an outboard motor.

A method occasionally used is to mount the engine amidships on a bracket projecting from the gunnel. This has several disadvantages, however, as well as looking unsightly, and a much more simple way out of the difficulty consists of bolting a narrow false transom above the waterline. Constructed of stout hardwood with an 'up-and-down' grain, it need project only an inch or two beyond the end of the boat.

One sea-going craft which does sometimes benefit from having the outboard motor mounted amidships is the sort with a projecting stern – 'saucer-lip stern' is the term used on some parts of the coast. This is because, when pitching to a rough sea, this type of boat has a habit of kicking up its heels, so that the screw is lifted clean out of the water.

Of course, a rigid outrigger motor bracket, fitted amidships, would prove troublesome when coming alongside a harbour wall, and it should therefore be of a quick-release design.

Many dinghies have a small area of stern decking to prevent pooping in a following sea. To fit an outboard in these circumstances it may be necessary to cut away a small square of the deck so that the engine can be clamped over the transom. A small hinged flap should be made to fit over the hole in the deck when the engine is not fitted.

If the dinghy is designed for use under sail, mount the engine well to starboard (for right-handed steering), to allow room to fit the rudder. When under power the boat can be steered either by swivelling the engine in the normal way (the rudder, of course, being previously removed), or by means of the rudder, with the engine locked in the straight ahead position.

Laying Up an Outboard Motor. As a general rule an outboard motor thrives on hard work. It is when it is lying idle for months on end that mechanical troubles are most likely to begin. With this fact in mind, I decided while writing this chapter to visit a well-known outboard motor factory to find out what the experts there had to say on the subject of maintaining and 'mothballing' these portable power units.

The first point to be stressed was that tinkering with an outboard should be kept to an absolute minimum. Over-enthusiastic amateur mechanics – the type who 'know all about engines' – are apt to make trouble for themselves and the manufacturer's Repairs Department by dismantling engine parts which were never meant to be taken to pieces. On the other hand, the outboard owner who knows little about engines, but who faithfully follows the maker's instructions, usually obtains years of trouble-free use.

As regards laying-up, one of the chief enemies of an outboard used on the sea is the encrustation of salt which will inevitably cover the motor – especially those parts which become heated in use. If you keep your boat in an estuary it is a good idea, where practicable, to motor her upstream into fresh water at the end of the season. Then, while still in fresh water, the motor should be unhitched and lifted aboard, and the boat rowed back to the lay-up place.

Alternatively, the motor can be flushed by clamping it to the side of a barrel filled with fresh water, and running it up in that for a few minutes. In this event, however, it will be necessary to remove the propeller to avoid overloading the engine.

Encrusted salt left for any length of time on the shaft or other exposed parts of the motor will eventually spoil its appearance. The salt may be removed by wiping the metal thoroughly with a sponge which has been dipped in fresh water and wrung almost dry again. The sponge will need to be rinsed at very frequent intervals.

When dry, the motor can be wiped over with an oily rag;

although some people prefer to apply two or three coats of transparent marine varnish. This is not an essential precaution, but it does help to preserve the appearance of a new motor, and ensures that a better price will be obtained should you ever decide to sell it.

It is recommended by most manufacturers that regular attention should be given to the gearbox throughout the season, topping it up with the correct lubricant whenever necessary. At the end of a season of hard use the gearbox can with advantage be emptied and refilled, and this should certainly be done before laying up if salt water has found its way into the box.

If the gearbox of your engine is designed to take oil (not grease), and you know that it leaks very slowly, it will naturally be better to postpone refilling until the end of the lay-up period. In this event, however, be sure to tie a label on your motor bearing the words: 'REFILL GEARBOX'. Otherwise you may forget this part of the job – with disastrous results.

The majority of outboard motors run on a petrol/oil mixture, and these should automatically finish the season with a film of lubricant inside the cylinder. However, to be on the safe side, the sparking-plug can be removed, and a few drops of light lubricating oil inserted around the edges of the piston. Then, if the flywheel is rotated once or twice, the cylinder walls will be smeared with a film of oil. Naturally, when carrying out this job it is most important to make sure that the spout of the oilcan is perfectly clean.

At this stage the sparking-plug can be cleaned, and the gap closed up slightly, if necessary. A single-edged razor blade is a handy tool when cleaning the plug points. Before replacing the sparking-plug, make sure that no specks of grit or metal filings, picked up from the work bench, are adhering to the screw threads.

Your outboard motor will now be ready for laying-up. For preference, it should be stored upright in the corner of a dry and airy shed or garage. Some sort of a cover should be provided to protect it from dust, and a rope hitched round it to prevent it from being knocked over accidentally.

16

Cooking the Catch

Just as the gardener is able to enjoy home-grown vegetables that are far superior to the shop-bought variety, so the salt-water angler has the benefit of knowing just how appetizing freshly-caught fish can be when properly cooked. There is, in fact, no comparison at all between the taste of fish cooked immediately after being taken from the sea, and those dull-eyed, flabby-fleshed things so often to be seen reposing on the fishmonger's slab.

Freshly-caught sea fish can be made to tickle any palate, and from the nutritional point of view compares favourably with butcher's meat. It also contains substances which are valuable in maintaining human health – the most important being calcium, phosphorus and iodine.

A deep-freeze cabinet, equipped with a quick-freeze compartment, is a worthwhile investment for the sea angler who regularly catches quantities of fish which are surplus to his immediate requirements. Most boat anglers, and quite a lot of shore anglers, come into this category.

Fish intended for the freezer should be killed and gutted as soon as possible after capture, and rinsed thoroughly in clean sea-water. Every effort should be made to keep them in a cool, shady place until it is time to return home with the catch.

Final preparation for the freezer entails removing the scales (where necessary) and fins, and dividing large fish into meal-sized portions. From personal experience I have learned that many sorts of fish, including bass, pollack, coalfish and cod, retain their sea-fresh flavour much better if divided into fillets rather than cutlets. The fillets should be placed in clean plastic bags, which are then compressed gently to remove all surplus air. Finally, the neck of the bag is folded tightly and sealed, and a label added showing the type of fish, date of freezing down, and the number of portions.

Provided these simple rules are followed, you will find that freshly-caught fish can be quick-frozen and stored for six to twelve months without any noticeable loss of flavour. Rays' wings take to freezing particularly well. Large wings are best divided into two or three individual portions before being bagged up, with each bag containing sufficient portions to provide one for each member of the family.

Another very useful item is a small portable fish-smoker, of the type often sold by fishing-tackle shops. Primarily intended for smoking trout and mackerel in small quantities, they also give delicious results with fillets of pollack and coalfish.

Now for a few recipes specially designed for the sea angler's wife, who – poor soul! – is liable to be called upon to deal with anything from a 7-foot long conger eel to a handful of whitebait. Here's hoping the next few pages will help to lighten her burden.

BASS

Baked. Clean and scale a fair-sized bass and divide into cutlets or fillets. Place these in a greased baking dish, and sprinkle with a little pepper and salt. Chop up one shallot, 4 skinned tomatoes and 3 or 4 sprigs of parsley, and spread these over the fish, together with a small dab of butter on each. Bake in a moderate oven for 20 minutes. Serve with a white sauce containing chopped-up prawns. *Note:* Freshly caught and boiled prawns store well in a deep-freezer.

BREAM

Grilled. Scale the bream, taking care not to prick your fingers on the sharp spines, which should be removed. Wash and dry the fish, and score the flesh on either side with a sharp knife to help the heat penetrate. Smear lightly with lard or cooking oil. Cover with a sheet of foil and place under the grill until nicely browned. Large fish need to be grilled more slowly than small ones.

Note: On no account should bream be boiled.

BRILL

These fish are very similar to turbot, and in the kitchen may be treated in the same way.

COALFISH AND POLLACK

Both these fish belong to the cod tribe, and so far as the larger specimens are concerned may be treated as such when being cooked. Fillets taken from scaled pollack are also delicious smoked in a portable smoker – the taste being very similar to 'Finnan Haddock'.

Small inshore pollack weighing about 1 to 2 lb. are best scaled, split down the middle and the backbone removed. The opened-out fish (or fillets, in the case of larger fish) should be rolled in flour, sprinkled with salt and grated nutmeg, and fried in a pan until both sides are golden brown.

COD AND CODLING

Baked Cod Steak. Take a middle cut from the cod, this being the best part of the fish for baking. Wash the fish and remove the fins, afterwards tying into shape if necessary. Place the steak into a greased baking dish and spread over the top a mixture comprising the following: 2 oz. of butter, 1 eggspoonful of dried herbs, 1 dessertspoonful of chopped parsley, 2 tablespoons of breadcrumbs. Afterwards add a liberal sprinkling of salt and pepper. Place a sheet of foil over the steak and cook in a moderate oven for 20 minutes. Serve with anchovy sauce.

Stuffed Cod. After cleaning and washing the fish, leave it to soak in a bowl of well-salted water for an hour. Then dry the fish and stuff it with the following mixture: $\frac{1}{2}$ lb. of oatmeal, 2 finely chopped onions, 2 oz. of dripping, seasoning, and $\frac{1}{2}$ pint of milk. Place the cod in a fireproof dish, and either pour another $\frac{1}{2}$ pint of milk over it or cover it liberally with dripping. Place in a slow oven and bake for 1 hour, basting at frequent intervals. Carry to the table in the dish in which it was cooked. Serve with white sauce; the sauce containing, for preference, a quantity of boiled and shelled prawns, chopped up fine.

Fried Cod. Fillets, sliced from the side of a codling, or the tail-end of a large cod, are the best parts for frying. Methods include deep-frying in batter, or dipped in egg and breadcrumbs and fried in a pan.

CONGER EEL

Baked. Skin and clean the fish in sea-water as soon as it has been killed, and cut slices between the 'shoulders' and the middle – this being the best part of the eel. Break the slices into pieces about the size of an egg, dredge in flour seasoned with pepper and salt. Place the pieces of fish, in layers, in a greased baking dish with chopped parsley, sliced hard-boiled egg, and a few dabs of butter between each layer. When the baking dish has been filled in this way, pour in sufficient milk to half-fill the dish, and then sprinkle breadcrumbs on top. Bake in a moderate oven until tender.

DABS

Fried. Dredge with flour seasoned with pepper and salt; dip in beaten egg and then in breadcrumbs, and fry until golden brown. Garnish with parsley and sliced lemon.

Alternatively, skin the dabs, dip in flour seasoned with salt and pepper, and fry in butter. Sprinkle with lemon juice.

FLOUNDERS

Fried. Clean the fish some two hours before they are required, and rub with salt all over, inside and out, to make them firm. Wash off salt before cooking and dry thoroughly. Then fry by the methods suggested above for DABS.

GARFISH

Fried. Clean and scale the fish immediately after capture. Remove heads, tails and bones; then cut their long, eel-like bodies into convenient lengths for the pan. Dip the fillets in flour and sprinkle with pepper and salt. Fry slowly in a pan until lightly browned. Serve with lemon juice or tomato ketchup.

GURNARD

Baked. Larger gurnards are excellent when baked. Clean and wash the fish, and slit down the back to allow the heat to penetrate when cooking. Prepare a stuffing by chopping up two medium-sized shallots, a rasher of bacon and a dessert-spoonful of parsley, and mixing well with a cupful of breadcrumbs, the grated rind of a lemon, a liberal pinch of mixed herbs, a dessertspoonful of Worcester Sauce, a beaten egg, and a sprinkling of salt and pepper. Force this into the belly of the fish and sew up the body with needle and thread; at the same time trussing the fish with the thread so that the tail is held in the mouth. Place the fish in a fireproof dish and add ½ pint of water and another dessertspoonful of Worcester Sauce. Smear the fish with 1 oz. of butter, then chop up two or more shallots and sprinkle the pieces over the fish. Spread a sheet of foil over the fish and bake in a quick oven for 20 or 30 minutes, according to size, basting it at frequent intervals. At the final basting add a teaspoonful of Bisto to the liquor in the dish. Serve the fish in the dish in which it was cooked, using the liquor as a sauce.

HADDOCK

Fried. Fillet the haddock and wash each piece in salty water. Thoroughly dry the fillets with a cloth and brush them over with well-beaten egg, then dip them in breadcrumbs. Fry until golden-brown. A few drops of lemon juice on each fillet will be to most people's taste.

Haddock Soufflé. Boil a large, freshly-caught haddock; afterwards removing the skin and bones. Pound up the flesh with a little melted butter, and pass it through a sieve into a basin. Mix in three egg yolks; then whisk up the whites to a stiff froth and stir in separately. Spoon the mixture into a soufflé dish or small china cups, and bake in a moderate oven for 20 minutes.

MACKEREL

These fish deteriorate very rapidly after being caught, and should therefore be gutted at sea and placed in the refrigerator as soon as they are brought home. In any event, it is unwise to eat mackerel after they have been out of the sea for more than 24 hours. When eaten fresh, however, they are most wholesome and appetizing.

Unlike most other fish, mackerel do not take very kindly to deep-freezing. The freezing process seems to spoil both the flavour and texture of the fish.

Fried. Gut the mackerel as soon as possible after capture and wash them in sea-water. Before cooking, remove the heads and tails, and remove the backbone by splitting down the middle. Dip in flour and sprinkle with pepper and salt. Fry slowly in a frying-pan until lightly browned.

Soused. Clean the fish as described above, and place them (minus their heads and tails) in a large heatproof dish. Sprinkle with pepper and salt; then cover with equal quantities of water and vinegar, and add a few cloves and peppercorns, together with one small shallot, sliced up, to each fish. Place in a slow oven and cook for 35 minutes; then allow the fish to cool in the liquor. Serve with cold beetroot and lettuce.

Smoked. Mackerel are delicious when cooked in a small fish-smoker – the sort sold by many fishing-tackle shops. Gut the fish by cutting off their heads – do not slit open their bellies. Also remove the tails and fins. Wash and thoroughly dry the fish, both inside and out, and rub salt well into the flesh and body cavity. Allow plenty of time for the salt to penetrate – an hour or two, if possible.

Most home smokers will accommodate about 4 to 6 mackerel, depending on their size. Just cover the bottom of the smoke container with the fine sawdust provided, close the lid tightly, and cook for approximately 15 minutes – or a few minutes longer if the mackerel were very cold from being stored in a refrigerator.

MULLET

Grilled. Scale, clean and dry the fish, afterwards replacing the liver. Lightly score the flesh once or twice along either side. Place on a dish; season with pepper and salt, and smear liberally all over with olive oil in which has been placed a pinch of mixed herbs and some chopped onion. Leave the fish to drain on the dish; allowing plenty of time for the oil and seasoning to be absorbed by the fish.

After about an hour, transfer to a well-greased gridiron and cook under the grill, turning the fish two or three times during the process.

Baked. To cook a mullet to perfection it should be baked. Prepare the fish as for the previous recipe, then wrap it in foil smeared with butter. Cook in a moderate oven for half an hour, and serve with a squeeze of lemon juice.

Note: Mullet should never be boiled.

PLAICE

Fried. Clean and fillet the fish, and dip the pieces in flour seasoned with pepper and salt. Then brush them with beaten egg, and cover with breadcrumbs. Fry until golden brown. Serve with a slice of lemon.

Alternatively, instead of treating the fillets with egg and breadcrumbs, they can be dipped into a thick flour and water batter before frying.

POLLACK

Use the recipes described under COALFISH.

POUTING

Pouting in Cider. Fair-sized pouting are caught around the West Country coasts – a district famous also for its draught cider. Anglers living in those parts who declare that pouting make uninteresting eating should try cooking these fish in a little rough cider, to which have been added some chopped up shallots and mushrooms, and a pinch of mixed herbs. The fish should be gutted and washed in sea-water immediately after capture. Prior to cooking, they should be filleted and placed with the vegetables and cider in a heatproof dish, then covered with greased foil and cooked in a moderate oven for about 20 minutes. This recipe is also good with whiting and pollack.

SKATE AND RAYS

The majority of so-called 'skate' which find their way on to the table are, in fact, rays – thornback rays and small-eyed rays for the most part.

Fried. Cut off the 'wings' of the skate, which – apart from the liver – are the only portions of the fish suitable for cooking. Remove the coarse skin by immersing the wings for about 3 or 4 minutes in a bowl of boiling water – it will be found that the skin can then be stripped off easily by rubbing gently with the blade of a knife. Divide the wings into individual portions.

This preliminary immersion in hot water also partly cooks the flesh, which will be found of great assistance when frying thick portions of wing from a large ray. Before frying, however, lay the portions of wing on a gridiron to allow the water to drain off; then dry with a paper towel or clean cloth.

Dip each portion in beaten egg, and then in breadcrumbs, and fry in plenty of oil.

SOLE

Grilled. Skin, clean, and remove the head, tail and fins of the sole. Score lightly with a sharp knife, and leave for an hour or more in a shallow covered dish containing cooking oil, a little vinegar and several slices of onion. Turn the fish once during this period, so that both sides make contact with the oil. Remove from the dish, allow the surplus oil to drain off, but do not wipe it off. Place under the grill and cook slowly. Serve with a squeeze of lemon juice.

SPRATS

These tasty morsels never form part of the angler's catch, but they merit some mention because during the 'spratting season' they may often be bought very cheaply down by the harbour. Also, it is not unusual for shoals of sprats, when chased by bass or mackerel, to become stranded in their hundreds on the beach at the angler's feet. They may be cooked in the same way as WHITEBAIT.

TOPE

These large fish are usually caught solely for the sport they provide, and are seldom eaten. Actually the flesh is quite wholesome; though its rather strong flavour is not to everyone's taste. Try it in the form of steaks, fried in the manner suggested for cod.

TURBOT

Turbot Pie. After filleting, cut the turbot into pieces and parboil. Put the partly-boiled pieces into a greased heatproof dish. Make a good rich white sauce, with butter if possible, and cover the fish with the sauce.

Sprinkle fine breadcrumbs on top of the white sauce, and around this add sliced tomatoes and hard-boiled eggs. Bake in a moderate oven for 30 minutes. This pie is really delicious, and can be served hot, or cold with salad.

WHITEBAIT

These small fry of the herring, although not caught by the angler, are often stranded at low tide in rock pools, or are hauled ashore in sandeel seines. They should be eaten within a few hours of being taken from the sea.

To prepare whitebait, first wash them whole and then *thoroughly* dry them in a paper kitchen towel. Next cover a sheet of paper with flour and gently toss the fish in this until well coated with flour. For best results they should be fried a few at a time in a wire basket immersed in smoking-hot fat or oil. Turn the fish out on to absorbent paper, then transfer them to heated plates and serve with sliced lemon.

WHITING

Fried. Gut and wash the fish, and wipe it dry with a cloth. Decent-sized whiting can either be fried as fillets, or the whole fish can be curled up, tail in mouth, and fried in a wire basket in deep fat. Serve with a slice of lemon.

Baked. Whiting are caught in large numbers during the autumn – the mushroom season – so here is a recipe which makes use of both these delicacies. Gut and fillet the fish, and place in a greased fireproof dish with a little draught cider, several small peeled mushrooms and a sliced shallot. Cover with foil and bake in a moderate oven for 20 minutes or more, according to the size of the fish. Transfer the fish and warmed vegetables to a warmed dish, and quickly concentrate the liquor by pouring it into a small saucepan, stirring in a little creamed-up flour and butter, mixed in equal proportions by weight, and boiling rapidly. Pour the concentrated liquor over the fish and mushrooms, and serve with mashed potatoes.

WRASSE

These fish are not normally kept for the table, but they are often caught by youthful anglers who expect them to be cooked and eaten by the family. Frying them with tomatoes and sliced onions is perhaps the best way of turning wrasse into a reasonably palatable dish.

British Record Sea Fish

British Record Sea Fish

The following list gives details of sea fish caught on rod and line in British waters which have been accepted by the British Record Fish Committee. Several uncommon or small, non-sporting species have been omitted. It should be noted that the term 'British waters' embraces all coastal areas around Great Britain and Northern Ireland, but excludes waters bordering the shores of the Irish Republic. The list was compiled in January, 1979. B = boat record; S = shore record.

Species		Weight			Date	Captor and Location
		lb	oz.	dr.		
Angler Fish	B	82	12	—	1977	K. Ponsford, off Mevagissey
	S	68	2	—	1967	H. Legerton, Canvey I.
Bass	B	18	6	—	1975	R. Slater, off Eddystone Reef
	S	18	2	—	1943	F. Borley, Felixstowe
Bream, Black	B	6	14	4	1977	J. Garlick, over wreck off Devon
	S	4	14	4	1977	R. Holloway, Dover
Bream, Gilthead	B	5	—	—	1978	A. Stratton-Knott, off St Mawes, Cornwall
	S	6	15	—	1977	H. Solomons, Salcombe
Bream, Red	B	9	8	12	1974	B. Reynolds, off Mevagissey
	S	3	—	—	1976	D. Berry, Alderney C.I.
Brill	B	16	—	—	1950	A. Fisher, Isle of Man
	S	5	12	4	1976	M. Freeman, Chesil Beach, Dorset
Bull Huss	B	21	3	—	1955	J. Holmes, Looe
	S	17	15	—	1977	M. Roberts, Trefusis Point, Cornwall
Coalfish	B	30	12	—	1973	A. Harris, Eddystone
	S	16	8	8	1977	N. Randall, Plymouth
Cod	B	53	—	—	1972	G. Martin, Start Point
	S	44	8	—	1966	B. Jones, Barry
Common Skate	B	226	8	—	1970	R. Macpherson, Shetland
	S	150	—	—	*Qualifying weight*	
Conger	B	109	6	—	1976	R. Potter, S.E. of Eddystone
	S	67	1	—	1967	A. Lander, Torquay

Species		Weight lb	oz.	dr.	Date	Captor and Location
Dab	B	2	12	4	1975	R. Islip, Gairloch
	S	2	9	8	1936	M. Watts, Port Talbot
Dogfish, Lesser Spotted	B	4	1	13	1976	B. Solomon, off Newquay
	S	4	8	—	1969	J. Beattie, off Ayr Pier, Scotland
Flounder	B	5	11	8	1956	A. Cobbledick, Fowey
	S	4	7	—	1976	M. King, Seaford
Garfish	B	2	13	14	1971	S. Claeskens, off Newton Ferrers, Devon
	S	2	8	—	1977	S. Lester, Pembroke Bay, Guernsey
Gurnard, Grey	B	2	7	—	1976	D. Swinbanks, Mull
	S	1	8	—	1977	S. Quine, Peel Breakwater, Isle of Man
Gurnard, Red	B	5	—	—	1973	B. Critchley, off Rhyl, Wales
	S	2	10	11	1976	D. Johns, Helford River, Cornwall
Gurnard, Yellow	B	11	7	4	1952	C. King, Wallasey
or Tubfish	S	12	3	—	1976	G. Reynolds, Langland Bay, Wales
Haddock	B	13	11	4	1978	G. Bones, Falmouth
	S	6	12	—	1976	G. Stevenson, Loch Goil, Scotland
Hake	B	25	5	8	1962	H. Steele, Belfast Lough, N. Ireland
	S	5	—	—	*Qualifying weight*	
Halibut	B	212	4	—	1975	J. Hewitt, off Dunnet Head, Scotland
	S	14	—	—	*Qualifying weight*	
Herring	B	1	1	—	1973	B. Barden, off Bexhill-on-Sea
	S	1	—	—	*Qualifying weight*	
John Dory	B	11	14	—	1977	J. Johnson, Newhaven
	S	4	—	—	*Qualifying weight*	
Ling	B	57	2	8	1975	H. Solomons, off Mevagissey
	S	15	5	11	1976	P. Sanders, Porthleven
Mackerel	B	5	6	8	1969	S. Beasley, N. of Eddystone
	S	4	—	8	1952	S/Ldr. P. Porter, Peel Breakwater, Isle of Man
Megrim	B	3	12	8	1973	Master P. Christie, Loch Gairloch, Scotland
	S	2	—	—	*Qualifying weight*	
Monkfish	B	66	—	—	1965	C. Chalk, Shoreham
	S	50	—	—	1974	R. Brown, Monknash Beach, Wales
Mullet, Golden Grey	B	1	9	15	1978	B. Morin, off Jersey, C.I.
	S	2	10	—	1976	R. Hopkins, Burry Port, Wales
Mullet, Red	B	3	8	—	*Qualifying weight*	
	S	3	10	—	1967	J. Martel, Guernsey, C.I.
Mullet, Thick-Lipped	B	10	1	—	1952	P. Libby, Portland
	S	10	—	12	1978	R. Gifford, Aberthaw, Wales

Species		Weight lb	oz.	dr.	Date	Captor and Location
Mullet, Thin-Lipped	B	4	—	—		*Qualifying weight*
	S	5	11	—	1975	D. Knowles, R. Rother, Sussex
Plaice	B	10	3	8	1974	Master H. Gardiner, Longa Sound, Scotland
	S	8	1	4	1976	Master N. Mills, Southend Pier
Pollack	B	25	—	—	1972	R. Hosking, off Eddystone
	S	16	—	—	1977	R. Raybould, Portland Bill, Dorset
Pouting	B	5	8	—	1969	R. Armstrong, off Berry Head
	S	3	4	—	1978	P. Weekes, Dover
Ray, Blonde	B	37	12	—	1973	H. Pout, off Start Point
	S	25	4	—	1975	S. Sangan, Jersey, C.I.
Ray, Cuckoo	B	5	11	—	1975	V. Morrison, off Causeway Coast, Northern Ireland
	S	4	8	—		*Qualifying weight*
Ray, Eagle	B	52	8	—	1972	R. Smith, off I. of Wight
	S	25	—	—		*Qualifying weight*
Ray, Small-eyed	B	16	4	—	1973	H. Pout, Salcombe
	S	13	8	15	1976	A. Jones, Trevose Head
Ray, Spotted	B	6	3	4	1977	P. England, off Caliach Point, Mull
	S	7	12	—	1977	P. Dower, Stoke Beach, South Devon
Ray, Sting	B	59	—	—	1952	J. Buckley, Clacton
	S	51	4	—	1975	A. Stevens, Sowley Beach, Hampshire
Ray, Thornback	B	38	—	—	1935	J. Patterson, Rustington, Sussex
	S	19	—	—	1976	A. Paterson, Mull of Galloway, Scotland
Ray, Undulate	B	19	6	13	1970	L. le Page, Herm, C.I.
	S	10	10	4	1968	G. Robert, Guernsey, C.I.
Scad	B	3	5	3	1978	M. Atkins, Torbay
(Horse Mackerel)	S	2	5	13	1977	W. Rail, North Cliffs, Cornwall
Shad, Allis	B	3	—	—		*Qualifying weight*
	S	4	12	7	1977	P. Gerrard, Chesil Beach, Dorset
Shad, Twaite	B	3	2	—	1949	T. Hayward, Deal
	B	3	2	—	1954	S. Jenkins, Torbay
	S	2	12	—	1978	J. Martin, Garlieston, S.W. Scotland
Shark, Blue	B	218	—	—	1959	N. Sutcliffe, Looe
	S	75	—	—		*Qualifying weight*
Shark, Mako	B	500	—	—	1971	Mrs J. Yallop, off Eddystone
	S	75	—	—		*Qualifying weight*
Shark, Porbeagle	B	465	—	—	1976	J. Potier, off Padstow
	S	75	—	—		*Qualifying weight*
Shark, Thresher	B	295	—	—	1978	H. Aris, S. of I. of Wight
	S	75	—	—		*Qualifying weight*

Species		Weight lb	oz.	dr.	Date	Captor and Location
Smooth-hound, Starry (*Mustelus asterias*)	B	20	15	12	1978	B. Allpress, Bradwell-on-Sea
	S	23	2	—	1972	D. Carpenter, Bradwell-on-Sea
Smooth-hound	B	28	—	—	1969	A. Chilvers, Heacham
(*Mustelus mustelus*)	S	14	14	12	1977	A. Peacock, St. Donats, Wales
Sole	B	4	—	—		Qualifying weight
	S	4	8	—	1978	H. Pike, Alderney, C.I.
Sole, Lemon	B	2	2	—	1976	J. Gordon, Loch Goil Head, Firth of Clyde
	S	2	2	15	1971	D. Duke, Douglas, I. of Man
Spurdog	B	21	3	7	1977	P. Barrett, off Porthleven, Cornwall
	S	16	12	8	1964	R. Legg, Chesil Beach, Dorset
Tope	B	74	11	—	1964	A. Harries, Caldy I.
	S	54	4	—	1975	D. Hastings, Loch Ryan, Scotland
Tunny	B	851	—	—	1933	L. Mitchell Henry, Whitby, Yorks
	S	100	—	—		Qualifying weight
Turbot	B	32	3	—	1976	D. Dyer, off Plymouth
	S	28	8	—	1973	J. Dorling, Dunwich Beach, Suffolk
Whiting	B	6	4	—	1977	S. Dearman, West Bay, Dorset
	S	3	2	—	1976	C. Kochevar, Dungeness, Kent
Wrasse, Ballan	B	7	8	5	1975	M. Hale, Herm, C.I.
	S	8	6	6	1976	R. Le Page, Guernsey, C.I.
Wrasse, Cuckoo	B	2	—	8	1973	A. Foley, Plymouth
	S	1	4	8	1973	R. Newton, Holyhead Breakwater, Wales

Index

Index

A bold-type page number indicates an illustration facing